Divine Presence

Divine Presence

Elements of Biblical Theophanies

MARK G. BOYER

WIPF & STOCK · Eugene, Oregon

DIVINE PRESENCE
Elements of Biblical Theophanies

Copyright © 2017 Mark G. Boyer. All rights reserved. Except for brief quotations in critical publications or reviews, no part of this book may be reproduced in any manner without prior written permission from the publisher. Write: Permissions, Wipf and Stock Publishers, 199 W. 8th Ave., Suite 3, Eugene, OR 97401.

Wipf & Stock
An Imprint of Wipf and Stock Publishers
199 W. 8th Ave., Suite 3
Eugene, OR 97401

www.wipfandstock.com

PAPERBACK ISBN: 978-1-5326-1751-5
HARDCOVER ISBN: 978-1-4982-4223-3
EBOOK ISBN: 978-1-4982-4222-6

Manufactured in the U.S.A.   FEBRUARY 23, 2017

Dedicated to
Vernon Meyer,
pastor, teacher, friend

"We must remember . . . that the metaphors of one historically conditioned period, and the symbols they innervate, may not speak to the persons who are living long after that historical moment and whose consciousness has been formed through altogether different experiences."

—Joseph Campbell

"The master always frowned on anything that seemed sensational. 'The divine,' he claimed, 'is only found in the ordinary.'"

—Anthony De Mello

"The earth is once and for all encircled by spirit."

—Pierre Teilhard de Chardin

"The world is charged with the grandeur of God,
It will flame out, like shining from shook foil."

—Gerard Manley Hopkins

Contents

Abbreviations | ix
Notes on the Bible | xi
Introduction | xiii

1	Mountain	1
2	Sacred Numbers	10
3	God's Voice	26
4	People's (Person's) Response	30
5	Cloud	34
6	Water	42
7	Thunder	49
8	Lightning	52
9	Trumpet Blast	55
10	Smoke	60
11	Fire	64
12	Earthquake	74
13	Terms of the Event (Covenant)	77
14	Sign	83
15	Transformation	89
16	Altar	96
17	Feast (Meal)	102
18	Wind	107
19	Light and Darkness	113
20	Jewels (Precious Stones)	121

21	Dream	124
22	Hermeneutic	129

Bibliography | *155*
Index of Major Biblical Theophanies | *161*
Other Books by Mark G. Boyer | *166*

Abbreviations

CB (NT) = CHRISTIAN BIBLE (NEW TESTAMENT)

Acts = Acts of the Apostles

1 Cor = First Letter of Paul to the Corinthians

2 Cor = Second Letter of Paul to the Corinthians

Gal = Letter of Paul to the Galatians

Heb = Letter to the Hebrews

Jas = Letter of James

John = John's Gospel

1 John = First Letter of John

Luke = Luke's Gospel

Mark = Mark's Gospel

Matt = Matthew's Gospel

1 Pet = First Letter of Peter

2 Pet = Second Letter of Peter

Rev = Revelation

Rom = Letter of Paul to the Romans

1 Thess = First Letter of Paul to the Thessalonians

2 Thess = Second Letter of Paul to the Thessalonians

HB (OT) = HEBREW BIBLE (OLD TESTAMENT)

Amos = Amos

1 Chr = First Book of Chronicles

2 Chr = Second Book of Chronicles

Dan = Daniel

Abbreviations

Deut = Deuteronomy
Eccl = Ecclesiastes
Exod = Exodus
Ezek = Ezekiel
Ezra = Ezra
Gen = Genesis
Hab = Habakkuk
Hos = Hosea
Isa = Isaiah
Jer = Jeremiah
Job = Job
Joel = Joel
Josh = Joshua
Judg = Judges
1 Kgs = First Book of Kings
2 Kgs = Second Book of Kings
Lam = Lamentations
Lev = Leviticus
Mal = Malachi
Mic = Micah
Nah = Nahum
Neh = Nehemiah
Num = Numbers
Obad = Obadiah
Prov = Proverbs
Ps = Psalm
Pss = Psalms
1 Sam = First Book of Samuel
2 Sam = Second Book of Samuel
Song = Song of Songs (Canticle of Solomon)
Zech = Zechariah
Zeph = Zephaniah

OT (A) = OLD TESTAMENT (APOCRYPHA)

Jdt = Judith
1 Macc = First Book of Maccabees
2 Macc = Second Book of Maccabees
Sir = Sirach (Ecclesiasticus)
Sg Three = Song of the Three Jews (Daniel)
Tob = Book of Tobit
Wis = Wisdom (of Solomon)

Notes on the Bible

THE BIBLE IS DIVIDED into two parts: The Hebrew Bible (Old Testament) and the Christian Bible (New Testament). The Hebrew Bible consists of thirty-nine named books accepted by Jews and Protestants as Holy Scripture. The Old Testament also contains those thirty-nine books plus seven to fifteen more named books or parts of books called the Apocrypha or the Deuterocanonical Books; the Old Testament is accepted by Catholics and several other Christian denominations as Holy Scripture. The Christian Bible, consisting of twenty-seven named books, is also called the New Testament; it is accepted by Christians as Holy Scripture. Thus, in this work:

—Hebrew Bible (Old Testament), abbreviated HB (OT), indicates that a book is found both in the Hebrew Bible and the Old Testament;

—Old Testament (Apocrypha), abbreviated OT (A), indicates that a book is found only in the Old Testament Apocrypha and not in the Hebrew Bible;

—and Christian Bible (New Testament), abbreviated CB (NT), indicates that a book is found only in the Christian Bible or New Testament.

In notating biblical texts, the first number refers to the chapter in the book, and the second number refers to the verse within the chapter. Thus, HB (OT) Isa 7:11 means that the quotation comes from Isaiah, chapter 7, verse 11. OT (A) Sirach 39:30 means that the quotation comes from Sirach, chapter 39, verse 30. CB (NT) Mark 6:2 means that the quotation comes from Mark's Gospel, chapter 6, verse 2.

Notes on the Bible

In the HB (OT) and the OT (A), the reader often sees LORD (note all capital letters). Because God's name (Yahweh or YHWH, referred to as the Tetragrammaton) is not to be pronounced, the name Adonai (meaning *Lord*) is substituted for Yahweh when a biblical text is read. When a biblical text is translated and printed, LORD (cf. Gen 2:4) is used to alert the reader to what the text actually states: Yahweh. Because some scholars referenced in this book use Yahweh or YHWH, the author has maintained their usage but presented LORD in parentheses after the divine name. Furthermore, when the biblical author writes Lord Yahweh, printers present Lord GOD (note all capital letters for GOD; cf. Gen 15:2) to avoid the printed ambiguity of LORD LORD. When the reference is to Jesus, the word printed is Lord (note capital L and lower case letters; cf. Luke 11:1). When writing about a lord (note all lower case letters; Matt 18:25) with servants, no capital L is used.

Introduction

THE GLORY OF THE LORD

"The glory of the LORD" is a phrase used over one hundred times in the Bible. It is, according to Ryken, "an image of his greatness and transcendence."[1] The Hebrew word for glory, *kabod*, "signifies weight or heaviness."[2] As McKenzie makes clear, the phrase "is a complex theological concept which exhibits several aspects"[3] or elements which will be explored below. Furthermore, the glory of the LORD "is an image of divine transcendence as it makes itself visible to people."[4] Naturally occurring phenomena are employed by biblical authors to portray the glory of the LORD. Natural phenomena collectively, and sometimes individually, are said to be a theophany, a representation of God's presence, a personification of God in the forces of nature, a visible manifestation of the invisible God.

THEOPHANY

Thus, a theophany can be defined as the appearance of a god in a visible form to a human being. It is the physical manifestation of the divine presence; some self-revelation occurs on the part of God. A theophany

1. Ryken, *Dictionary*, 330.
2. McKenzie, *Dictionary*, 313.
3. Ibid.
4. Ryken, *Dictionary*, 330.

Introduction

is usually, but not always, presented in biblical literature as a scene that portrays a manifestation of a divine being in the natural order. Using the word *epiphany*—meaning the manifestation of a divine being, that is, a manifestation or appearance; in particular, the appearance of God or a divine being—Bergmann states, "Nature serves as a source and place of epiphany...."[5] He explains: "God has made himself at home on earth."[6] McKenzie says that the "one natural phenomenon with which Yahweh [the LORD] is most frequently associated is the storm."[7] He explains:

> The theophany is an Israelite confession of the power of Yahweh [the LORD] in nature; but this power is not seen as blind, irrational force. Most frequently Yahweh [the LORD] appears in the theophany as the savior of his people from their enemies.... [T]he power of Yahweh [the LORD] in nature is also manifested as a power of judgment, an act of his moral will that affects all evildoers, whether they be Israelites or others. [And] [t]he supreme manifestation of the power of Yahweh [the LORD] in nature is eschatological. Nature as the instrument of judgment finds expression in the expectation of the Day of Yahweh [the LORD], i.e., the cataclysmic encounter of Yahweh [the LORD] with the powers of evil. The annihilating judgment of Yahweh [the LORD] will reduce the earth to the primitive chaos that it was before the creative action.[8]

Matthews states that the glory of the LORD "serves as both a sign and a means of generating power which can awe and destroy the beholder."[9] Thus, according to Bergmann, "... [T]he earth and the life of its inhabitants are interpreted [in the Bible] as divine gift that humans can never reproduce or control, but only humbly adapt."[10]

Savran understands the word *theophany* to imply "the presence of a visual component in addition to verbal interaction."[11] Robinson states that he sees little difference "between saying that someone sees God and saying that God appears to, or is seen by, someone."[12] Furthermore, as Robinson

---

5. Bergmann, *Religion*, 283.
6. Ibid., 416.
7. McKenzie, "Aspects," 1294.
8. Ibid.
9. Matthews, "Theophanies," 308.
10. Bergmann, *Religion*, 283.
11. Savran, "Theophany," 120.
12. Robinson, "Theophany and Meal," 158.

notes, "Talk of seeing God is a bold usage but it needs no emending nor explaining away, despite the existence of texts which express the view that it is impossible, or nigh impossible, to see God without dying."[13] The various "theophany narratives reveal to the reader something of the shock and surprise of the encounter with the divine," states Savran. "In these texts, the individual is jolted sharply out of his normal existence in the face of something that he at first does not fully grasp but that ultimately induces a sense of self-awareness (and awareness of the Other) that is nothing short of transformative."[14]

MODEL OF THEOPHANY

Of all the biblical accounts that illustrate the glory of the LORD, the narrative of Moses' encounter with God on Mount Sinai (Horeb) contains nineteen of the twenty-one elements that reveal the glory of the LORD. McKenzie states, "In the theophany of Sinai [Horeb], Yahweh [the LORD] comes as the deliverer who makes a covenant with Israel; his power in nature is a warrant of his power and will to save Israel."[15] Thus, the theophany on Mount Sinai (Horeb) will serve as a model for uncovering the meaning of the phrase "the glory of the LORD" and the elements that comprise it. There are other biblical, theophanic manifestations which contain some of the same elements as Moses' Sinai (Horeb) experience, and they will be presented in each of the following chapters to support the list of common elements of a theophany. Biblical theophanies will be examined in light of the common elements. Miller states that "all the theophany narratives in the second half of Exodus are related to the initial theophany of chapter 19 and to God's covenant choice of the Israelites as 'a royal priesthood and a holy nation' (19:6)."[16] All the elements of a theophany listed below are not present in all theophanies. However, a model of a theophany that reveals the glory of the LORD in its fullness is needed, and Moses' experience on Mount Sinai (Horeb) has been chosen to serve this purpose.

Some biblical scholars used to think that the Mount Sinai (Horeb) experience of Moses was modeled on a description of a volcanic eruption.

---

13. Ibid.
14. Savran, "Theophany," 119.
15. McKenzie, "Aspects," 1294.
16. Miller, "Seeing the Glory," 507.

Introduction

Clifford states that "the theophany is not [a] volcano."[17] Likewise, Gray states that the "description of the theophany strongly suggests a volcano in eruption" but it "is evidently a thunderstorm."[18]

Theophany is a broad category involving many literary forms. Not only do biblical scholars discuss these literary forms elsewhere, but they also discuss sources or strands of biblical narrative. Here, the perspective is from that of a completed, written, biblical narrative, no matter its literary form or sources. In other words, this examination is from the perspective of the finished, written, and handed on text. The final composition describing a theophany probably developed through repeated oral storytelling until it was written. Various written versions of the same theophanic narrative were ultimately redacted to form the canonical version of today. Even written versions of theophanies undergo development through reflection by other biblical authors. The interest here is not the source or sources of biblical theophanies; the interest here is exposing the elements common to biblical theophanic narratives. Thus, this author readily acknowledges that there are inconsistencies in biblical accounts. For example, in the model of Moses on Mount Sinai (Horeb) employed below, Moses often ascends the mountain and may never descend before ascending again! There is no doubt that various written—and before that oral—sources have been combined into a single narrative. The task here is to identify and describe the elements of a theophany that occur in all sources.

Savran notes that "theophany narratives exhibit a set number of recurrent motifs around which the story is based."[19] The motif of setting the scene for a theophany, although it is not considered to be an element of them, is important to note. "In theophany stories," Savran writes, "the primary function of such a *mise-en-scene* is to separate the protagonist from family or others in preparation for what, in nearly every case, is a solitary experience."[20] The first function of setting the scene is so that the recipient of the experience can "separate himself from his everyday reality as a precondition for the encounter."[21] While Savran underscores the point that the Moses-on-Mount-Sinai (Horeb) narrative is an exception to this rule, he explains that the second significant function of the setting of the scene

---

17. Clifford, "Exodus," 52.
18. Gray, "Exodus," 53.
19. Savran, "Theophany," 125.
20. Ibid., 126.
21. Ibid., 127.

INTRODUCTION

"is the determining of location,"[22] which may be a mountain, a sanctuary, a well, a tree, etc. Savran states that "the setting of the scene is not simply a formal requirement of the narrative structure, but is essential to the purpose and experience of the theophany that follows."[23]

ELEMENTS OF THEOPHANIES

Twenty-one elements are found in biblical theophanies: mountains, sacred numbers, God's voice, people's (person's) response, cloud, water, thunder, lightning, trumpet blast, smoke, fire, earthquake, terms of the event, sign, transformation of witnesses, altar, feast, wind, light and darkness, jewels (precious stones), and dreams. Each of these or some of them grouped together reveal the glory of the LORD. In the following chapters, each element is examined more closely using biblical texts that best illustrate the element, keeping in mind that the narrative concerning Moses on Mount Sinai (Horeb) serves as a model for other theophanic experiences that reveal the glory of the LORD. Where necessary, specific subsections will explain what elements have been gathered by a biblical author to narrate a theophany.

As a guide and a point of reference for the reader, the narrative of Moses on Mount Sinai (Horeb) is presented below with the element identified with the chapter number and title in parenthesis indicating where the particular element is examined. It would be helpful to read the entire narrative before beginning the individual parts of it: Exodus 19:1–5a, 7–11, 13b–15a, 16–20; 20:1–4, 7–10, 12–18, 21; 24:1, 3–11, 15–18; a reading guide follows the biblical text below which has the biblical notation and chapter number and chapter title for ease of reference. All biblical quotations and references are from the New Revised Standard Version of the Bible.

MOSES ON MOUNT SINAI (HOREB)

> On the third (**2 Sacred Numbers**) new moon after the Israelites had gone out of the land of Egypt, on that very day, they came into the wilderness of Sinai. They had journeyed from Rephidim, entered the wilderness of Sinai, and camped in the wilderness; Israel

22. Ibid.
23. Ibid., 128.

camped there in front of the mountain (**1 Mountain**). Then Moses went up to God; the LORD called to him from the mountain, saying, "Thus you shall say to the house of Jacob, and tell the Israelites: You have seen what I did to the Egyptians, and how I bore you on eagles' wings and brought you to myself. Now therefore, if you obey my voice and keep my covenant, you shall be my treasured possession out of all the peoples . . ." (**15 Transformation, 3 God's Voice**).

So Moses came, summoned the elders of the people, and set before them all these words that the LORD had commanded him. The people all answered as one: "Everything that the LORD has spoken we will do" (**4 People's [Person's] Response**). Moses reported the words of the people to the LORD. Then the LORD said to Moses, "I am going to come to you in a dense cloud, in order that the people may hear when I speak with you and so trust you ever after" (**3 God's Voice, 5 Cloud**).

When Moses had told the words of the people to the LORD, the LORD said to Moses: "Go to the people and consecrate them today and tomorrow (**3 God's Voice**). Have them wash their clothes (**6 Water**) and prepare for the third day (**2 Sacred Numbers**), because on the third day (**2 Sacred Numbers**) the LORD will come down upon Mount Sinai (**1 Mountain**) in the sight of all the people. When the trumpet sounds a long blast (**9 Trumpet Blast**), they may go up on the mountain." So Moses went down from the mountain to the people. He consecrated the people, and they washed their clothes (**6 Water**). And he said to the people, "Prepare for the third day . . ." (**2 Sacred Numbers**).

On the morning of the third day (**2 Sacred Numbers**) there was thunder (**7 Thunder**) and lightning (**8 Lightning**), as well as a thick cloud (**5 Cloud**) on the mountain (**1 Mountain**), and a blast of a trumpet so loud that all the people who were in the camp trembled (**9 Trumpet Blast**). Moses brought the people out of the camp to meet God. They took their stand at the foot of the mountain (**1 Mountain**). Now Mount Sinai was wrapped in smoke (**10 Smoke**), because the LORD had descended upon it in fire (**11 Fire**); the smoke went up like the smoke of a kiln (**10 Smoke**), while the whole mountain shook violently (**12 Earthquake**). As the blast of the trumpet grew louder and louder (**9 Trumpet Blast**), Moses would speak and God would answer him in thunder (**7 Thunder**). When the LORD descended upon Mount Sinai, to the top of the mountain, the LORD summoned Moses to the top of the mountain, and Moses went up (**1 Mountain**).

Introduction

Then God spoke all these words (**3 God's Voice**): I am the LORD you God, who brought you out of the land of Egypt, out of the house of slavery; you shall have no other gods before me (**13 Terms of the Event [Covenant]**). You shall not make for yourself an idol, whether in the form of anything that is in heaven above, or that is on the earth beneath, or that is in the water under the earth. You shall not make wrongful use of the name of the LORD your God, for the LORD will not acquit anyone who misuses his name (**13 Terms of the Event [Covenant]**).

Remember the sabbath day, and keep it holy. Six days you shall labor and do all your work. But the seventh day is sabbath to the LORD your God' you shall not do any work—you, your son or your daughter, your male or female slave, your livestock, or the alien resident in your towns (**13 Terms of the Event [Covenant]**).

Honor your father and your mother, so that your days may be long in the land that the LORD your God is giving you. You shall not murder. You shall not commit adultery. You shall not steal. You shall not bear false witness against your neighbor. You shall not covet your neighbor's house; you shall not covet your neighbor's wife, or male or female slave, or ox, or donkey, or anything that belongs to your neighbor (**13 Terms of the Event [Covenant]**).

When all the people witnessed the thunder (**7 Thunder**) and lightning (**8 Lightning**), the sound of the trumpet (**9 Trumpet Blast**), and the mountain smoking (**10 Smoke**), they were afraid and trembled and stood at a distance (**4 People's [Person's] Response**) . . . while Moses drew near to the thick darkness where God was (**19 Light and Darkness**).

Then [the LORD] said to Moses (**3 God's Voice**), "Come up to the LORD, you and Aaron, Nadab, and Abihu, and seventy (**2 Sacred Numbers**) of the elders of Israel, and worship at a distance." Moses came and told the people all the words of the LORD and all the ordinances; and all the people answered with one voice and said, "All the words that the LORD has spoken we will do" (**4 People's [Person's] Response, 15 Transformation**). And Moses wrote down all the words of the LORD (**14 Sign**). He rose early in the morning, and built an altar (**16 Altar**) at the foot of the mountain (**1 Mountain**), and set up twelve pillars (**2 Sacred Numbers**), corresponding to the twelve tribes of Israel. He sent young men of the people of Israel, who offered burnt offerings and sacrificed oxen as offerings of well-being to the LORD. Moses took half of the blood and put in it basins (**14 Sign**), and half of the blood he dashed against the altar (**14 Sign, 16 Altar**). Then he took the books of covenant (**13 Terms of the Event [Covenant]**), and read

Introduction

it in the hearing of the people; and they said, "All that the LORD has spoken we will do, and we will be obedient" (**4 People's [Person's] Response, 15 Transformation**). Moses took the blood and dashed it on the people (**14 Sign**), and said, "See the blood of the covenant that the LORD has made with you in accordance with all these words" (**15 Transformation**).

Then Moses and Aaron, Nadab, and Abihu, and seventy (**2 Sacred Numbers**) of the elders of Israel went up, and they saw the God of Israel. Under his feet there was something like a pavement of sapphire stone (**20 Jewels [Precious Stones]**), like the very heaven for clearness. God did not lay his hand on the chief men of the people of Israel; also they beheld God, and they ate and drank (**17 Feast [Meal]**).

Then Moses went up on the mountain (**1 Mountain**), and the cloud (**5 Cloud**) covered the mountain (**1 Mountain**). The glory of the LORD settled on Mount Sinai, and the cloud (**5 Cloud**) covered it for six days (**2 Sacred Numbers**); on the seventh day (**2 Sacred Numbers**) he called to Moses out of the cloud (**5 Cloud**). Now the appearance of the glory of the LORD was like a devouring fire (**11 Fire**) on the top of the mountain (**1 Mountain**) in the sight of the people of Israel. Moses entered the cloud (**5 Cloud**), and went up on the mountain (**1 Mountain**). Moses was on the mountain for forty days and forty nights (**1 Mountain, 2 Sacred Numbers**). (Exodus 19:1–5a, 7–11, 13b—15a, 16–20; 20:1–4, 7–10, 12–18, 21; 24:1, 3–11, 15–18)

READING GUIDE WITH CHAPTER NUMBER AND TITLE REFERENCES

Exod 19:1 = 2 Sacred Numbers

Exod 19:2–3 = 1 Mountain

Exod 19:3–6 = 3 God's Voice

Exod 19:4–6 = 15 Transformation

Exod 19:5–6 = 13 Terms of the Event (Covenant)

Exod 19:8 = 4 People's (Person's) Response

Exod 19:9a = 3 God's Voice; 5 Cloud

Exod 19:10 = 3 God's Voice; 6 Water

Exod 19:11 = 2 Sacred Numbers; 1 Mountain

Exod 19:13 = 9 Trumpet Blast; 1 Mountain

Exod 19:14 = 6 Water

INTRODUCTION

Exod 19:15 = 2 Sacred Numbers

Exod 19:16 = 2 Sacred Numbers; 7 Thunder; 8 Lightning; 5 Cloud; 1 Mountain; 9 Trumpet Blast

Exod 19:18 = 1 Mountain; 10 Smoke; 11 Fire; 12 Earthquake

Exod 19:19 = 9 Trumpet Blast; 7 Thunder

Exod 19:20 = 1 Mountain

Exod 20:1 = 3 God's Voice

Exod 20:2–17 = 13 Terms of the Event (Covenant)

Exod 20:18 = 7 Thunder; 8 Lightning; 9 Trumpet Blast; 10 Smoke; 4 People's (Person's) Response; 15 Transformation

Exod 20:21 = 19 Light and Darkness

Exod 24:1 = 3 God's Voice

Exod 24:3 = 4 People's (Person's) Response; 15 Transformation

Exod 24:4 = 14 Sign; 16 Altar; 2 Sacred Numbers

Exod 24:6 = 14 Sign; 16 Altar

Exod 24:7 = Terms of the Event (Covenant); 4 People's (Person's) Response; 15 Transformation

Exod 24:8 = 14 Sign; 13 Terms of the Event (Covenant); 15 Transformation

Exod 24:10 = 20 Jewels (Precious Stones)

Exod 24:11 = 17 Feast (Meal)

Exod 24:15 = 1 Mountain; 5 Cloud

Exod 24:16 = 1 Mountain; 5 Cloud; 2 Sacred Numbers

Exod 24:17 = 11 Fire

Exod 24:18 = 5 Cloud; 1 Mountain; 2 Sacred Numbers

INDEX

At the end of this book, the reader will find an extensive index. It contains the major theophanies covered in this book in their biblical book order with a list of the chapters in which the reader can find more information about the specific theophany. A third element in the index presents where the theophanies appear in the Roman Catholic Lectionary on Sundays throughout the three year cycle of Scripture texts. And it contains the notations of where the theophanies appear in the Common Lectionary's Sunday three-year cycle of biblical texts. These latter two items are included here for the convenience of those who use a lectionary in worship, such as

Introduction

Catholics, Anglicans, Episcopalians, Disciples of Christ, Lutherans, Presbyterians, and Methodists, to name but a few.

It is the author's hope that this book not only functions academically to help the reader understand the elements of theophanies, but that it also aid the preacher's preparation of sermons or homilies on them. Furthermore, this author hopes to open the hermeneutic door to foster the presentation of ancient images that display the glory of the LORD and the glory of the Lord (Jesus) to modern readers and hearers in new and exciting ways.

A word of thanks is due to Victor H. Matthews, Dean of the College of Humanities and Public Affairs at Missouri State University, Springfield, for his help in locating some of the resources used in this book. His knowledge and expertise assisted in the development of this work, and his insightful discussions helped guide the author in organizing the material in this book.

Mark G. Boyer
Memorial of St. Jerome
September 30, 2016

1

Mountain

MANY THEOPHANIES TAKE PLACE on a mountain, an elevated terrain. This makes a mountain, in particular a named mountain, an element of a theophanic experience. According to Harrington, "Mountains are the usual settings for supernatural revelations and theophanies."[1] Viviano states that a mountain is "symbolic of revelation."[2] There are several mountains in biblical literature that get more attention than others. For example, there is Mount Horeb, "the mountain of God" (Exod 3:1), where Moses encounters the LORD in a burning bush, and later is described as the place where God stands before giving his people water to drink (Exod 17:6). Mount Horeb is also known as Mount Sinai. Thus, the narrative of Moses on Mount Sinai after leading the Israelites out of Egypt is filled with references to the mountain place (Exod 19:11, 18, 20, 23; 24:16; 31:19; 34:2, 4, 29, 32). Of the thirty-eight times Mount Sinai is mentioned in biblical literature, ten of those occur in the Book of Exodus; four in the Book of Leviticus (7:38, 25:1, 26:46, 27:34); twelve in the Book of Numbers (1:1, 19; 3:1, 4, 14; 9:1, 5; 10:12; 26:64; 28:6; 33:15, 16); two each in the books of Deuteronomy (33:2, 16), Psalms (68:8, 17), Acts (7:30, 38), and Galatians (4:24, 25); and one each in the books of Judges (5:5), Nehemiah (9:13), Judith 5:14), and Sirach (48:7).

Bergmann notes that "the Old Testament uses place as an important category in the three-way relationship of God, people, and place. . . ."[3] He

---

1. Harrington, "Mark," 615.
2. Viviano, "Matthew," 660.
3. Bergmann, *Religion*, 374.

explains, "... [T]he mystery of God takes place in specific localities...."[4] He says that Abrahamic religions view "the world as creation, a space in which the Creator acts in liberating synergy with the creatures...."[5] While Bergmann doesn't call this theophany, he means the same thing by his word *inhabitation*. "Inhabitation," he writes, "is an ongoing and dynamic process in which God comes into and goes beyond the world and transforms it from within."[6] In other words, "the Creator, in an act of salvation, draws the creation toward its fulfillment, toward new heavens and a new earth."[7]

Mount Sinai, "territory sacred to Yahweh [the LORD],"[8] is the place where thunder, lightning, and thick cloud appear (Exod 19:16) along with smoke, fire, earthquake (Exod 19:18), and thunder (Exod 19:19)—all other elements of a theophany. Without God's presence, the mountain is a place of wildness, distance, and alienation; however, once these other elements of a theophany are present, the mountain becomes a place for religious experience indicating permanence and solidity. Clifford states: "The entire mountain becomes sacred by the coming of Yahweh [the LORD]; anyone who strays into it becomes charged with holiness. Such a dangerous person must be removed lest his contagion infect others."[9] Ryken states that a mountain's "inaccessibility makes [it] unknown and gives [it] an aura of mystery. [Its] visible immensity makes [it] the benchmark for enormity."[10]

In contrast to Mount Sinai, Mount Horeb is mentioned only eighteen times. After noting that Horeb is the mountain where Moses first encounters God (Exod 3:1), the author of the Book of Exodus does not refer to it again until 17:6, and after that not again until 33:6. The Book of Deuteronomy mentions it nine times (Deut 1:2, 6, 19; 4:10, 15; 5:2; 9:8; 18:16; 29:1), while the First Book of Kings refers to it two times (1 Kgs 8:9; 19:8), and it is mentioned one time each in the Second Book of Chronicles (5:10), Psalms (106:19), Sirach (48:7), and Malachi (4:4). In this work, when Mount Horeb is a point of reference, it will be noted as Mount Horeb (Sinai) to indicate that it is the same mountain with two different names. Likewise, when Mount Sinai is referenced, it will be indicated as Mount Sinai (Horeb) to

---

4. Ibid., 377.
5. Ibid., 5.
6. Ibid., 41, 417.
7. Ibid., 43.
8. Clifford, "Exodus," 52.
9. Ibid.
10. Ryken, *Dictionary*, 573.

indicate the same. No matter what name is used for the mountain, Psalm 114 captures the joy of the exodus in poetry: "When Israel went out from Egypt, . . . [t]he mountains skipped like rams, the hills like lambs . . . at the presence of the LORD" (Ps 114:1a, 4, 7a).

The prophet Elijah, modeled after Moses, experiences theophanies on two different mountains. The first is Mount Carmel, which means *vineyard of El* (El is the Canaanite word for *God*) to which Elijah invites the prophets of Baal to a duel (1 Kgs 18:19). Once they assemble there (1 Kgs 18:20), Elijah proposes that both they and he offer a sacrifice to their gods (1 Kgs 18:23-24). The god who consumes the sacrifice with fire will demonstrate who the real God is in Israel. The elements of a theophany are altar (1 Kgs 18:30, 32); the sacred numbers twelve (1 Kgs 18:31), four (1 Kgs 18:33b), and three (1 Kgs 18:33b-34); water (1 Kgs 18:33b); and fire (1 Kgs 18:38) (see Altar, Sacred Numbers, Water, and Fire). Mount Carmel is also mentioned three times in two other biblical books: the Second Book of Kings (2:25) and as the residence of Elisha, Elijah's successor (2 Kgs 4:25), and the Song of Songs (7:5).

The second mountain with which Elijah is associated and makes him look even more like Moses is Mount Horeb (Sinai). After killing the prophets of Baal on Mount Carmel, the prophet flees to Mount Horeb (Sinai); it takes him the sacred number of forty days to get there, just like it took Moses forty years of wandering in the desert to get the Israelites to the promised land (1 Kgs 19:8). The LORD, who speaks to Elijah four times (1 Kgs 19:9b, 11, 13b, 15-19) to indicate the importance of his mission for those who live on the earth, stands on the mountain, and he passes by (1 Kgs 19:11a). The narrator states:

> Now there was a great wind, so strong that it was splitting mountains and breaking rocks in pieces before the LORD, but the LORD was not in the wind; and after the wind an earthquake, but the LORD was not in the earthquake; and after the earthquake a fire, but the LORD was not in the fire; and after the fire a sound of sheer silence. When Elijah heard it, he wrapped his face in his mantle and went out and stood at the entrance of the cave. (1 Kgs 19:11b-13a)

The usual elements of a theophany (see Wind, Earthquake, and Fire) are not the harbingers of the Divine Presence this time on Mount Horeb (Sinai). For the only time in biblical literature, it is sheer silence that serves as the indicator of the LORD's presence. Walsh says that "[t]he whole scene, including Elijah's veiling his face, recalls the theophany promised to Moses."[11] Psalm 50, however, takes the opposite position, describing a theophany as God coming and not keeping silence (Ps 50:3).

The most-mentioned mountain in biblical literature is Mount Zion, upon which was built the temple, and around which was enclosed Jerusalem. Clifford says, "Mount Zion in Jerusalem later became the heir of the Sinai [Horeb] traditions."[12] The one-hundred eighty references to Mount Zion in biblical literature begin with the narrative of how King David captured the Jebusite fortress of Zion (2 Sam 5:7; 1 Chr 11:5) and made Jerusalem his capital city. Psalm 48 declares that Mount Zion is beautiful in elevation (Ps 48:2). After Solomon, David's son and successor to his throne, builds the temple, the ark of the covenant of the LORD is transferred from the tent David had built for it to the Holy of Holies in the temple (1 Kgs 8:1; 2 Chr 5:2). When Solomon finished placing the ark in the Holy of Holies, a theophany occurred (see Cloud). This indicated that the LORD had taken residence in Zion (Pss 9:11; 74:2; 76:2; 78:68), that out of Zion, "the perfection of beauty, God shines forth" (Ps 50:2), that "the God of gods will be seen in Zion" (Ps 84:7), that "the LORD is great in Zion; he is exalted over all the peoples" (Ps 99:2), that "the LORD will build up Zion; he will appear in his glory" (Ps 102:16), and that the "LORD has chosen Zion; he has desired it for his habitation" (Ps 132:13). Toombs comments on Psalm 50, writing: "The theophany of the LORD from the temple is accompanied by light and storm."[13] Toombs says that Psalm 76 is "a hymn of Zion" that "celebrates the theophany of God in his temple . . . , his point of contact with the world."[14] This makes Zion "more majestic than the everlasting mountains" (Ps 76:4). Psalms 125 and 146 say it best: "Those who trust in the LORD are like Mount Zion, which cannot be moved, but abides forever" (Ps 125:1). "The LORD will reign forever, your God, O Zion, for all generations" (Ps 146:10).

In time of turmoil and war, the prophet Isaiah speaks words of hope about and to Zion. He envisions many people coming and saying: "'Come, let us go up to the mountain of the LORD, to the house of the God of Jacob; that he may teach us his ways and that we may walk in his paths.' For out of Zion shall go forth instruction, and the word of the LORD from Jerusalem"

---

11. Walsh, "1–2 Kings," 172.
12. Clifford, "Exodus," 52.
13. Toombs, "Psalms," 277.
14. Ibid. 283.

(Isa 2:3; cf. Mic 4:2). Later, he explains that there will be a theophany on Mount Zion: "[T]he LORD will create over the whole site of Mount Zion and over its places of assembly a cloud by day and smoke and the shining of a flaming fire by night. Indeed over all the glory there will be a canopy" (Isa 4:5). For those who had any doubt of the Divine Presence residing in Zion, Isaiah says, "Shout aloud and sing for joy, O royal Zion, for great in your midst is the Holy One of Israel" (Isa 12:6; cf 52:8; 59:20; 62:11). Isaiah can express such hope because he believes that the LORD founded Zion (Isa 14:32; 28:16); it is the place of the name of the LORD of hosts (Isa 18:7; 24:23); from Zion good tidings flow forth (Isa 40:9; 41:27; 52:7).

There are many references to Mount Zion in the prophet Jeremiah and the minor prophets; most of these are references to restoring Jerusalem and the temple after the Babylonians destroy both in 587 BCE. In the CB (NT), there are only seven references to Mount Zion. The author of Matthew's Gospel, quoting inaccurately from the prophet Zechariah, understands Jesus' entry into Jerusalem as fulfillment of Zechariah's words. By so doing, he indicates that a theophany is taking place (Matt 21:5; Zech 9:9). The author of John's Gospel does the same (John 21:15). The author of the Letter to the Hebrews, tells his readers that they have not come to Mount Sinai (Horeb), "a blazing fire, and darkness, and gloom, and a tempest, and the sound of a trumpet, and a voice whose words made the hearers beg that not another word be spoken to them" (Heb 12:18–19). They have come

> to Mount Zion and to the city of the living God, the heavenly Jerusalem, and to innumerable angels in festival gathering, and to the assembly of the firstborn who are enrolled in heaven, and to God the judge of all, and to the spirits of the righteous made perfect, and to Jesus, the mediator of a new covenant, and to the sprinkled blood that speaks a better word than the blood of Abel. (Heb 12:22–24)

The Book of Revelation presents a similar theophany with the Lamb (Jesus) standing on Mount Zion with those who bear his name and his Father's name (Rev 14:1).

With about five hundred references to mountains in biblical literature, it is not hard to see how they become "the standard of ancient existence against which God's everlasting existence is measured."[15] In fact, Psalm 90 makes this point very clear. "Before the mountains were brought forth, or ever you [, Lord,] had formed the earth and the world, from everlasting to

---

15. Ryken, *Dictionary*, 573.

everlasting you are God" (Ps 90:2). Once God chooses a mountain upon which to manifest himself, the mountain's chaos is tamed; it moves from barrenness to fruitfulness and from isolation to community gathering place. In a three-storied world, a mountain, located on the middle story, is as close as one can get to God, who lives above the dome of the sky on the top story. Because mountains are so close to the glory of the LORD, they melt like wax before him (Ps 97:5; Mic 1:4; Jdt 16:15); in other words, God's fiery appearance melts the mountains.[16]

Other named biblical mountains are Hermon (Deut 3:8), known for its snow-capped summit, its waterfalls (Ps 42:7), and its dew (Ps 133:3). Psalm 89 states that Hermon's mere existence praises the LORD's name (Ps 89:12b). Mount Hermon is mentioned in the Book of Joshua six times (Josh 11:3, 17; 12:1, 5; 13:5, 11). It also appears in the First Book of Chronicles (5:23), in the Song of Songs (4:8), and in the OT (A) Book of Sirach (24:13). It is also mentioned using one of its others names—Sirion—in Psalm 29 in which it skips like a young wild ox (Ps 29:5; cf. Deut 4:48). Deuteronomy mentions that it is called Senir (Deut 3:9), and that name appears in three other biblical books (1 Chr 5:23; Song 4:8; Ezek 27:5).

Aaron, Moses' brother, dies on the sacred mountain named Hor (Num 20:22, 28; 33:38; Deut 32:50). Moses dies on Mount Nebo (Deut 32:48, 49; 34:1). Both Aaron and Moses die on mountains to indicate their closeness to God. Other named mountains include Ararat (Gen 8:4), Baalah (Josh 15:11), Baal-hermon (Josh 11:17; 13:5; Judg 3:3; 1 Chr 5:23), Bashan (Ps 68:15–16), Destruction (2 Kgs 23:13), Ephraim (Jer 4:15), Ephron (Josh 15:9), Eval (Deut 27:4, 13; Josh 8:30, 33),Gassh (Josh 24:30; Judg 2:9), Gerizim (Deut 11:29; 27:12; Josh 8:33; 9:7), Gilboa (1 Sam 31:1, 8; 2 Sam 1:6; 1 Chr 10:1, 8), Gilead (Gen 31:23; Judg 7:3; Song 4:1), Halak (Josh 11:17; 12:7), Jearim (Josh 15:10), Mizar (Ps 42:6), Moriah (2 Chr 3:1; Gen 22:2), Paran (Deut 33:2; Hab 3:3), Perazim (Isa 28:21), Seir (Deut 1:2, 2:1, 5, 33:2; Josh 11:17, 12:7, 15:10; 1 Chr 4:42; 2 Chr 20:10, 20, 22, 23; Ezek 35:2, 3, 7, 15), Shepher (Num 33:23, 24), Tabor (Judg 4:6, 12, 14; Jer 46:18), Zalmon (Judg 9:48), and Zemaraim (2 Chr 13:4).

In the CB (NT), the major mountain mentioned is that of the Mount of Olives. McKenzie notes the "[t]he name indicates the number of olive trees which grew on its slopes in ancient times."[17] Murphey adds, "The villages of Bethany and Bethpage flanked its slopes with Gethsemane at the

---

16. Ortlund, "Intertextual Reading," 278.
17. McKenzie, *Dictionary*, 626.

foot of the hill."[18] The word *Gethsemane* means *oil press*, and refers to the place where olives were pressed for their oil. The Mount of Olives is first mentioned in the Second Book of Samuel when King David is fleeing from his son, Absalom. David went up the ascent of the Mount of Olives, weeping as went, with his head covered and walking barefoot (2 Sam 15:30). The prophet Zechariah also mentions it when describing the day of the LORD. The prophet writes: "On that day his feet shall stand on the Mount of Olives, which lies before Jerusalem on the east; and the Mount of Olives shall be split in two from east to west by a very wide valley; so that one half of the Mount shall withdraw northward, and the other half southward" (Zech 14:4). While the prophet Ezekiel does not mention it by name, it is clear that he is referring to the Mount of Olives when he describes the cherubim as stopping on the mountain east of the city of Jerusalem (Ezek 11:23).

In the CB (NT), the Mount of Olives is the place where Jesus begins riding the donkey that will take him to Jerusalem (Mark 11:1; Matt 21:1; Luke 19:29, 37). It is also the place where he delivers his apocalyptic discourse in which he explains why Jerusalem fell to the Romans in 70 CE (Mark 13:3; Matt 24:3). After Jesus celebrates the Passover with his disciples, he goes out to the Mount of Olives (Mark 14:26; Matt 26:30; Luke 22:39), specifically Gethsemane (Mark 14:32; Matt 26:36), to pray. The author of Luke's Gospel and the Acts of the Apostles states that Jesus would go out and spend the night on the Mount of Olives (Luke 21:37) and that his ascension occurred there, because his disciples returned to Jerusalem from the mount called Olivet (Acts 1:12). Before the woman caught in adultery is brought to Jesus in John's Gospel, the narrative states that he had gone to the Mount of Olives (John 8:1). All of these references to Mount Olivet indicate that it is a place of theophany.

Unnamed mountains in the CB (NT) are also important places for theophanies. Because he is portrayed as a new Moses in Matthew's Gospel, Jesus gives his first discourse, commonly called the Sermon on the Mount, after going up a mountain (Matt 5:1) from which he descends when he is finished (Matt 8:1). He also heals many people while sitting on a mountain (Matt 15:29) or near a mountain (Mark 5:11). In Mark's Gospel, he goes up a mountain and then names his twelve apostles (Mark 3:13), as he also does in Luke's Gospel (Luke 6:12–13). He compares faith to the ability to command a mountain to be taken up and thrown into the sea (Mark 11:23; Matt 21:21; cf. Rev 8:8). Jesus prays on mountains (Mark 6:46; Matt 14:23;

---

18. Murphey, *Dictionary of Biblical Literacy*, 201.

Luke 6:12). His major theophany, commonly called the transfiguration, occurs on an unnamed mountain (Mark 9:2–8; Matt 17:1–8; Luke 9:28–36) (see Sacred Numbers).

Several other biblical items serve the same purpose that mountains do as theophanic elements. For example, in the HB (OT) the patriarch Isaac's son, Jacob, dreams about a ladder that reaches from the earth to the heaven with God's angels ascending and descending (Gen 28:12). Clifford notes that the word *ladder* should be translated as *stairway* or *ramp* "set in the ground and arching toward heaven."[19] The ladder or stairway is a link between heaven and earth;[20] it connects the top story of the universe, the heaven, with the middle story, the earth, and provides a means for God to manifest himself to Jacob. "The meaning of the dream," according to Clifford, "is the contact between God and creatures on earth."[21] According to the Book of Genesis, " . . . [T]he LORD stood beside [Jacob] and said, 'I am the LORD, the God of Abraham your father and the God of Isaac'" (Gen 28:13). In this theophany, according to Clifford, "the LORD appears and renews the promises—land, descendants, and through the descendants blessings to all nations of the earth."[22] After awakening, Jacob declares that the LORD is in that place (Gen 28:16) and calls it the house of God and the gate of heaven (Gen 28:17). He names the place Bethel (Gen 28:19), which means *house of God*. "The appearance of the Lord on earth, as at Bethel, provides an approach to the continuous presence in heaven," states Clifford.[23] Later in the same book he will meet angels—God—twenty years later and name the place God's camp (Gen 32:1–2). The author of John's Gospel references the experience of Jacob's ladder or stairway when he portrays Jesus telling Nathanael that he would see "heaven opened and the angels of God ascending and descending upon the Son of Man" (John 1:51). According to Clifford, angels on the ladder or stairway are another sign of heaven's contact with earth.[24] In other words, according to the author of John's Gospel, Jesus is the new ladder or stairway connecting heaven to earth.

Another item that serves the same purpose as a mountain is a tower. In the HB (OT) Book of Genesis, there is a story about people who built a tower with its top reaching into the heavens (Gen 11:4a). The tower, built

19. Clifford, "Genesis," 30.
20. Ibid.
21. Ibid.
22. Ibid.
23. Ibid.
24. Ibid.

on the earth, reached God, in the heavens. Most likely, the author of this story is alluding to a very high pyramid-like structure called a ziggurat, which functioned as a temple in Babylon. The purpose of building the tower was for the builders to make a name for themselves (Gen 11:4b). However, they didn't think that it might become a means for the LORD to descend from the heavens to the earth! Nevertheless, the LORD came down to see the tower (Gen 11:5). Once upon the earth, the LORD confuses the people's language and scatters them over the face of the earth (Gen 11:6–9). The purpose of a tower should have been to get close to God for worship; that purpose has been abrogated by the builders' desire to make a name for themselves. Other biblical references clarify this perspective. For example, the psalm imbedded in the Second Book of Samuel declares the LORD to be a tower of salvation (2 Sam 22:51). Psalm 61 declares God to be a strong tower (Ps 61:3), and the Book of Proverbs states, "The name of the LORD is a strong tower" (Prov 18:10a). Finally, the prophet Micah calls Mount Zion a tower where the LORD reigns (Mic 4:7–8).

Thus, many theophanies take place on a mountain, making both named and unnamed mountains an element of theophanic experiences. In the HB (OT) Mount Horeb, also called Mount Sinai, is identified as God's mountain. Mount Carmel becomes the place for the revelation of the true God in Israel. Once the Israelites enter the promised land and have a king, Mount Zion becomes the place for the Divine Presence which comes to rest in the temple built in Jerusalem. In the CB (NT) Mount Olivet becomes the point for Jesus' triumphal entry into Jerusalem. Furthermore, in order to connect him to theophanies of the past, evangelists portray him teaching and praying on unnamed mountains, not to mention being transfigured on one of them. A ladder and a tower serve to same function as a mountain: to connect the world above to the world below so that a theophany may occur.

As already noted above, Bergmann refers to this as a space in which the Creator acts in liberating synergy with the creatures,[25] naming this theophanic element as "inhabitation."[26] This does not mean that the world is God; it does mean that God dwells in the world.[27] In a biblical three-storied universe, God needs a means from getting from the top story to the middle story, and that means is usually a mountain, but it can also be a ladder, a stairway, or a tower. Thus, a mountain is an element of a theophany.

25. Bergmann, *Religion*, 5.
26. Ibid., 416.
27. Ibid.

2

Sacred Numbers

A NUMBER OF STUDIES have been done on the significance of sacred numbers. A sacred number's focus is not on quantity, even though a number may indicate such, but on quality. In other words, biblical numbers mean something; they have referents. Collins, quoted by Parsons, observes that "[n]umerical symbolism is part of the activity of discovering order in environment and experience."[1] Numbers are "used to order the experience of time" and to express "order in the experience of space."[2] Thus, a number in a theophany serves to bring order out of the chaos of the experience of the Divine Presence.

THREE

Three refers to the spiritual order; it gives a sense of order to chaos. Verman notes that "threefold constructs . . . represent a foundational reality."[3] Thus, the Torah is threefold—Torah, Prophets, and Writings; Adam and Eve procreate three sons: Cain, Abel, and Seth; Noah and his wife have three sons: Shem, Ham and Japeth; the names of Abraham, Isaac, and Jacob appear together frequently, especially as ancestors of Moses; three kings of all Israel often are named together: Saul, David, and Solomon.[4]

---

1. Parsons, "Exegesis," 26.
2. Ibid.
3. Verman, "Power of Threes," 171.
4. Ibid., 172–3.

Sacred Numbers

One element of Moses' experience on Mount Sinai (Horeb) that reveals the glory of the LORD is the sacred number three. The account of the narrative in Exodus 19 begins: "On the third new moon after the Israelites had gone out of the land of Egypt, on that very day, they came into the wilderness of Sinai" (19:1). Clifford explains the three new moons: "The first month is Nisan, the time of Passover and Unleavened Bread. The second month is the entry into the wilderness of Sin, where the manna was given (16:1); it was the time of cereal harvest. Here the third month is the feast of Weeks, Pentecost."[5] Three refers to the spiritual order; it is one of the elements of a theophany. The number three generates a sense of expectation; "something new and unexpected is likely to happen," states Ryken.[6] This motif "points to further developments yet to unfold" while also conveying "a sense of completeness or thoroughness to the episode itself."[7] The latter point is illustrated by the LORD's instructions to Moses to have the Israelites "prepare for the third day, because on the third day the LORD will come down upon Mount Sinai in the sight of all the people" (Exod 19:11). Thus, "on the morning of the third day" (Exod 19:16) God manifests himself on Mount Sinai (Horeb) in a variety of natural phenomena yet to be explored. It is also important to note at this early point in the narrative that the number three is intensified by its use three times, namely, the third new moon, preparation for the third day, and the LORD's arrival on the morning of the third day.

The number three is used extensively in biblical literature to indicate the Divine Presence. In the covenant-making ceremony with Abram, the LORD God tells the patriarch to bring and prepare, among other animals, "a heifer three years old, a female goat three years old, [and] a ram three years old" (Gen 15:9). As noted above, the three, three-year-old animals indicate that something new and unexpected is about to occur; a new order to the chaos is about to be given. Similarly, in the contest with the prophets of Baal on Mount Carmel, Elijah instructs the people gathered around him to "fill four jars with water and pour it on the burnt offering and on the wood" (1 Kgs 18:33) three times (1 Kgs 18:34–35). Not only does the prophet use the number three to indicate that God is about to do something new, unexpected, and ordered, but he also uses the number four, which indicates the created order, the world. Four is a universal number, appearing across

---

5. Clifford, "Exodus," 51.
6. Ryken, *Dictionary*, 866.
7. Ibid.

cultures, particularly in the four cardinal directions: north, south, east, and west. The number three is employed in Mark's Gospel in the CB (NT) in the narrative commonly referred to as Jesus' transfiguration, which, as in the HB (OT) examples given above, takes place on a mountain. Jesus takes only three disciples with him: Peter, James, and John (Mark 9:2). Once he is transfigured, Elijah and Moses appear and talk to Jesus; this makes another set of three. And Peter wants to make three dwellings (Mark 9:5), one each for Jesus, Elijah, and Moses. The parallel accounts of this event in Matthew's Gospel (Matt 17:1–8) and in Luke's Gospel (Luke 9:28–36) contain the same three sets of three to indicate Jesus' glory as a son of God. In other words, not only is God manifest in Jesus, but he is also going to do something new, unexpected, and ordered: raise Jesus from the dead. Other examples could be given, but these three are enough to prove that sacred numbers, especially the number three, is an element of theophanies.

THREE AND A HALF

While three represents the spiritual order, three and one-half represents evil. It does so because three and one-half is more than three and less than four, which represents the created order. Since it falls in between three and four and is half of seven (see below), its referent is whatever is not of God and of the earth. In other words, it is a third thing. In the CB (NT) the author of the Book of Revelation refers to forty-two months (Rev 11:2) as the time allowed for the nations to trample the city of Jerusalem. Prophecy for one thousand two hundred sixty days follows (Rev 11:3). For three and a half days (Rev 11:9) dead bodies will lie unburied. Forty-two months is three and a half years; one thousand two hundred sixty days is three and a half years (ancient people calculated 360 days to a year). The period of evil, signified by three and a half, refers to incompleteness, brokenness, evil—the lack of order in the spiritual and the created order.

FOUR

The number four, as already indicated above, signifies the created order. It is another way to write about the earth, which is conceived of as four cardinal directions: north, south, east, and west. As early as Genesis 2:10, the biblical reader is told that the river in Eden divides into four branches. Then, there are four kings (Gen. 14:9), four hundred years (Gen 15:13), four hundred shekels (Gen. 23:16), four hundred men (Gen 32:6), four cubits (Exod 26:2), four pillars (Exod 26:32), four towns (Joshua 19:7; 21:18, 22, 24, 29, 31, 35, 37, 39). The number four appears in biblical literature almost three hundred times. Space does not permit the listing of all the references. Indeed, a book could be written on the occurrences of four in the Bible! It is sufficient for purposes here to indicate that it is a sacred number referring to the created order. Multiples, as in four hundred or four thousand, merely intensify the number's importance.

FIVE

The number five is also a sacred number, used over three hundred times in biblical literature. There are five books in the Pentateuch: Genesis, Exodus, Leviticus, Numbers, and Deuteronomy. Together these five books of the HB (OT) form the Torah, whose writing is traditionally credited to Moses. Because he portrays Jesus as a new Moses, the author of Matthew's Gospel portrays Jesus giving five major discourses (Matt 5:1—7:29; 10:1—11:1; 13:1–52; 18:1–35; 24:1—25:46). Just as Moses saw the face of God, the author of Matthew's Gospel considers Jesus to be the revelation of God, a new way to see God face to face.[8] Furthermore, the HB (OT) Book of Psalms is divided into five parts or five books (Pss 1-41, 42-72, 73-89, 90-1-6, 107-150). Five represents God's grace, goodness, and unmerited gift. Thus, it often appears in a person's age; Noah becomes the father of three sons (note the number) after he was five hundred years old (Gen 5:32). Before Noah, Seth lived one hundred five years before becoming the father of Enosh (Gen 5:6). Abram left his home country when he was seventy-five (see Seven below) years old (Gen 12:4) and bargained with God in multiples of five (Gen 18:22–33). When Isaac is born to Abraham, the patriarch is one hundred years old (Gen 21:5), that is, he has reached a state of totality (ten, a multiple of five, multiplied by itself, see Ten below). Joseph increases his brother's portion fivefold (Gen 43:34; 45:22). Jesus feeds five thousand men with five loaves (Mark 8:38–44). Five or any of its multiples is a referent to abundance, grace, goodness, gift, or a severe lack thereof.

8. Duran, "Memory," 78.

SIX

Six is an important biblical number because it represents incompleteness.[9] Used over two hundred times in biblical literature, the first story of creation explains how God created everything in six days (Gen 1:1—2:3); creation will not be complete until there is rest on the seventh day! The great flood occurs in the six hundredth year of Noah's life (Gen 7:11). Abraham is eighty-six years old when Ishmael is born (Gen 16:16). Sixty-six people belonging to Jacob go to Egypt (Gen 46:26). Pharaoh takes six hundred chariots in pursuit of the Hebrews after they leave Egypt (Exod14:7). A Hebrew slave serves only six years (Exod 21:2). On Mount Sinai (Horeb), the glory of the LORD settles on the clouded mountain for six days (Exod 24:16). And while the CB (NT) Book of Revelation uses the number six repeatedly, the author's stroke of genius appears when he refers to the beast as the number six hundred sixty-six (Rev. 13:18), indicating that he is divinely (three) incomplete (sixes). Thus, six represents incompleteness.

SEVEN

The number seven refers to completion. It is the sum of three, the divine order, and four, the created order. Thus, while creation occurs in six days, the first week is not finished until God rests on the seventh day (Gen 2:2–3). Noah takes seven pairs of animals with him into the ark (Gen 7:2, 3) to repopulate and re-create the world after the flood. Furthermore, Noah lives another three hundred fifty years (Gen 9:29) (note the use of three and five); in other words, he was favored by God with a long life. In the CB (NT) the Book of Revelation loves the number seven. There are seven spirits (Rev 1:4)—showing a connection "with the seven planets, which in [this] time were held to be heavenly beings"[10]—seven lampstands (Rev 1:12), seven stars (Rev 1:16), seven horns and eyes (Rev. 5:6), seven seals (Rev. 6:1), seven angels with seven trumpets (Rev. 8:6), seven crowns and seven heads of the dragon (Rev. 12:3), seven angels with seven plagues (Rev. 15:1), seven bowls of wrath (Rev. 16:1), seven hills (Rev 17:9), and seven kings (Rev 17:10). Part of John's Gospel is structured around seven signs (John 2:1–11; 4:46–54, 5:1–15; 6:1–15; 6:16–21; 9:1–41; and 11:1–57), while John 21:2 presents seven disciples. In the Acts of the Apostles, seven men are cho-

---

9. Parsons, "Exegesis," 30.
10. Collins, "Apocalypse," 1000.

sen to wait on tables (Acts 8:35); "their number may reflect the institution of the Jewish town council (Deut 16:18),"[11] states Dillon. Jesus feeds four thousand with seven loaves and collects seven basketfuls of leftovers. (Mark 8:1–11). While Parsons lists several pages of data on the number seven,[12] suffice it here to note that the number represents completeness.

EIGHT

Eight represents fullness because it is one more than seven, and it is an octave. Seven is complete, but eight makes it even more complete! Before Arabic numerals were invented around 500 CE, zero did not exist. Thus, counting was not done in a linear method, presuming zero and moving to one. Without zero, the first number is always one. Thus, from one Sabbath (Saturday) to another Sabbath is eight days. Many biblical people lived over eight hundred years (Gen 5:7, 10, 13, 16, 17), that is, they reached fullness in God's presence. Seth is born to Adam when he was eight hundred years old (Gen 5:4); Jared lived eight hundred years after Enoch was born (Gen 5:19); circumcision was to be done on the eighth day (Gen 17:12; 21:4; Luke 2:21). Abdon not only judged Israel for eight years (Judg 12:14), but he also had forty sons: eight multiplied by five! Jesse had eight sons (1 Sam 17:12). In Luke's Gospel, Jesus is transfigured on the eighth day (Luke 9:28). And the First Letter of Peter reminds the reader that eight people in Noah's ark survived the great flood (1 Pet 3:20). Thus, eight—used almost one hundred times in the Bible—represents fullness, perfection, in God's sight either alone or in combination with another sacred number that adds even more meaning to it.

TEN

Ten, or any of its multiples (one hundred, one thousand), signifies totality. The Bible contains over two hundred direct references to ten, which is a double of five. There are ten years (Gen 16:3), ten camels (Gen 24:10), ten gold shekels (Gen 24:22), ten bulls (Gen 32:15), ten brothers (Gen 42:3), and ten donkeys (Gen 45:23). Joseph lives to be one hundred ten years old (Gen 50:22, 26)—which is ten multiplied by itself with ten more added

11. Dillon, "Acts," 740.
12. Parsons, "Exegesis," 27–30.

on! Using number symbolism, Williams thinks that Joseph's age "brings the ancestral narratives of Genesis to completion."[13] He says that Joseph's symbolic age "symbolizes the divine providence that will bring the story of Israel to a blessed conclusion" in the Book of Genesis.[14] God gives ten commandments (Exod 34:28; Deut 10:4). In the CB (NT), the Matthean Jesus tells parables featuring ten bridesmaids (Matt 25:1) and ten talents (Matt 25:28). The Lukan Jesus mentions ten silver coins (Luke 15:8), ten lepers (Luke 17:12), ten slaves and ten pounds (Luke 19:13, 16), and ten cities (Luke 19:17). The Book of Revelation mentions ten days (Rev 2:10), ten horns (Rev 12:3, 17:3, 7, 16; 13:1), and ten diadems (Rev. 13:1). Thus, the number ten, along with any of its multiples, represents totality.

TWELVE

The number twelve, arrived at in various ways, usually represents the twelve sons of Israel (Jacob) (Gen 35:22), referred to as the twelve tribes (Gen 49:29). However, it is important to note that there were never twelve tribes. Joseph was never a tribe; his two sons formed the half-tribe of Manasseh and the half-tribe of Ephraim. Pfeifer notes that "Old Testament lists of the twelve tribes, like the lists of the Twelve [apostles], reflect tendencies of re-ordering and substitution."[15] In other words, whose name is on the list pales in comparison to having a list of twelve. Occurring over one hundred seventy times in the Bible, the number twelve refers to Ishmael becoming the father of twelve princes (Gen 17:20, 25:16). Seth lives to be nine hundred twelve years old (Gen 5:8) (note the use of three multiplied by itself times ten multiplied by itself plus twelve). There are twelve springs (Exod 15:27), twelve pillars (Exod 24:4), twelve stones (Exod 28:21; 39:14), twelve loaves (Lev. 24:5), twelve oxen (Num 7:3), twelve silver plates, basins, and gold dishes (Num 7:84), and twelve bulls, rams, male lambs, and male goats (Num 7:87). The two Books of Chronicles employ the use of twelve thirty-three times.

In the CB (NT), Jesus chooses twelve apostles, disciples, or followers (Mark 3:14–19; Matt 10:2–4; Luke 6:12–16); he also heals a woman with hemorrhages for twelve years (Mark 5:25; Matt 9:20); Luke 8:43) and raises a little girl who is twelve years old (Mark 5:42; Luke 8:42). After feeding

13. Williams, "Number Symbolism," 86.
14. Ibid., 87.
15. Pfeifer, "Which Came First," 446.

many people, twelve basketfuls of leftovers are collected (Mark 6:43; Matt 14:20; Luke 9:17; John 6:13). Luke narrates a story of Jesus when he was twelve years old (Luke 2:42). And, of course, the Book of Revelation presents twenty-four elders (Rev 4:4), that is, twelve doubled; "their placement in a circle around the deity symbolize cosmic order and governance."[16] There are twelve stars (Rev. 12:1), twelve gates, angels, and names (Rev 21:12), twelve foundations (Rev 12:14), twelve gates with twelve pearls (Rev 12:21), and twelve kinds of fruit (Rev 12:22). Twelve times itself and then intensified by a thousand (itself a multiple of ten) yields the number sealed—one hundred forty-four thousand (Rev 7:4–8). Collins writes about the forty-four thousand: "The use of the traditional element of the twelve tribes makes the impression of closeness. The 12,000 for each tribe intensifies the sense of chosenness; a remnant survives, a minority is loyal. . . . The membership in the twelve tribes is probably also meant symbolically and not literally; membership in the Jewish people is not primarily a matter of birth."[17] She also writes about the twelve tribes and twelve apostles (Rev 21:12, 14): "The mention of the twelve tribes and the twelve apostles suggest that the [new Jerusalem] symbolizes a people; but there is no simple equation of the new Jerusalem and the people of God. Rather, the city represents a transcendent and future reality: God dwelling with people, face to face."[18]

One can arrive at twelve by adding seven (completion) and five (grace), by multiplying three (divine) by four (earth), or by taking two sixes (imperfect) and adding them together. Twelve represents God's people in their transcendent fullness. The twelve sons of Jacob represent the families that became the nation of Israel in the HB (OT).[19] Pfeifer states, "Jesus' choice of twelve distinct followers evoked the symbolism of the twelve tribes;"[20] the twelve, also known as the twelve apostles and disciples, designate the new people of God in the CB (NT) as those who follow Jesus.

FORTY

The last sacred number needing examination is that of forty. Forty refers to a lifetime in the ancient world; it represents the life of an average human

16. Collins, "Apocalypse," 1004.
17. Ibid., 1005
18. Ibid., 1015.
19. Pfeifer, "Which Came First," 445.
20. Ibid., 447.

generation. According to Karris, it "refers to a sufficiently long period of time."²¹ It also refers to a period of testing, trial, or temptation, which occurs during that average generation. The Bible contains over one hundred sixty references to the number forty. Isaac is forty years old when he marries Rebekah (Gen 25:30), and Essau is forty years old when he marries (Gen 26:34). It took forty days to embalm a body (Gen. 50:3); the Israelites ate manna for forty years in the desert (Exod 16:35) while they wandered in the desert for forty years (Num 32:13; Deut 2:7; 8:2, 17) after Moses spent forty days and forty nights with the LORD on Mount Horeb (Sinai) (Exod 34:28, Deut 9:9). The spies spent forty days looking over the land of Canaan (Num 13:25; 14:34). Every one of the census totals in the Book of Numbers contains the number forty (Num 1:21, 25, 33, 41; 2:11, 15, 19, 28; 26:7, 18, 41, 50). Jacob lived to be one hundred forty-seven years old (Gen 47:28), that is, ten times ten (totality) plus forty (a lifetime) plus seven (complete). In the CB (NT) Jesus spends forty days in the wilderness (Mark 1:13; Matt 4:2; Luke 4:2); Jesus' forty-day fast is meant to connect him to Moses and Elijah in the desert.²² According to the Acts of the Apostles, there are forty days between Jesus' resurrection and ascension (Acts 1:3); Dillon says that the "number is symbolic" and the author, Luke, may have "derived it from an existing tradition . . . or invented it himself."²³ The Book of Revelation presents the new Jerusalem with a wall one hundred forty-four cubits high (Rev 21:17); ten times ten (totality) plus forty (a generation) plus four (the earth) equals one hundred forty-four. Thus, the number forty represents a human lifetime of trial.

MISCELLANEOUS

Because numerology deals with the meaning of numbers and not their quantitative value, sacred numbers are signs needing to be decoded by modern readers. There is little difference between the number ten (totality), one hundred (ten times ten), and one thousand (ten times one hundred); the intensification of ten attempts to indicate that one totality is more total than another! Likewise, twelve (the number of God's people), one hundred forty-four (twelve times twelve), and one hundred forty-four thousand (twelve times twelve times a thousand) emphasize in greater degrees the

---

21. Karris, "Luke," 688.
22. Viviano, "Matthew," 638.
23. Dillon, "Acts," 727.

importance of God's people in both the HB (OT) and the CB (NT). Thus, multiples and repetitions serve to intensify the meaning of a text.

Finally, before Arabic numerals were invented letters of alphabets were used to represent numbers. About the only remnant of that today is Roman Numerals. So, I represents one; V represents five; X represents ten, etc. Sometimes when letters representing numbers are presented, they also spell a word. Such is the case with MID (1,499) using Roman Numerals. Hebrew and Greek letters functioned in the same way. For example, the author of Matthew's Gospel presents three sets of fourteen names each—even though the third set contains only thirteen (Matt 1:2–17)—because the Hebrew letters that spell David also represent the number fourteen. By dividing Jesus' ancestors into three sets, the author of this work is declaring that what each person did was directed by God. The sacred number's focus is not on quantity, even though a number may indicate such, but on quality. Biblical numbers meant something to the intended audiences of biblical texts; the task today is to figure out what they meant, especially in theophanic texts.

DETAILED ANALYSIS: THREE THEOPHANIES EMPLOYING SACRED NUMBERS

This section is not intended to be a detailed analysis of every number in the Bible; that would take volumes. This is an attempt to ascertain the meaning of sacred numbers that appear in theophanic texts in order to understand them. Thus, the narrative of God's covenant-making ceremony with Abram (Genesis 15:7–21), which developed in oral tradition over a long period and contains details of an ancient covenant-making ceremony, begins with the Lord GOD telling the patriarch to gather a heifer three years old, a female goat three years old, and a ram three years old (Gen 15:9). God's voice is an element of a theophany. Three, three-year-old animals signal a super theophany, even before they are cut in two! In other words, God is written all over this story. One three-year-old animal would have been enough, but three, three-year-old animals cubes and intensifies the number representing the divine. Abram's response is to do as the LORD instructs. Then, "a deep sleep fell upon Abram, and a deep and terrifying darkness descended upon him" (Gen 15:12). The deep sleep or dream state is another element of a theophany. The terrifying darkness is the thick cloud or thick darkness that is another element of a theophanic experience. God's voice is heard again (Gen 15:13–16). Then "a smoking fire pot and a flaming torch passed between [the] pieces [of the animals]" (Gen 15:17). And there are two more elements of a theophany: smoke and fire. God walks between the two halves of the three, three-three-year old animals and promises that he will be cut in two if he does not fulfill his words. Then, just to be sure, God's voice is heard again, telling Abram that he will give his descendants the land he promised (Gen 15:18–21). Thus, in this narrative of a theophany, the elements are three, three-year-old animals, God's voice heard three times, Abram's response, a dream, and cloud, smoke, and fire.

Sacred numbers are highlighted in the narrative of the theophany involving Elijah on Mount Carmel. In order to prove the all-powerfulness of his God, the LORD, Elijah proposes a contest between the LORD and Baal, the male Canaanite fertility deity. Elijah, prophet of the LORD, and Baal's prophets each take a bull, a very strong fertility animal, and prepare it by cutting it and placing the pieces upon wood. The prophets of Baal slaughtered and readied their bull first. Then, they called upon Baal, but there was no voice, no answer, and no response (1 Kgs 18:29); in other words, there was not the element of God's voice. Then it was Elijah's turn. The first thing he did was to repair the LORD's altar (1 Kgs 18:30); here, the altar is the first element of the theophany. The sign of twelve stones in honor of the twelve sons of Jacob are used to (re)build the LORD's altar (1 Kgs 18:31–32); twelve is a sacred number representing God's people. An additional sign is given, namely, a trench is dug around the altar. After placing the wood on the altar, Elijah then cuts up the bull and places it on top of the wood. Next comes the element of water coupled with more sacred numbers. The prophet directs that four jars of water (representing the earth) are to be filled three times (representing the Divine) and poured over the bull, the wood, and the altar until the trench is filled (1 Kgs 18:33–35). In the context of the story, the land has been in a three-year drought; Walsh refers to this action as "a priceless libation."[24] It is also important to note that Elijah addresses the people three times (1 Kgs 18:33–34) as a part of the theophany. Walsh notes that Elijah is "gradually drawing [the people] away from Baal toward Yahweh."[25] Using the number three again, Elijah addresses the LORD as the God of Abraham, Isaac, and Israel in a prayer requesting that he manifest himself to the people (1 Kgs 18:36). The element of fire now enters the picture; the narrator states that "the fire of the

24. Walsh, "1–2 Kings," 172.
25. Ibid., 171.

LORD fell and consumed the burnt offering, the wood, the stones, and the dust, and even licked up the water that was in the trench" (1 Kgs 18:38); this fire is lightning. The final element is the people's response: "The LORD indeed is God" (1 Kgs 18:39), which they repeat twice. Nothing is left to do now except for Elijah to kill the four hundred fifty prophets of Baal (1 Kgs 18:40); the killing of Baal's prophets is the sign of transformation that has occurred in the Israelites. Finally, Walsh notes: "The entire passage recalls the covenant sacrifice on Sinai [Horeb] (Exod 24:4–8), where Moses builds a similar altar, involves the people in offering sacrifice, and pours precious liquid (the blood of the sacrificial animals) over altar and people."[26]

Elijah next tells King Ahab to feast—another element of a theophany—because the drought is about to be ended (1 Kgs 18:41). The sound of rushing rain that Elijah hears proves who the real fertility God is: Yahweh! the LORD! Walsh states, "The meal atop Mt. Carmel parallels the covenant meal following the sacrifice on Sinai, where Moses and the elders of the people 'saw God and ate and drank' (Exod 24:9–11)."[27] Employing another sacred number, Elijah sends his servant to look out to the sea seven times (1 Kgs 18:43); seven is the sum of three (the divine) and four (the earth), representing completion of the drought because the rain is about to fall. However, several more elements of a theophany are presented. First, there is the mention of a little cloud or a wisp of cloud, an element of a theophany. Second, the heavens grow black; there is a contrast of light and darkness. Third, the clouds arrive, not only to herald the rain but to herald more of the Divine Presence. Fourth, there is wind, and the heavy rain begins (1 Kgs 18:45). Thus, this theophany is not only rich in sacred numbers—twelve, four, three sets of three, and seven—but it also contains the elements of mountain, altar, water, fire, lightning, people's response, transformation, feast, light and darkness, clouds, and wind.

The final theophany to be examined in this chapter on sacred numbers is the narrative usually labeled Jesus' transfiguration. The narrative appears in the gospels of Mark, Matthew, and Luke, and is referenced in the Second Letter of Peter. With the presupposition that Mark's Gospel is the source of the narrative for Matthew and Luke, the author of Mark sets the narrative six days (Mark 9:2) after Peter had identified Jesus as the Messiah, after Jesus had foretold his death and resurrection and rebuked Peter, and after Jesus had taught the crowd and his disciples about discipleship

26. Ibid., 172
27. Ibid.

(Mark 8:27—9:1). By using the sacred number six, the author of this work is indicating clearly that Jesus' mission is not yet complete, but the divine is very much present. God's presence is clearly signaled by the use of the sacred number three three times. Jesus takes only three disciples with him—Peter and James and John (Mark 9:2). Elijah and Moses appear talking with Jesus (Mark 9:4), another set of three. And Peter wants to make three dwellings—one for Jesus, one of Elijah, and one for Moses (Mark 9:5). There is a two-fold transformation; Jesus is transfigured (Mark 9:2); Peter didn't know what to say, and he, James, and John were terrified (Mark 9:6). The narrators description of Jesus' clothes becoming "dazzling white, such as no one on earth could bleach them" (Mark 9:2–3) is paralleled with the cloud—another theophanic element—that overshadows them, and then God's voice is heard from the cloud identifying Jesus as his son (Mark 9:7). Just as suddenly as the theophany began, it comes to an end (Mark 9:8). The three disciples' response is to say nothing to anyone even though they questioned the meaning of resurrection from the dead (Mark 9:9–10). Because Mark's Gospel contains no post resurrection appearances of Jesus, this is the author's description of resurrection;[28] he is declaring that Jesus' resurrection is a theophany, a manifestation of God which occurs on an unidentified high mountain (Mark 9:2)—an element of a theophany; it is a transfiguring experience which leaves Jesus changed from dead to alive. Harrington notes that in Mark's account of the transfiguration Jesus' disciples "are granted a glimpse of him in his glorious state."[29] He adds, "Given the allusions to Exodus in this account, it is best to take the cloud as the vehicle for God's presence as in Exod[us] 16:10; 19:9; 24:15–16; 33:9."[30]

When the author of Matthew's Gospel copies this narrative from Mark's Gospel, he changes very little of it. For example, he indicates that the place is a high mountain (Matt 17:1) and states that Jesus "face shone like the sun, and his clothes became dazzling white" (Matt 17:2) and parallels that with the "bright cloud [that] overshadowed them" (Matt 17:5). This gospel makes clear that the disciples "were overcome by fear" (Matt 17:6) in their response to this event, omitting the note about them questioning the meaning of the resurrection because Matthew will supply two post-resurrection appearances of Jesus at the end of his gospel. As far as sacred numbers go, Matthew keeps Mark's six days, and three sets of three: Peter,

---

28. Pherigo, "Mark," 659.
29. Harrington, "Mark," 615.
30. Ibid.

James, and John; Moses, Elijah, and Jesus; and three dwellings. Matthew understands Mark's transfiguration narrative as a type of metamorphosis, which will not be complete and proven until Jesus appears after his crucifixion, death, and resurrection. Kee states that "this story [is] a kind of advanced viewing of the glory of the risen Christ."[31]

When Luke rewrites the transfiguration narrative he finds in Mark's Gospel, he turns it into a full-blown theophany. Furthermore, Miller argues: "The mountain, cloud, and heavenly voice of Luke's transfiguration account are widely regarded as stage pieces, designed to recall biblical theophany narratives associated with Mount Sinai [Horeb] and to set up a comparison demonstrating Jesus' superiority to Moses."[32] Luke's account of Jesus' transfiguration occurs eight days (Luke 9:28) after Jesus teaches about discipleship; it narrates the fullness of Jesus' divinity. Miller writes: "Luke wraps the entire transfiguration in a series of allusions to the wilderness theophany narratives associated with Mount Sinai"[33] [Horeb]. Luke keeps the three disciples who accompany Jesus, but they go up the mountain to pray (Luke (9:28), a unique feature of the Lukan Jesus. Like the Mount Sinai (Horeb) narrative, the Lukan transfiguration narrative is located in proximity to a mountain; in other words, the author keeps his Markan source, having "recognized many of the similarities between the transfiguration and the wilderness theophany narratives that were present already in his Markan source."[34] Luke notes that it is while they are praying that Jesus' face changes and his clothes become dazzling white (Luke 9:29) to parallel the cloud that comes and overshadows them (Luke 9:34). The change in Jesus' face is intended to echo the change that occurs to Moses' face (Exod 34:30). Miller thinks "that Luke saw in Jesus' glorious appearance a parallel with the glorified face of Moses."[35] Moses and Elijah now appear in glory—the glory of the LORD—and if that were not enough to indicate Luke's theophanic understanding, they speak to Jesus about his departure, which he would accomplish in Jerusalem (Luke 9:31); in other words, they speak about the exodus—a direct reference to the escape of the Hebrews from the Egyptians and the theophany at Mount Sinai (Horeb) that followed[36]—he will make

31. Kee, "Matthew," 630.
32. Miller, "Seeing the Glory," 498.
33. Ibid., 499.
34. Ibid., 505.
35. Ibid., 504.
36. Ibid., 516.

both through death to resurrection and through ascension to the glory of the LORD. Miller notes that "it is surely significant that both Moses and Elijah had theophany experiences on a mountain."[37]

Luke notes that even though Peter, James, and John are sleepy, they see Jesus' glory and the two men who stand with him (Luke 9:32). Baird writes that this fact "suggests that the transfiguration occurred at night—a setting which would magnify the radiance of the raiment which became dazzling white."[38] Peter wants to erect three dwellings, but he and his companions are terrified (Luke 9:34). Again, this is the same response given to Moses when the Israelites saw his face after he descended from the mountain. Just as in Mark, the voice of the LORD is heard from the cloud, indicating that Jesus is his chosen one (Luke 9:35). The descending cloud and the voice that comes from it are found in the Sinai (Horeb) narrative. Miller notes that this is the "more important function" of the transfiguration narrative, namely, "to connect the voice from the cloud with the voice on Mount Sinai [Horeb], and to set the requirement to hear Jesus within the framework of God's covenant relationship with the people."[39] Then, after the voice all returns to as it was before. Miller notes: "Jesus' superiority to Moses and Elijah is visually displayed when the lawgiver and prophet depart, leaving Jesus alone as the one who must now be heard."[40] The Lukan disciples' response is to keep silent of what they had seen (Luke 9:36). Thus, Luke transforms his Markan source into a full-blown theophany using the number eight, three sets of three, the cloud, and specifically the glory of the LORD that surrounds Moses, Elijah, and Jesus. The Lukan disciples, like Moses and Elijah before them, get to see the glory and live! Miller notes that "the heavenly glory experienced by Moses, Elijah, and Jesus is . . . precisely God's own glory . . . , which is associated . . . with anything belonging to God's realm."[41] Furthermore, "Both the text of Exodus and early Jewish reflections on the wilderness theophanies suggest that the theophany imagery in the transfiguration account would have recalled the theophany in which God initiated the covenant with the Israelites at Sinai."[42]

---

37. Ibid., 501.
38. Baird, "Luke," 687.
39. Miller, "Seeing the Glory," 517.
40. Ibid.
41. Ibid., 503.
42. Ibid., 512; cf. 515.

The Second Letter of Peter seems to have Luke's account of the transfiguration in mind, especially with his reference to Jesus' majesty (2 Pet 1:16), "which was then revealed and which will again be known at his return in glory."[43] However, he also knows Matthew's version of the story, writing, "... [H]e received honor and glory from God the Father when that voice was conveyed to him by the Majestic Glory, saying, 'This is my Son, my Beloved, with whom I am well pleased'" (2 Pet 1:17; cf. Matt 17:5). The Second Letter of Peter also mentions that the event took place on a mountain, and that the author, pseudonymously named Peter, heard the voice of God from heaven (2 Pet 1:18). According to Neyrey, "Peter describes a holy mountain, apostolic eyewitnesses, Peter in particular, Jesus' glorious appearance, God's numinous presence, and God's proclamation."[44] He adds, "The apocalypse ends with Jesus' glorification in the presence of Moses and Peter.... [T]he transfiguration functions not only as the occasion on which Peter was instructed about Jesus' parousia and future judgment, but also as a prediction of that future event."[45] Thus, this account employs the elements of majesty, another word for glory, the voice of God, and the setting of a mountain to convey its theophanic importance. Missing is any mention of any sacred number.

---

43. Thompson, "Second Letter of Peter," 932.
44. Neyrey, "Second Epistle of Peter," 1019.
45. Ibid.

3

God's Voice

ANOTHER ELEMENT THAT MANIFESTS the glory of the LORD in a theophany is God's voice. Savran refers to this as the appearance and speech of Yahweh.[1] Ryken states that voice "implies a spoken utterance, usually in the form of language."[2] He adds, "The voice of God is a major biblical motif, mentioned three dozen times (NRSV)."[3] God must speak because humans do. Of course, it is very important to note at the onset that God, being a spirit, does not have a voice! However, because God is both anthropomorphized and a voice is the primary way that humans communicate—and is so reflected in biblical literature—God's voice is an element of a theophany.

Furthermore, because a human is writing the text, he is limited by his humanness. There is no other way than to depict God with human characteristics. Thus, God speaks. God speaks in the language of the writer of the biblical text. Thus, God speaks in Hebrew, Aramaic, and Greek. His words can represent God's transcendent power, stir up great fear, connote power, and render judgment. In the twenty-five verses of chapter 19 in the Book of Exodus, the LORD speaks to Moses five times; it is a time of grace. He reminds Moses that both he and the Israelites have already seen what he did to the Egyptians, and he informs him that if the people obey his voice and keep his covenant, they shall be his treasured possession of all peoples (Exod 19:3–6). He speaks again to Moses in Exodus 19:9 explaining the vehicle of his manifestation. Then, the LORD tells Moses how to prepare

---

1. Savran, "Theophany," 128.
2. Ryken, *Dictionary*, 918.
3. Ibid.

for his manifestation on Mount Sinai (Horeb) (Exod 19:10–13). Once the LORD is present on Sinai (Horeb), he humorously summons Moses to the top of the mountain and immediately sends him down with another message for the people about not breaking through the established barriers to get a look at God (Exod 19:21–22); this is the biblical prohibition that no one can see God's face and live. After Moses informs God that the people know their limits, God tells Moses to go down and get Aaron and bring him to the top of the mountain (Exod 19:24). A little later in the story, after God delivers the Ten Commandments, a chorus of the people tells Moses not to let God speak to them or they will die (Exod 20:19). This prohibition is similar to that of seeing God's face and dying. The biblical author presents a boundary of holiness surrounding the LORD's presence that cannot be crossed without dire consequences.

Hearing God's voice with fear and trembling occurs in the call narrative of the judge-priest-prophet Samuel. Saying only his name, the LORD calls Samuel three times (1 Sam 3:4, 6, 8). Not only is God's voice heard, but the theophany is confirmed by the number three. Finally, after some instruction by the priest Eli, Samuel understands who is calling him the fourth time and responds by listening to the LORD's instructions (1 Sam 3:11–14). Isaiah hears the LORD's voice after having experienced a theophany. The voice asks for someone to go on a mission, and Isaiah readily volunteers (Isa 6:8). Two more times Isaiah hears the voice (Isa 6:9–10; 6:11–13) for a total of three auditory experiences of the glory of the LORD. In the CB (NT) Book of Acts, Saul, who will later be known as Paul, hears the voice of Jesus two times directly (Acts 9:4–6) and one time through Ananias (Acts 9:17), who, after also hearing the voice of the Lord three times (Acts 9:10; 9:11–14; 9:15–16), fulfills the mission entrusted to him. Thus, another element of a theophany is hearing God's voice; this is a moment when the Divine and the human in the world meet.[4]

In the HB (OT) Book of Deuteronomy, Moses recalls the Mount Horeb (Sinai) theophanic experience for the Israelites. His focus is on reminding the people of their rebellion against the LORD and God's pardon given to them. After being on the mountain for forty days and nights, the LORD gives Moses the two stone tablets, which he breaks after coming down the mountain and discovering the golden calf. However, the narrator also recounts the LORD's words to him: "Get up, go down quickly from here, for your people whom you have brought from Egypt have acted corruptly.

---

4. Ibid., 919.

They have been quick to turn from the way that I commanded them; they have cast an image for themselves" (Deut 9:12). God continues to speak to Moses, explaining how the people are stubborn, that he desires to destroy them, and he will make a great nation out of Moses and his descendants (Deut 9:13–14). Moses descends the mountain, breaks the tablets when he sees the golden calf, and intercedes for the people before the LORD.

In what might be characterized as an anti-theophany in some ways, the prophet Elijah hears the voice of God as silence (1 Kgs 19:12). After leaving Mount Carmel, the prophet traverses the wilderness for forty days. He feasts on a cake baked on hot stones and drinks from a jar of water which are provided by an angel of the LORD (1 Kgs 19:5–8). Drawn after the pattern of Moses, Elijah climbs Mount Horeb (Sinai) upon which he finds a cave. "Then the word of the LORD came to him, saying, 'What are you doing here, Elijah?'" (1 Kgs 19:9b) After explaining why he was there, God speaks to him a second time, telling him, to go out and stand on the mountain before the LORD, who is about to pass by (1 Kgs 19:11). At this point the narrator takes over and describes "a great wind, so strong that it was splitting mountains and breaking rocks in pieces before the LORD, but the LORD was not in the wind" (1 Kgs 19:11b). One of the usual elements of a theophany is hereby negated. The narrator continues: " . . . [A]fter the wind an earthquake, but the LORD was not in the earthquake" (1 Kgs 19:11c). For the second time a usual element of a theophany is negated. Because numerology plays an important role in theophanies, there is a third negation: " . . . [A]fter the earthquake a fire, but the LORD was not in the fire" (1 Kgs 19:12). Thus, in a manner of speaking, while the divine is present—signaled by the three elements in which the LORD is not—the sound of sheer silence, the fourth element, signals it. And then for the third time Elijah again hears God's voice, asking him again, "What are you doing here, Elijah?" (1 Kgs 19:13b) Now that the (anti-)theophany has occurred, Elijah answers the LORD, who proceeds to give directions as to three individuals he is to anoint (1 Kgs 19:15–16). Finally, God tells him that he has counted seven thousand people in Israel who have not abandoned the LORD (1 Kgs 19:18); (the reader will note the number seven). Thus, in this narrative there is not only the voice of God, but the theophanic elements of feast (meal), mountain, wind, earthquake, fire, and sheer silence in addition to the sacred numbers forty, multiple threes, and seven.

Almost all of Psalm 29 is about the voice of the LORD. The hymn attributes a number of the elements of a theophany to God's voice using the following repeated refrain to begin each strophe: "The voice of the LORD." The voice of the LORD is mentioned seven times, indicating its completeness of his power in this song which uses a thunderstorm as a metaphor for God's glory. Kselman states that the expression "is meant to suggest peals of thunder crashing in rapid succession."[5] The first theophanic elements of the storm are water and thunder (Ps 29:3); God battles the watery chaos. Then, God's voice breaks the cedars, causing the Lebanon and Mount Hermon (Sirion) to skip (Ps 29:5–6), a reference to gusty winds. A reference to sharp lightening and fire follows: "The voice of the Lord flashes forth flames of fire" (Ps 29:7). More wind follows; it shakes the wilderness (Ps 29:8); it causes the oak trees to whirl and leaves the forest bare of leaves (Ps 29:9). In seven verses of Psalm 29, the theophanic elements of water, thunder, wind, lightening, and fire appear in addition to the voice of the LORD. Thus, this song is meant to capture a theophany in poetry.

There are biblical theophanies that consist mainly of hearing God's voice. Such is the case of Abraham's son, Isaac. All the biblical text says is that the LORD appeared to him, saying, "I am the God of your father Abraham; do not be afraid, for I am with you and will bless you and make your offspring numerous for my servant Abraham's sake" (Gen 26:24). Clifford says that the theophany makes Isaac the "vehicle of the promises to Abraham of land, people, and blessing."[6] There are other theophanic elements present, such as the narrator's mention of the fact that Isaac built an altar there, called on the name of the LORD there, and had his servants dig a well (water) there (Gen 26:25). The primary element, however, is God's voice, which is an element of a theophany.

---

5. Kselman, "Psalms," 531.
6. Clifford, "Genesis," 28.

4

People's (Person's) Response

THE NEXT ELEMENT OF a theophany to be investigated is the response made by the people or the person who hear(s) the voice of the LORD. Savran says that "responses are characterized by an unusual display of humility or fear, an awareness of 'creature consciousness'"[1] displayed by bowing, hiding the face, or exclamation. Such expressions "are coupled with a sense of thankfulness for not having perished as a result of the [en]counter with the divine" because "visual contact with the divine is lethal."[2] After presenting the words of God to the elders of the people, the narrator of the account about Moses on Mount Sinai (Horeb) states: "The people all answered as one: 'Everything that the LORD has spoken we will do'" (Exod 19:8). Then, Moses relays the people's response to God. In other words, once God's voice is heard, a dialogue—which may be as short as a call and a one-word response—ensues. Something new and unexpected is taking place. God is speaking from heaven (Exod 20:22), the world above, to people on earth, the middle of the presumed three-storied universe. Moses reminds the people in the Book of Deuteronomy: "The LORD spoke with you face to face at the mountain" (Deut 5:4). Later, Moses reminds the people that they said, "Look, the LORD our God has shown us his glory and greatness, and we have heard his voice. . . . Today we have seen that God may speak to someone and the person may still live" (Deut 5:24). After hearing the voice of God, the people respond by saying that they will listen and do what the LORD tells them (Deut 5:27). They are given a means to determine whether

1. Savran, "Theophany," 130.
2. Ibid., 130–31.

People's (Person's) Response

or not they should respond: If a prophet speaks in the LORD's name, but the thing does not take place or prove true, it is a word that God has not spoken (Deut 18:21–22).

There are many responses of people to God's voice. Samuel states, "Speak, for your servant is listening" (1 Sam 3:10). Isaiah responds, "Here am I; send me!" (Isa 6:8) And in the CB (NT) Acts of the Apostles, Saul asks, "Who are you, Lord?" (Acts 9:5) And the reply comes, "I am Jesus, whom you are persecuting" (Acts 9:5). A reaction occurs by the people or the person hearing the unexpected voice of the LORD, and this response is an element of a theophany.

While fear is the usual response, it is not the only response. Three call narratives are examined here, the one found in the prophets Isaiah, Jeremiah, and Ezekiel. Matthews has indicated the importance of paying attention to the elements in this literary form. He states:

> Prophetic call narratives generally include the following steps: a theophany, the appearance of a divine being to a human; a demur or excuse made by the frightened or intimidated person who is called to serve; an empowering event and reassurance that puts aside all such excuses; and a charge that provide explicit instructions for the newly called prophet.[3]

The interest here is on the theophanic element of response while also acknowledging the other elements of a theophany.

Isaiah describes the theophany he experiences using a kingly metaphor. He writes that he "saw the Lord sitting on a throne, high and lofty; and the hem of his robe filled the temple" (Isa 6:1). Six-winged seraphs attend him and praise him in a single chorus of song (Isa 6:2–3). Because he is divine, they sing the word *holy* three times. Next follow the theophanic elements of shaking (earthquake) and smoke (Isa 6:4). Once the LORD of hosts has appeared to Isaiah, the prophet bemoans his fate for having seen God (Isa 6:5), the king. Fire, in the form of a live coal, is brought from the altar, another element of a theophany, by a seraph and touched to the prophet's lips to purify him (Isa 6:6–7). Then the voice of the Lord asks, "Whom shall I send, and who will go for us?" (Isa 6:8). Isaiah's response is this: "Here am I; send me!" (Isa 6:8) In the verses that follow, God gives instructions to Isaiah (Isa 6:9–13).

Jeremiah's call begins with hearing God's voice, that is, the word of the LORD (Jer 1:4), telling him that God has known him and called him before

3. Matthews, *Old Testament*, 51.

he was conceived (Jer 1:4–5). Jeremiah's response, like that of Isaiah, is to declare that he barely knows how to speak because he is only a boy (Jer 1:7). However, God insists that the prophet accept his mission (Jer 1:7): "Do not be afraid . . . , for I am with you to deliver you, says the LORD" (Jer 1:8). Jeremiah's mouth is not touched with a burning coal, but the LORD himself puts out his hand, a theophanic sign, and touches his mouth, a gesture indicating that God's words are now Jeremiah's words (Jer 1:9–10). With the LORD's words in his mouth, the prophet has no choice but to move forward with the mission entrusted to him. Besides Jeremiah's response, the theophanic element of God's voice pervades this narrative.

The prophet Ezekiel begins his book with a cryptic date involving the fourth month, a reference to the earth, on the fifth day of the month (stated twice), a reference to grace, while being near water (Chebar River). He experiences a theophany: "As I looked, a stormy wind came out of the north: a great cloud with brightness around it and fire flashing forth continually, and in the middle of the fire, something like gleaming amber" (Ezek 1:4). Present are the theophanic elements of wind, cloud, and fire. Then the prophet sees four living creatures, which he spends a lot of time describing (Ezek 1:5–12). More elements follow: fire and lightening (Ezek 1:13–14). Using the metaphor of a chariot, Ezekiel portrays each of the living creatures as a wheel on what becomes the LORD's throne chariot (Ezek 1:15–21). Above the chariot is a dome, echoing Genesis 1:6–8, and above the dome is a throne which appears to be like sapphire or lapis lazuli, a jewel or precious stone (Ezek 1:22–26). The glory of the LORD is like fire (Ezek 1:27) or like the bow in a cloud (Ezek 1:28); the rainbow is a sign of God's covenant with Noah never to destroy the earth again with a flood. However, the rainbow is also a bridge between the heavens and the earth for God; in other words, the LORD walks over the multi-light bridge from heaven to earth, from the world above to the world below. The (rain)bow is also God's means to launch his lightning arrows to the earth! Thus, the theophanic elements of sacred numbers, wind, cloud, fire, lightening, jewels or precious stones, and signs are present. Brownlee notes that underlying this vision "was undoubtedly a simpler original in which Ezekiel told of seeing Yahweh's [the LORD's] glory in a storm cloud."[4] Brownlee explains that he thinks Ezekiel saw "a real storm approaching. Its dark cloud flashed with lightning and perhaps glowed on the edges from the setting sun. . . . Others who saw the storm may have been simply frightened; only Ezekiel

---

4. Brownlee, "Ezekiel," 414.

People's (Person's) Response

was aware of the glory of Yahweh [the LORD] in it."[5] And after all this the prophet has not yet made his response! Finally, he writes, "When I saw it, I fell on my face, and I heard the voice of someone speaking" (Ezek 1:28c).

Ezekiel now hears God's voice detailing his mission and exhorting him not to fear (Ezek 2:1–8). God's spirit or wind enters into the prophet (Ezek 2:2). "In the power of the wind he feels the might of Yahweh's [the LORD's] hand, which is to sustain him in his whole ministry in the face of the opposition he will meet," writes Brownlee.[6] The sign God gives to the prophet is a scroll with writing on it. The LORD tells Ezekiel to eat the scroll, and he does (Ezek 2:9–11). Thus, he interiorized the message and is commissioned to go to the Israelite exiles. Next, Ezekiel sees the LORD and his chariot leave (Ezek 3:12–13), and the prophet is completely stunned for seven days before beginning his mission (Ezek 3:14–16). The wind, the sign of the scroll, and another sacred number bring this theophany to an end.

While Ezekiel's message is lamentation, mourning, and woe (Ezek 2:10), the unique theophany narrated by the author of Luke's Gospel is good news of great joy for all people (Luke 2:10). The angel of the Lord appears to shepherds, who live in fields and keep watch over their sheep at night. Luke is specific is stating that "the glory of the Lord shone around" the angels (Luke 2:9) which causes the shepherds to be terrified—their first response to the divine presence. God, in the disguise of an angel, sends the shepherds to Bethlehem to see the Savior. They are given a sign: "a child wrapped in bands of cloth and lying in a manger" (Luke 2:12). The shepherds' second response is to travel to Bethlehem, find the sign, and then proclaim what they had heard from the angel about this child (Luke 2:15–18). And their third response is to glorify and praise God for all they had heard and seen (Luke 2:20). Thus, in eleven verses Luke has narrated a theophany, using light (shine) and darkness (night), God's voice, a sign, and a three-fold response by shepherds in a field.

---

5. Ibid., 415.
6. Ibid.

5

Cloud

"I AM GOING TO come to you in a dense cloud, in order that the people may hear when I speak with you and so trust you ever after," says the LORD to Moses (Exod 19:9). "On the morning of the third day there was . . . a thick cloud on the mountain" (Exod 19:16). Gray states that a cloud is "a sign of the Divine Presence."[1] After God speaks the Ten Commandments to Moses, the narrator declares, "[T]he people stood at a distance, while Moses drew near to the thick darkness where God was" (Exod 20:21). Later, the narrator records: " . . . Moses went up on the mountain and the cloud covered the mountain. The glory of the LORD settled on Mount Sinai [Horeb], and the cloud covered it for six days; on the seventh day he called to Moses out of the cloud. Moses entered the cloud, and went up on the mountain." (Exod 24:15–16, 18a). Milgrom states that the word "glory generally refers to a cloud which often contains fire."[2] Guthrie puts it this way: "[T]he cloud is connected with the 'glory' of Yahweh [the LORD], i.e. his presence."[3] Schwartz notes that "the visible manifestation of the residing deity remains in full view of the people day and night."[4] McKenzie considers a cloud "an almost universal element of the theophany."[5] Ryken thinks that the cloud represents "God's presence but also his hiddenness. No one can see God and live, so the cloud shields people from actually seeing the form of

---

1. Gray, "Exodus," 47; cf. 67.
2. Milgrom, "Leviticus," 74.
3. Gutherie, "Numbers," 87.
4. Schwartz, "Priestly Account," 115.
5. McKenzie, *Dictionary*, 145.

God."⁶ Faley notes that the cloud indicates the "might and transcendence" of the glory of the LORD.⁷ It is also important to note that the cloud covers the mountain for six incomplete days; on the seventh complete day, God calls Moses into the Divine Presence.

The cloud is found in other theophanies. Among those is the description of the cloud that descended on the tent of meeting, which serves as a type of portable Mount Sinai (Horeb).⁸ When Moses would enter the tent, "the pillar of cloud would descend and stand at the entrance of the tent, and the LORD would speak to Moses. Thus the LORD used to speak to Moses face to face, as one speaks to a friend" (Exod 33:10–11a). Once the ark is built and the tabernacle constructed to house it is finished, the cloud covers "the tent of meeting, and the glory of the LORD [fills] the tabernacle" (Exod 40:34). Faley notes that the "tent was primarily a place of revelation from which Yahweh [the LORD] as head of the covenant assembly directed the activity of his people. . . . Moses does not enter the tent as this time, covered as it is by the cloud and filled with the Lord's glory."⁹ Indeed, the biblical narrator states:

> Moses was not able to enter the tent of meeting because the cloud settled upon it, and the glory of the LORD filled the tabernacle. Whenever the cloud was taken up from the tabernacle, the Israelites would set out on each stage of their journey; but if the cloud was not taken up, then they did not set out until the day that it was taken up. (Exod 40:35–37)

Schwartz says that "the portable abode of the deity" does not replace "the mountain on which he temporarily rested during his descent to earth but [is] rather his heavenly palace and throne room."¹⁰ In the CB (NT), the cloud appears in all three versions of Jesus' transfiguration. It overshadows Peter, James, and John and Elijah, Moses, and Jesus (Mark 9:7; Matt 17:5; Luke 9:34). All of them and the reader of the stories hear a voice that speaks from the cloud, just as Moses did in the narratives above. Harrington writes: "Given the allusions to Exodus in this account, it is best to take the cloud as the vehicle for God's presence as in Exodus 16:10; 19:9; 24:15–16; 33:9."¹¹

6. Ryken, *Dictionary* 157.
7. Faley, "Leviticus," 67.
8. Miller, "Seeing the Glory," 507.
9. Faley, "Leviticus," 62.
10. Schwartz, "Priestly Account," 124.
11. Harrington, "Mark," 615.

Divine Presence

Thus, one element of theophanies that reveals the glory of the LORD is a cloud.

The most extensive use of the cloud element in theophanies is usually identified as "a pillar of cloud." The event that gives rise to its use as a theophanic element is the account of the Israelites' escape from Egypt. The LORD goes "in front of them in a pillar of cloud by day" (Exod 13:21) which never leaves its place in front of the people (Exod 13:22). After arriving at the Red Sea, the pillar of cloud moves from its place in front of the Israelites to behind them in order to separate them from the oncoming Egyptian army (Exod 14:19). The next morning, the Book of Exodus states, the LORD in the pillar of cloud looks down upon the Egyptian army, and throws it into a panic (Exod 14:24). This allowed the Israelites to cross the Red Sea while the Egyptian army struggled to unclog the mud in their chariot wheels, after which they raced into the parted waters which flowed back to their normal depth and drowned them. The Israelites, almost immediately desiring better food than they had, complained to Moses. However, while looking "toward the wilderness, . . . the glory of the LORD appeared in the cloud" (Exod 16:10) and assured them that they would have meat and bread.

Keeping in mind that the tent of meeting serves as a type of portable Mount Sinai (Horeb), once the tent is finished being made Moses enters the tent and, as already indicated above, the pillar of cloud would descend and stand at the entrance of the tent, and the Lord would speak with Moses (Exod 33:9). When the Israelites saw the pillar of cloud standing at the entrance of the tent, they would bow down at the entrances of their tents (Exod 33:10). As a summary paragraph at the end of the Book of Exodus, the narrator records: "Then the cloud covered the tent of meeting, and the glory of the LORD filled the tabernacle. Moses was not able to enter the tent of meeting because the cloud settled upon it, and the glory of the LORD filed the tabernacle" (Exod 40:34–35). Milgrom thinks that the cloud may be caused by burning incense in order "to hide the symbol of God's presence from . . . human gaze."[12] Just as the cloud had led the Israelites out of Egypt, it continues to lead them during their journey to the promised land. The narrator of the Book of Numbers states: "Whenever the cloud lifted from over the tent, then the Israelites would set out; and in the place where the cloud settled down, there the Israelites would camp. As long as the cloud rested over the tabernacle, they would remain in camp"

---

12. Milgrom, "Leviticus," 77–8; cf. North, "Chronicler," 373.

(Num 9:17, 18b; cf. Neh 9:12, 19). After Solomon builds the first temple in Jerusalem, "a cloud fills the house of the LORD, so that the priests could not stand to minister because of the cloud; for the glory of the LORD filled the house of the LORD" (1 Kgs 8:10b–11; cf. 2 Chr 5:14). Now, Mount Zion becomes the new Mount Horeb (Sinai), just like the tent of meeting had been before. Walsh states that the narrative "recounts a theophany."[13] Toombs, commenting on verse 7 of Psalm 99—"[The LORD] spoke . . . in the pillar of cloud"—states: "The pillar of cloud, symbol of God's presence, was associated with the tabernacle, the place of revelation in the time of Moses (cf. Exod 33:9–10; 40:34). It was transferred successively to Samuel's shrine at Shiloh and the Jerusalem temple, the heirs of the tabernacle as Israel's central shrine."[14]

As fast as the prophet Isaiah proclaims the destruction of Jerusalem he also writes about its restoration using the image of the pillar of cloud: " . . . [T]he LORD will create over the whole site of Mount Zion and over its places of assembly a cloud by day. . . . Indeed over all the glory there will be a canopy" (Isa 4:5). The prophet Ezekiel describes the temple being "filled with the cloud" and the court "full of the brightness of the glory of the LORD" (Ezek 10:4) which leaves the temple (Ezek 10:18–19; 11:22–23) while the Israelites are in Babylonian exile. Zimmerli states that "the glory of Yahweh abandons the sanctuary"[15] and "departs from the city area."[16] Ezekiel narrates "how the LORD in Jerusalem abandoned his dwelling place there in order to leave the city and temple to their destruction."[17] Once Jerusalem is purified, the glory of the LORD returns to Jerusalem (Ezek 43:1–12). Zimmerli states, "The vision of the return of the divine glory into the reconstructed sanctuary represents the climax of the vision of the temple of the future."[18] He continues, "Yahweh himself appears in his majesty."[19]

This sign of the Divine Presence is referred to in various other HB (OT) Books. For example, in Leviticus the LORD tells Moses to tell his brother Aaron not to enter the sanctuary of the tent at just any time

13. Walsh, "1–2 Kings," 167.
14. Toombs, "Psalms," 290.
15. Zimmerli, *Ezekiel 1*, 251.
16. Ibid., 252.
17. Ibid., 253.
18. Ibid., *Ezekiel 2*, 412.
19. Ibid., 413.

because, states God, "I appear in the cloud upon the mercy seat" (Lev 16:2). The Book of Numbers states: "[O]n the day the tabernacle was set up, the cloud covered the tabernacle, the tent of the covenant; and from evening until morning it was over the tabernacle . . . " (Lev 9:15). It is understood that the LORD comes down in the cloud (Num 11:25; 12:5); the cloud covers the tent of meeting and the glory of the LORD appears (Num 16:42). The Book of Deuteronomy reminds the people that at Horeb (Sinai) the mountain was shrouded in dark clouds (Deut 4:11); it also explains that "the LORD appeared at the tent in a pillar of cloud; the pillar of cloud stood at the entrance to the tent" (Deut 31:15). Psalm 99 mentions the fact that the LORD spoke to Moses, Aaron, and Samuel in the pillar of cloud (Ps 99:7a). In the OT (A) Book of Sirach, personified wisdom tells of her glory as coming forth from the mouth of the Most High, and having her throne in a pillar of cloud (Sir 24:4).

In the HB (OT), God is often described as riding on the clouds. Psalm 68 unseats the Canaanite god Baal, who was described as a warrior god riding on the clouds of his chariot. The psalmist exhorts singers to "lift up a song to [the LORD] who rides upon the clouds" (Ps 68:4). "Amid rain and earthquake God comes from his traditional home on Mount Sinai [Horeb] to conquer a homeland for his people," states Toombs.[20] Psalm 104 specifically declares that he makes the clouds his chariot (Ps 104:3b). However, it is Psalm 18 that exploits the use of the theophanic cloud; Shnider states that it is "one of the principal theophanies of the Hebrew Bible" (OT).[21] The theophany described by the song begins with an earthquake; the psalm declares that "the earth reeled and rocked; the foundations also of the mountains trembled and quaked" (Ps 18:7; cf. 2 Sam 22:8). Smoke, devouring fire, and glowing coals (Ps 18:8; cf. 2 Sam 22:9) are more elements present in this theophany. The bow is mentioned as the means for God to come from the top level of the universe to the earth (Ps 18:9; cf. 2 Sam 22:10); Toombs says that "the LORD thrusts his way through the dome of the sky."[22] Besides serving as a bridge from the world above to the world below, the (rain)bow, "a symbol of divinely endowed power,"[23] is also used by God to shoot his arrows of lightening (Ps 7:12–13). The LORD flies on the wings of the wind (Ps 18:10; 2 Sam 22:11). Then, the LORD makes "dark-

---

20. Toombs, "Psalms," 281.
21. Shnider, "Psalm XVIII," 386.
22. Toombs, "Psalms," 267.
23. Shnider, "Psalm XVIII," 392.

ness his covering around him, his canopy thick clouds dark with water" (Ps 18:11; cf. 2 Sam 22:12). Brightness or light breaks through the clouds and hailstones and coals of fire fall (Ps 18:12; cf. 2 Sam 22:13). Thunder is heard, and the Most high utters his voice (Ps 18:13; cf. 2 Sam 22:14). He sends his arrows, lightnings (Ps 18:14; cf. 2 Sam 22:15), with his bow—"the instrument of God's wrath"[24]—which reveal both the channels of the sea and the foundations of the earth (Ps 18:15; cf. 2 Sam 22:16). Thus, Psalm 18 presents the theophanic elements of earthquake, smoke, fire, (rain)bow, wind, clouds, thunder, God's voice, lightning, and water. The clouds are presented as thick darkness under his feet, covering him, serving as a canopy over his chariot. Toombs refers to these elements collectively as the "upheavals of nature traditionally associated with a theophany."[25] He explains:

> Attended by earthquake and . . . fire, the LORD thrusts his way through the dome of the sky. Surrounded and supported by storm clouds and carried along by the wind, preceded by hail and thunder and with his arrows of lightning striking down his enemies, the LORD cleaves his way through the sea . . . and the foundations of the world to Sheol itself and lifts the beleaguered king to safety through the subterranean waters. The cosmology involved in this description is the ancient Mesopotamian conception of the three-storied universe; heaven, the abode of God, above the dome of the sky (the firmament); the inhabited world, a flat disk, anchored or founded over the subterranean waters; and Sheol, the realm of the dead, within the waters and far below the earth.[26]

The prophet Nahum develops "the ancient theme of Yahweh's [the LORD's] power (wrath) in nature,"[27] declaring that "the clouds are the dust of [the LORD's] feet" (Nah 1:3b). Psalm 97 further emphasizes that "clouds and chick darkness are all around" the LORD (Ps 97:2). Toombs refers to this verse as part of "the standard imagery of the theophany" describing "God's coming to reign over his people."[28] Ortlund writes:

> The theophanic description begins with Yahweh's [the LORD's] veiling in cloud and thick darkness; but the significance of these clouds has not just to do with Yahweh's [the LORD's] hiddenness,

---

24. Ibid., 394.
25. Toombs, "Psalms," 267.
26. Ibid.
27. De Vries, "Nahum," 491.
28. Toombs, "Psalms," 289.

> but the destruction of his enemies, for out of this storm-cloud flashes fire and lightning which destroys Yahweh's [the LORD's] enemies and convulses the earth (vv. 3–4).[29]

In a similar vein, Shnider thinks that Psalm 18:8–16 is "an extended battle scene involving God and the king."[30] This is supported by the superscription, which states that David "addressed the words of this song to the LORD on the day when he LORD delivered him from the hand of all his enemies . . . " (Psalm 18; cf. 2 Sam 22:1). In this battle scene, "God in a chariot scatter[s] the enemies of Israel."[31] Like any other warrior, the arrows, lightnings, shot from his chariot are signs of God's power used on behalf of the king. No matter which psalm is used to portray the LORD as a mighty warrior, his heavenly reign is assured; readers are granted "a revelation of Yahweh [the LORD] on his throne in overwhelming glory, coming to the glad expectation of the entire world."[32]

It is no small leap from God riding in his chariot on the clouds to Jesus—once he is declared to be the Son of God—coming on the clouds in judgment. The HB (OT) Book of Daniel 7:13 is the origin of the CB (NT) books' depictions. In one of his visions, the prophet sees "one like a human being coming with the clouds of heaven" (Dan 7:13); this one, in some translations called a "son of man," is presented to the Ancient One, God. Knight states that the human being coming on the clouds is in some sense divine. "This is suggested at once by his coming with the clouds of heaven. In Canaanite mythological texts from the middle of the second millennium the gods are said to ride on the clouds, and such language is used of Yahweh [the LORD] in a number of poetic passages of the [HB] OT (e.g. Pss 18:10–11; 68:4; 104:3; Isa 19:1)."[33] The human being or son of man is the hoped-for Davidic descendant who would conquer Israel's enemies and restore the kingdom of Judah. When this did not happen, the image was applied to Jesus by the writers of the books of the CB (NT). For example, the author of Mark's Gospel portrays Jesus, using the unspecified "they," stating to four of his disciples, "Then they will see 'the Son of Man coming in clouds' with great power and glory" (Mark 13:26). Later in the narrative, he tells the high priest, "[Y]ou will see the Son of Man seated at the right

---

29. Ortlund, "Intertextual Reading," 278.
30. Shnider, "Psalm XVIII," 386.
31. Ibid., 388.
32. Ortlund, "Intertextual Reading," 283.
33. Knight, "Daniel," 445.

hand of the Power, and 'coming with the clouds of heaven'" (Mark 14:62). Because the author of Matthew's Gospel and Luke's Gospel borrowed material from Mark's Gospel, it should be no surprise that similar verses are found there (Matt 24:29; 26:64; Luke 21:27). In the Acts of the Apostles, the second volume of Luke's Gospel, the author understands Jesus' ascension as a theophany, stating that as "he was lifted up; . . . a cloud took him out of [the] sight" of his disciples (Acts 1:9). When he returns as judge, "he will come in the same way as [they] saw him go into heaven" (Acts 1:11). Dillon notes the comparison of the cloud at Jesus' ascension with that of the one at his transfiguration:

> Jesus transfigured, attended by the once-translated Elijah (and Moses?), was thus already a prefiguration of the ascended Christ: the ultimate prophet, the ultimate apotheosis. The point of the comparison seems to be the transportation by the cloud, which was also to be the conveyance of the Son of Man at his coming. . . .[34]

In his First Letter to the Thessalonians, Paul makes a reference to being caught up in the clouds to meet the Lord in the air (1 Thess 4:17) on judgment day, but he does not quote Daniel word-for-word as does Mark and Matthew. Collins notes that clouds typically are "a means for heavenly transport."[35] The author of the Book of Revelation presents more urgency in his apocalypse, while clearly referring to Daniel's vision and writing, "Look! He is coming with the clouds . . . " (Rev 1:7a). He goes into more detail later in his narrative, writing that there was a white cloud, and seated on the cloud was one like the Son of Man (Rev 14:14). In the two succeeding verses he mentions that the one seated on the cloud (Rev 14:15–16) has come to judge the world. This same author understands the appearance of angels in his story as theophanic experiences since some of them are wrapped in a cloud (Rev 10:1; 11:12); this echoes Psalm 105 which describes Israel's God as spreading a cloud for a covering over the Israelites as they escaped Egypt (Ps 105:39a). Paul employs this, too, when he tells the Corinthians that their ancestors were all under the cloud (1 Cor 10:1) and all of them were baptized into Moses in the cloud (1 Cor 10:2).

---

34. Dillon, "Acts," 728.
35. Collins, "1 Thessalonians," 778.

6

Water

ANOTHER FREQUENT ELEMENT OF theophanies is water. While it may be a bit hard to detect, it is, nevertheless, present in the account of Moses on Mount Sinai. The LORD says to Moses: "Go to the people and . . . [h]ave them wash their clothes" (Exod 19:10). They did so (Exod 19:14). Here, water is a purifying or cleansing agent. Clifford notes that the Israelites must be separated from the profane world and that is why their clothing is to be washed of earthly grime.[1] Nothing that is unclean can come in contact with God. Ryken acknowledges that "the spiritual principles underlying the need for cleansing in the Mosaic laws are universal."[2] While there is a lot more to this concept, suffice it to be said for now that God, who is holy and clean, can contact only those who are clean—minimally having washed their clothes in this story—in order to bestow upon them his presence. McKenzie notes: "The concepts of holy and unclean resemble each other only in the fact that neither is to be touched and that holiness and uncleanness are both incurred by contact."[3] Most uncleanness "is removed simply by bathing. Uncleanness is therefore conceived as a physical entity, not a moral state."[4] That is why uncleanness must be removed by the physical action of the Israelites washing their clothes in order for the people to participate in the experience of the Divine at Mount Sinai (Horeb).

1. Clifford, "Exodus," 52.
2. Ryken, *Dictionary*, 156.
3. McKenzie, *Dictionary*, 142.
4. Ibid.

The same idea is found in the story of the LORD's appearance to Abraham by the oaks of Mamre. After spying three men coming toward his tent, Abraham greets them, bows to them, and says, "My lord, if I find favor with you, do not pass by your servant. Let a little water be brought, and wash your feet, and rest yourselves under the tree" (Gen 18:3–4). After Abraham and Sarah prepare a lavish feast (an element of a theophany) for the three men (the reader will note the use of three as a sacred number element of a theophany), they give the couple the promise of a son. The promise follows the washing of the feet; the three men (God in disguise) must be clean or holy in order to deliver a clean or holy promise.

If water can be used to cleanse, it can also be used to contaminate. Such is the case with the first plague. Moses lifts up his staff in the sight of Pharaoh and all his officials and strikes the water of the Nile River, "and all the water in the river was turned into blood" (Exod 7:20b). The fish died, and the river stank. And whatever came in contact with the unclean water became unclean.

In the CB (NT), Jesus' baptism in the Jordan River by John serves to make him clean for the theophany of which it is an element (Mark 1:9; Matt 3:13; Luke 3:21; John 1:31). After emerging from the water, Jesus sees the heavens open, a dove fly by, and hears a voice (note another element of a theophany) identify him. Thus, water, which can either make a person clean or unclean, is an element of a theophany that reveals the glory of the LORD.

Water in all its forms—liquid or frozen—represents chaos that only God can create and tame.[5] In a three-storied universe, water is located above the dome of the sky and on the earth. In the second verse of the opening chapter of the HB (OT) Book of Genesis, "darkness cover[s] the face of the deep, while a wind from God [sweeps] over the face of the waters" (Gen 1:2). In other words, chaos reigns in the first account of creation. However, God first creates a dome that separates the waters that are under it from the waters that are above it (Gen 1:7). Then, he sets more boundaries by gathering the waters under the dome in one place, called seas, so that dry land can appear and life can flourish (Gen 1:9). In three days of creating (note the sacred number), God has not only controlled the water, but he has also created a three-storied world. This provides the basis "for believing that the world is a stable, secure, and ordered universe," states Habel. "The

---

5. Kselman, "Psalms," 541, 545.

earth is ruled by a divine monarch who established the world as a cosmic empire and still holds dominion."[6]

In a poem the prophet Habakkuk describes a theophany in which the LORD's glory covers the heavens and the earth (Hab 3:3b). Then, Habakkuk presents the mythic battle between God and the powers of chaos represented by turbulent and uncontrollable water.[7] The prophet refers to the LORD's wrath and anger against the rivers and his rage against the sea (Hab 3:8). After God splits the earth with rivers, torrents of water sweep by the mountains (Hab 3:8–10). God wins the battle, trampling the sea, churning the mighty waters (Hab 3:15). De Vries states that this "theophany, or divine self-revelation, becomes a new revelation of Yahweh's [the LORD's] power."[8] Using battle imagery, it also echoes the first story of creation.

In the second account of creation, the Book of Genesis narrates that out of Eden flows a river that divides into four branches (Gen 2:10–14). The use of the sacred number four indicates that from the lush garden the whole world is watered and given life. The OT (A) Book of Sirach reflects on the water of creation, stating that at the LORD's word the waters stood in a heap, and the reservoirs of water at the word of his mouth (Sir 39:17c). Likewise, the author of the CB (NT) Book of Revelation proclaims the God who made the sea and the springs of water (Rev 14:7), and the author of the Second Letter of Peter makes clear "that by the word of God . . . earth was formed out of water and by means of water" (2 Pet 3:5). Psalm 65 emphasizes that water is an element of a theophany. The psalmist declares that God visits the earth and waters it. God's river is full of water which fills the earth's furrows, settles its ridges, and softens it with showers (Ps 65:9–10).

Chaos is calmed by God at Rephidim, where the Israelites camped, but there was no water. Furthermore, the people quarreled with Moses, telling him to give them water to drink; Moses interprets this as testing the LORD. After listening to the grumbling of the Israelites, Moses asks God what he should do.

> The LORD said to Moses, "Go on ahead of the people, and take some of the elders of Israel with you; take in your hand the staff with which you struck the Nile, and go. I will be standing there in front of you on the rock at Horeb. Strike the rock, and water will

---

6. Habel, *Land*, 27.
7. Wahl, "Zephaniah, Nahum, Habakkuk," 263–4.
8. De Vries, "Habakkuk," 495.

WATER

come out of it, so that the people may drink." Moses did so, in the sight of the elders of Israel. (Exod 17:5–6)

Once the water flows from the rock, the chaos is ordered. Similarly, is the narrative about Samson killing a thousand men with the jawbone of a donkey and then being thirsty. He calls on the LORD, and "God split open the hollow place, . . . and water came from it" (Judg 15:19). Psalm 114 makes it very clear that it is the LORD "who turns the rock into a pool of water, the flint into a spring of water" (Ps 114:8). It is God who brings order out of chaos.

Once God's glory returns to the temple (see Cloud), the prophet Ezekiel describes the water flowing from the temple as the new source of life (Ezek 47:1–2); it is a new garden of Eden. As the prophet walks through the water four times—indicating that it gives life to the whole world—it gets deeper and deeper (Ezek 47:3–6). This water even transforms the Dead Sea into fresh water (Ezek 47:8). This water is the theophanic element of the presence of God. The author of the CB (NT) Book of Revelation recognizes this. The One seated on the throne in his vision gives "water as a gift from the spring of the water of life" (Rev 21:6). Instead of flowing from the temple, as it does in Ezekiel's vision, the water flows from the throne of God in John of Patmos's vision, because there is no temple in the new Jerusalem. The water of life, bright as crystal, flows from God's throne and spreads life everywhere (Rev 22:1–5).

Noah and the flood, considered to be two separate and somewhat different stories which have been woven into one final biblical account, represent the destructive and reconstructive qualities of water. God tells the patriarch that he intends to "bring a flood of waters on the earth to destroy from under heaven all flesh in which is the breath of life" (Gen 6:17). The forty-day flood—forty represents the life of an average human generation—will come both from the earth and from the heavens (Gen 7:4). The fountains of the great deep burst forth and the windows or floodgates of the heavens are opened (Gen 7:11); thus, water flowed from both the earth and above the dome of the sky, returning the world to a state of chaos. The Book of Genesis describes this return to chaos: "The waters swelled so mightily on the earth that all the high mountains under the whole heaven were covered; the waters swelled above the mountains . . . " (Gen 7:19–20). God blotted out every living thing except for Noah and his family (Gen 7:23), of whom the CB (NT) author of the First Letter of Peter writes that "eight persons were saved through water" (1 Pet 3:20); the number represents fullness. All of "the world at that time was deluged with water and perished" (2 Pet 3:6). Once the water abated and Noah and his family and the animals emerged from their protective ark, God commissioned all to start over, to repopulate the earth (Gen 8:1—9:10). Noah's three sons (note the divine number) become the ancestors of all people. God even enters into covenant with Noah and every living creature that the waters would never again become a flood to destroy all life (Gen 9:11–17). And, thus, the chaos of water was once again tamed by God; its boundaries were once again established.

If water can paradoxically give life and destroy it, its destructive characteristics are highlighted by the various plagues in the HB (OT) Book of Exodus. Keeping in mind that the staff that Moses wields is referred to as "the staff of God" (Exod 4:20; 17:9), when Aaron strikes the water in the Nile River, the water turns to blood (Exod 7:14–24) after which a period of seven days (note the sacred number) passes (Exod 7:25). As a result of the bloody water, there emerge frogs (Exod 8:1–15) gnats (Exod 8:16–19), flies (Exod 8:20–32), disease (Exod 9:1–7), and boils (Exod 9:8–12). In other words, the plagues are theophanies. There are a total of six plagues to indicate that there are more to come. There are five that result from the bloody Nile to indicate God's grace, goodness, and unmerited gift to the Hebrew slaves. Furthermore, the plague of the Nile River turning to red blood is echoed by the crossing of the Red Sea which is itself another creation story.

Lifting up the staff of God, Moses stretches out his hand over the sea, and it divides; a new boundary—like that in the first creation account and in the Noah story—is created. God separates the water from the land. According to Exodus narrator, Moses stretches out his hand over the sea. The LORD drives the sea back by a strong east wind all night, turns the sea into dry land, and the waters are divided (Exod 14:21). Chaos is again tamed. Once the Israelites cross through the sea, the usual boundary is restored as Moses stretches out his hand again, and the sea returns to its normal depth, covering Pharaoh's chariots and chariot drivers (Exod 14:26–29). Psalm 114 captures this is song; the lyrics state that when Israel went out from Egypt, the sea looked and fled (Ps 114:1a, 3a). The OT (A) Book of Wisdom refers to this as "the rhythm of violently rushing water" (Wis 17:18c). Continuing, the author states, " . . . [D]ry land emerg[ed] where water had stood before, an unhindered way out of the Red Sea, and a grassy plain out of the raging waves, where those protected by [God's] hand passed through as one nation" (Wis 19:7–8). Paul, in his First Letter to the Corinthians states that his ancestors passed through the sea, and all were baptized into Moses in the sea (1 Cor 10:1–2).

This altering of the boundary of water is reenacted by Joshua (Josh 3:1–17), Elijah (2 Kgs 2:8), and Elisha (2 Kgs 2:13–14) when they cross the Jordan River. The theophany of divided waters occurs when Joshua heeds the LORD's instructions to select twelve men (note the sacred number), one from each tribe (even though there are not twelve tribes!). When the soles of the priests who carry the ark of the LORD, the sign of God's presence, touch the water of the Jordan, the waters stop, standing in a heap. Each of the twelve men takes a stone from the Jordan River bed, and Joshua erects them as a memorial of the crossing. Then, once all have crossed, the Jordan River returns to its usual flow (Josh 3:7—4:18). Psalm 114 expresses this in poetic form; when Israel went out from Egypt, the Jordan turned back (Ps 114:1a, 3b).

With his own type of flair, the prophet Elijah rolls up his mantle and strikes the water of the Jordan and it parts so that he and Elisha can pass (2 Kgs 2:8). Once the theophany of "a chariot of fire and horses of fire" appears and "Elijah ascended in a whirlwind into heaven" (2 Kgs 2:11), Elisha picks up Elijah's mantel, goes to the Jordan, and strikes the water, which parts for him just as it had done for Elijah (2 Kgs 2:13–14). Thus, it is not difficult to see that water—especially divided water—is a theophanic element in biblical literature.

In the CB (NT), it is the water associated with baptism that is theophanic. The author of Mark's Gospel declares that Jesus is baptized by John the Baptist in the Jordan River, reenacting the Red Sea crossing and the Jordan River crossing by Joshua, Elijah, and Elisha. For Jesus the theophany occurs as he is coming up out of the water; he sees the heavens torn apart, the Spirit descends like a dove on him, and he hears a voice from heaven (Mark 1:10–11). The author connects this theophany to the one that follows Jesus' crucifixion and death when the curtain of the temple is torn in two (Mark 15:38). Because God was understood to live above the dome of the sky, when the heavens are torn apart, God falls to the earth. Likewise, when the temple curtain is torn in two, God escapes from the holy place. Matthew tones down his Markan source for Jesus' baptism and theophany at the Jordan; he writes that "as [Jesus] came up from the water, suddenly the heavens were opened to him" (Matt 3:16). Luke does the same, stating that it was while Jesus was praying after his baptism that "the heaven was opened" (Luke 3:21). The other elements of the theophany—Holy Spirit like a dove and voice of God—remain the same. In the Acts of the Apostles, Philip is directed by an angel of the Lord, that is, a theophany, to meet an Ethiopian eunuch and explain the prophet Isaiah to him. After so doing, they come to some water, in which Philip baptized the eunuch. "When they came up out of the water, the Spirit of the Lord snatched Philip away" (Acts 8:39a). Thus, Philip experiences a second theophany as he emerges from water. The purifying water of baptism, which is itself a drowning and rebirth—a redrawing of boundaries—is an element of a theophany.

7

Thunder

THUNDER IS AN ELEMENT in theophanies. The HB (OT) Book of Exodus clearly states that there was thunder on Mount Sinai (Horeb) (Exod 19:16; 20:18). Furthermore, in their dialogue, "Moses would speak and God would answer him in thunder" (Exod. 19:19). As McKenzie makes clear, "the voice of Yahweh [the LORD] . . . is one of the motifs of the theophany."[1] Ryken explains: "The primal imagination links thunder with the presence, power, and wrath of deity."[2] Going into more depth, he states: "The image of thunder in the Bible is based on a paradox: it is a force of nature that consistently images forth something beyond nature, namely, the presence, power, and judgment of deity, evoking primarily awe and dread."[3]

Thunder is very prominent in the narrative about the seventh plague in Egypt. That plague, hail and fire, begins with Moses stretching out his staff and the LORD sending thunder (Exod 9:23). Pharaoh tells Moses and Aaron to ask God to stop the thunder (Exod 9:28), and Moses explains that he will extend his staff and the thunder will stop (Exod 9:29)—and it does (Exod 9:33). However, when Pharaoh sees that it has stopped, he refuses to let the Hebrews leave Egypt (Exod 9:34). In this narrative fire is an element of a theophany, and hail, frozen water, is still another one. Clifford notes, "The hail is part of a thunderstorm, the appropriate context for the revelation of the storm-god Yahweh" (the LORD)[4] What he means is that the

1. McKenzie, *Dictionary*, 889.
2. Ryken, *Dictionary*, 869.
3. Ibid.
4. Clifford, "Exodus," 48.

plagues represent a battle taking place between the LORD and Pharaoh. Thunder—along with hail and lightning or fire—demonstrates God's superior power. "God's manipulation of natural elements is a narrative way of revealing his sole divinity," states Clifford.[5] Psalm 78 interprets the seventh plague as God giving over the Egyptians' cattle to the hail and their flocks to thunderbolts (Ps 78:48). The OT (A) Book of Wisdom refers to the seventh plague as "the violence of thunder" (Wis 19:13b). And should anyone doubt that thunder is an element of a theophany, the prophet Isaiah tells the citizens of Jerusalem that "in an instant, suddenly, [they] will be visited by the LORD of hosts with thunder . . . " (Isa 29:5–6). It seems that Isaiah had experienced the suddenness of a thunderstorm!

The element of thunder in the HB (OT) First Book of Samuel represents divine judgment. In what is commonly known as the song of Hannah, the shattering of the LORD's adversaries, that is, his judgment of them, is equated with the Most High thundering in heaven (1 Sam 2:10a). Later in the same book, Hannah's son, Samuel, after he establishes Saul as Israel's first king, gives a lengthy speech recounting Israel's history. He addresses all Israel about the evil of the people's demand for a king. Samuel makes clear that the people have done great wickedness in demanding a king for themselves. However, as long as they continue to worship their God, the monarchy is acceptable. The last judge concludes by declaring that he will ask God to send thunder to validate his words (1 Sam 12:17). Then, Samuel calls upon the LORD to demonstrate his superior power and judgment, "and the LORD sent thunder and rain that day; and all the people greatly feared the LORD and Samuel" (2 Sam 12:18). This theophany of thunder demonstrates both the LORD's response to Samuel's request for a sign and God's judgment of his people's desire for a king. Repeatedly the psalmists declare that the skies thunder (Ps 77:17b), and that at the sound of thunder the waters take to flight (Ps 104:7). The OT (A) Book of Sirach declares: "The voice of [the Most High's] thunder rebukes the earth" (Sir 43:17a). Thus, thunder serves as an element of theophanies and reveals the glory of the LORD.

As an element of a theophany, thunder often is equated with God's voice in biblical literature, even though the LORD often speaks in human words, too. Psalm 18 merges these two elements: "The LORD also thundered in the heavens, and the Most High uttered his voice" (Ps 18:13). In Psalm 77, the singer declares, "The crash of your thunder was in the whirlwind"

---

5. Ibid.

(Ps 77:18a). In Psalm 81, God declares that he answered the singer "in the secret place of thunder" (Ps 81:7b). Sirach, too, combines God's voice and thunder writing, "The voice of his thunder rebukes the earth" (Sir 43:17a). The author of the HB (OT) Book of Job proposes thunder as God's voice as a powerful element of a theophany; he refers to the thunder of his power (Job 26:14c), the thunder of his voice and the rumbling that comes from his mouth (Job 37:2), and thunder with a voice like his (Job 40:9). In the CB (NT), John's Gospel merges a voice from heaven that glorifies God's name in the person of Jesus with thunder (John 12:28–29). And the author of the Book of Revelation several times writes about the rumblings and peals of thunder that come from God's throne (Rev 4:5, 11:19), that describe a voice of thunder (Rev 6:1; 14:2), and that merely describe peals of thunder (Rev 8:5, 16:18), not to mention the "seven thunders" (Rev 10:4)!

8

Lightning

LIGHTNING IS ANOTHER ELEMENT of theophanies revealing the glory of the LORD. Lightning appears on Mount Sinai (Horeb) (Exod 19:16; 20:18). While it is often paired with thunder, according to Ryken it "symbolizes at once both the untamable power and unapproachable presence of God."[1] In other words, lightning serves a paradoxical purpose; it is both frightening and awesome. It is frightening because it is potent and blinding. It is awesome because is serves "as a sign of the active presence of God."[2]

In one of the prophet Daniel's visions, he sees a man whose face is like lightning (Dan 10:6), signaling divine revelation. In one of the prophet Ezekiel's visions, he describes lightning issuing from a fire and four living creatures darting "to and fro like a flash of lightning" (Ezek 1:14). The author of the CB (NT) Book of Revelation, who loves to borrow imagery from Ezekiel, describes his vision of God's temple in heaven with the ark of his covenant and "flashes of lightning" (Rev. 11:19).

The OT (A) Book of Sirach states, "Lightning travels ahead of the thunder" (Sir 32:10). It is primarily understood to be God's arrows which are launched with his bow, that is, his rainbow! The HB (OT) Book of Job exploits this element. Elihu, a character who suddenly enters the book three-fourths of the way through, describes God's greatness in a theophanic thunderstorm (Job 36:26–29) during which "he scatters his lightning around him" (Job 36:30). Elihu states, "He covers his hands with the lightning, and commands it to strike the mark" (Job 36:32). And he adds, "Under the

---

1. Ryken, *Dictionary*, 512.
2. McKenzie, *Dictionary*, 511.

whole heaven he lets it loose, and his lightning to the corners of the earth" (Job 37:3); "he does not restrain the lightnings when his voice is heard" (Job 37:4). "He loads the thick cloud with moisture; the clouds scatter his lightning" (Job 37:11) and his command "causes the lightning of his cloud to shine" (Job 37:15b).

Psalm 77 recalls the events surrounding the Exodus, mentioning God's arrows that flashed on every side (Ps 77:17) and his lightnings that lit up the world (Ps 77:18). Psalm 105 also refers to the lightning that flashed through the land of Egypt (Ps 105:32). Psalm 18 is more explicit, declaring that God "sent out his arrows, and scattered [his enemies]; he flashed forth lightnings, and routed them" (Ps 18:14). Shnider says that the arrows are a sign of God's power.[3] However, the most explicit statement equating lightning and arrows is found in 2 Samuel 22:15, a part of a version of Psalm 18 that was inserted into the Second Book of Samuel: "He sent out arrows, and scattered [his enemies]—lightning, and routed them." Echoing Psalm 18, Psalm 144 includes a plea to the LORD to make the lightning flash and to send out his arrows to rout his enemies (Ps 144:6). In describing God's care of the righteous, the OT (A) Book of Wisdom states: "Shafts of lightning will fly with true aim, and will leap from the clouds to the target, as from a well-drawn bow" (Wis 5:21). In a hymn praising God's rule, the prophet Habakkuk describes a theophany in which the moon stood still as the light of God's arrows and the gleam of his flashing spear sped by (Hab 3:11). Wahl says that God "is depicted in heroic terms as a giant striding the earth and using the very lightning as one of his weapons."[4] Likewise, the prophet Zechariah describes the LORD's appearance in which his arrow goes forth like lightning (Zech 9:14).

While Psalm 135 is very clear that it is the LORD who makes lightnings for the rain (Ps 135:7; cf. Jer 10:13; 51:16), Psalm 97 presents a theophany which includes the elements of clouds and thick darkness (Ps 97:2), fire (Ps 97:3), mountains (Ps 97:5), and the LORD's "lightnings [that] light up the world," causing the earth to see and tremble (Ps 97:4). Ortlund notes that this psalm begins "with a standard description of Yahweh's [the LORD's] appearance in smoke, fire, and lightning."[5] The OT (A) Book of Sirach considers these to be the lightnings of God's judgment (Sir 43:13). According to Ortlund, these elements are combined by the psalmist to cre-

3. Shnider, "Psalm XVIII," 389.
4. Wahl, "Zephaniah, Nahum, Habakkuk," 264.
5. Ortlund, "Intertextual Reading," 273.

ate "the standard imagery . . . to depict Yahweh's [the LORD's] presence."[6] Addressing himself specifically to lightning, Ortlund says that God is depicted as a warrior, wielding his weapons of lightning: "Yahweh's appearance in the storm . . . occurs in order for him to do battle as a Divine Warrior, using the elements of the storm as weapons leveled against his enemies."[7] However, as Ortlund notes, there is a paradoxical understanding present. Lightning, along with the other elements present in the theophany in Psalm 97, is "used by that deity to nurture the earth in blessed fecundity."[8] In both cases of the paradox, the LORD produces order; he defeats both the chaos caused by war (his enemies) to restore divine rule and that caused by the earth's lack of rain by making it fertile and fruitful.[9]

In the CB (NT), lightning is used to describe Jesus' transfiguration by the author of Matthew's Gospel (Matt 28:3). Once Jesus is given the titles Son of God and God, lightning is attributed to his coming in glory. For example, in material referred to as Q (from *Quelle*, meaning *source*), indicating that it comes from a common source used by the author of Matthew's Gospel and the author of Luke's Gospel, Jesus speaks about his return to the earth comparing it to a lightning flash: " . . . [A]s the lightning comes from the earth and flashes as far as the west, so will be the coming of the Son of Man" (Matt 24:27). Luke records Jesus saying: " . . . [A]s the lightning flashes and lights up the sky from one side to the other, so will the Son of Man be in his day" (Luke 17:24). The pseudonymous author of the Book of Revelation loves lightning to indicate both the presence of God and the Lamb and to indicate judgment. From God's throne come flashes of lightning (Rev. 4:5), and lightning accompanies the revisited plagues (Rev 8:5; 16:18). Thus, lightning serves as an element of theophanies in both the HB (OT) and the CB (NT) to reveal the glory of the LORD.

---

6. Ibid., 276.
7. Ibid., 277.
8. Ibid.
9. Ibid, 277–8.

9

Trumpet Blast

WHILE NOT USED EXTENSIVELY, another element of a theophany is a trumpet blast. Trumpets, "straight metal tubes blown by priests in concert,"[1] are used to summon the Israelites to meet their God. From Mount Sinai (Horeb) is heard "a blast of a trumpet so loud that all the people who were in the camp trembled" (Exod 19:16). The "blast of the trumpet grew louder and louder" (Exod 19:19), according to the narrative. In fact the sound of the trumpet makes the people afraid and causes them to tremble and stand at a distance (Exod 20:18). The author of the Letter to the Hebrews in the CB (NT) refers to the sound of the trumpet as one of the terrifying events that took place on Mount Sinai (Horeb) (Heb 12:19). And the author of the Book of Revelation, echoing the events of Sinai (Horeb), portrays John of Patmos hearing "a loud voice like a trumpet" (Rev 1:10; cf. 4:1).

The HB (OT) Book of Numbers records the LORD's words to Moses which authorize the making of trumpets and explains their purpose: "Make two silver trumpets; you shall make them of hammered work; and you shall use them for summoning the congregation.... When both are blown, the whole congregation shall assemble before you at the entrance of the tent of meeting" (Num 10:2–3). This is the last act before leaving Mount Sinai (Horeb) states Guthrie.[2] L'Heureux says that trumpets are the means of signaling the people. The trumpet of beaten metal replaced in part the earlier use of the ram's horn.[3]

---

1. Toombs, "Psalms," 289.
2. Guthrie, "Numbers," 87.
3. L'Heureux, "Numbers," 84.

> When both trumpets are sounded, the community assembles at the tent, whereas a single trumpet summons just the chiefs. . . . [A] different manner of blowing the trumpets provides a signal for setting out on the march. . . . The two modalities will also be characteristic after Israel has settled in the land: the first manner will announce liturgical convocation; the alarm modality will be used in warfare.[4]

In biblical literature besides being used to summon the congregation (Joel 2:15–16) and to sound the alarm to go to war (Num 10:9; 31:6; Judg 7:8–22; Neh 4:20; Jer 4:19, 51:27; Ezek 33:3–6; Hos 5:8; Amos 3:6; 1 Macc 3:54; 4:13, 4:40, 5:31, 33, 6:33, 7:45, 9:12, 16:8; 2 Macc 5:25) and to stop the battle (1 Sam 13:3; 2 Sam 2:28, 18:16, 20:22; Jer 6:1), trumpets are also used to break camp (Num 10:2), to announce days of rejoicing, festivals, and at the beginning of months (Num 10:10; Ps 81:3), on the first day of the seventh month to announce a holy convocation (Num 29:1; Lev 23:24), on the tenth day of the seventh month to announce the day of atonement (Lev 25:9), to proclaim Solomon as king (1 Kgs 1:34, 39), and to proclaim that "the day of the Lord is coming" (Joel 2:1). Of importance here is the use of the trumpet in theophanies. Besides the model theophany presented in the HB (OT) Book of Exodus and referred to by the author of the Letter to the Hebrews (Heb 12:19), trumpets are also featured in the account of Joshua at Jericho. Since Joshua is portrayed as a new Moses, it should not come as a surprise that there is a story about him using trumpets in a theophanic event.

The story begins after all the Israelites have crossed the Jordan River into the promised land. The LORD speaks directly to Joshua, telling him to march around the city of Jericho for six days with seven priests bearing seven trumpets of rams' horns before the ark of the LORD, the portable Horeb (Sinai). On the seventh day they will march around the city seven times with the priests blowing the trumpets (Josh 6:4). The six days of marching around the city indicate incompleteness. The march is complete on the seventh day when God will hand over the city to Joshua and his army. Specific directions are given for the last day, namely, a long blast on the trumpet followed by a great shout of all the people before the walls fall (Josh 6:5). The long blast signals the attack, and the great shout initiates it. Armed men lead the procession, followed by the seven priests with the seven trumpets. After the priests comes the ark, then the rear guard (Josh

---

4. Ibid.

6:8–9). This ceremonial procession before the LORD takes place in silence, except for the blowing of the trumpets, for six days (Josh 6:10—14); however, the story is not yet finished.

On the seventh day the procession takes place as it has done on the previous six days. However, the completeness is indicated by the fact that this is the seventh day and the procession circles the outer walls of Jericho seven times (Josh 5:15) while blowing the seven trumpets. The three sets of seven indicate a theophany. After the seventh complete circumambulation Joshua instructs all the people to shout (Josh 5:16). "So the people shouted, and the trumpets were blown. As soon as the people heard the sound of the trumpets, they raised a great shout, and the wall fell down flat" (Josh 6:20). Thus, the LORD, whose presence was signified by the portable Horeb (Sinai) ark, handed over the city of Jericho to the Israelites with trumpet blasts.

The divine presence is heralded with trumpet blasts. Echoing the shouts of the people in the story of the fall of the Jericho above, Psalm 47 declares: "God has gone up with a shout, the LORD with the sound of a trumpet" (Ps 47:5). God is enthroned as Israel's king; this is made clear in Psalm 98: "With trumpets and the sound of the horn," all the earth is exhorted to make a joyful noise before the King, the LORD (Ps 98:6). The last song in the Book of Psalms also announces God's reign and tells the singer: "Praise him with trumpet sound" (Ps 150:3a). As already noted above, God, the King, is also the LORD, the mighty warrior who defends his people. The prophet Zechariah presents him bending Judah as his bow, making Israel his arrow (Zech 9:13a), and sounding the trumpet before beginning the march to war (Zech 9:14b).

Trumpets herald the bringing of the ark to Jerusalem (2 Sam 6:15; 1 Chr 13:8, 15:28). Seven priests, echoing the seven priests in the account of the fall of Jericho, are appointed to blow trumpets before the ark of the LORD (1 Chr 15:24). Once David brings the ark to Jerusalem and settles it into the tent he made, he appoints two priests to blow trumpets regularly before the ark of the covenant of God (1 Chr 16:6). Through much of the Second Book of Chronicles there is mention of trumpets being blown before the ark of the LORD (2 Chr 5:13, 7:6, 20:28, 28:13, 29:26–27). When Ezra begins the rebuilding of the temple destroyed by the Babylonians, priests blow trumpets when the foundation is laid (Ezra 3:10); when the walls of Jerusalem are dedicated nine—the sacred number three squared—priests with trumpets are named (Neh 12:35–36) along with seven—the sum of the number for the divine plus the number for the earth—other named trumpeters giving thanks (Neh 12:41). Reflecting upon these events, the OT (A) Book of Sirach states: " . . . [T]he sons of Aaron shouted; they blew their trumpets of hammered metal; they sounded a mighty fanfare as a reminder before the Most High" (Sir 50:16).

The trumpet blast will send out the Son of Man's angels to gather his elect, according to the author of Matthew's Gospel (Matt 24:31). This unique Matthean detail echoes the HB (OT) prophet Isaiah's declaration that a great trumpet will be blown to summon God's people when he restores Israel (Isa 27:13) and that God gathers the exiles (Deut 30:4; Zech 2:6). Before Matthew, it was Paul who used the trumpet as one of the elements of the theophanic and apocalyptic end of the world. In his First Letter to the Thessalonians, the oldest piece of literature in the CB (NT), he describes it this way: " . . . [T]he Lord himself, with a cry of command, with the archangel's call and with the sound of God's trumpet, will descend from heaven, and the dead in Christ will rise first" (1 Thess 4:16). Paul has most likely borrowed that image from the prophet Joel, who describes the coming of the day of the LORD with the blowing of a trumpet (Joel 2:1, 15), a "part of Jewish apocalyptic imagery."[5] He refers to this eschatological theophany again in his First Letter to the Corinthians, writing: "Listen, I will tell you a mystery! We will not all die, but we will all be changed, in a moment, in the twinkling of an eye, at the last trumpet" (1 Cor 15:51–52a). Collins explains that the trumpet, along with the cry of command and the archangel's call, "stress the divine initiative in the event."[6] He also explains the origin of the imagery. " . . . [T]he solemn entrance of kings into a (conquered) town [is] the model for the scenario."[7] However, he also adds, " . . . [T]he biblical description of the theophany at Sinai [Horeb] provides the exemplar for this description of the parousia,"[8] that is, Christ's return in glory.

Many of the uses of the trumpet are brought together in the Book of Revelation. John of Patmos records that he was in the spirit on the Lord's day (Rev 1:10), another way to say that he was experiencing a theophany, when he heard "a loud voice like a trumpet" (Rev. 1:10) telling him to record what he sees in a book. When he looks through the open door of heaven, he hears the voice like a trumpet again (Rev 4:1). When the Lamb opens

---

5. Murphy-O'Connor, "First Letter to the Corinthians," 814.
6. Collins, "First Letter to the Thessalonians," 778.
7. Ibid.
8. Ibid.

the seventh seal, John sees seven angels who stand before God with seven trumpets (Rev 8:2). The reader will immediately notice the three sets of seven, sacred number elements of a theophany. The seven angels with seven trumpets—called "trumpets of doom"[9] by Gilmour—begin another series of seven; these events mirror seven plagues of the HB (OT) Book of Exodus. Collins states: "The content of the trumpet series is a free adaption of the ten plagues against the Egyptians which preceded the exodus."[10] The first angel blows the trumpet and hail, fire, and blood comes forth (Rev 8:7; Exod 9:13–35; 7:14–25). The second angel blows the trumpet and a great mountain of burning fire was hurled into the sea (Rev 8:8; Exod 14:1–31). After the third angel blows the trumpet, a great star falls from heaven (Rev. 8:10; Exod 7:14–25). A third of the sun is struck, and a third of the moon, and a third of the stars by the blast of the fourth angel's trumpet (Rev 8:12; Exod 10:21–29). Collins notes that "the first four trumpets form a group. Together they affect the cosmos as a totality. . . . The last three trumpets affect humanity more directly."[11] The fifth angel blows the trumpet and a star falls from heaven to earth with a key to the bottomless pit from which locusts emerge (Rev. 9:1; Exod 10:12–20). The sixth angel blows the trumpet to release four angels to kill a third of humankind (Rev. 9:13–21; Exod 12:29–32). When the seventh angel blows the trumpet, voices in heaven proclaim that the kingdom of the world has become the kingdom of the Lord and his Messiah (Rev. 11:15). The end has arrived, as John declares that "God's temple in heaven was opened, and the ark of his covenant was seen within his temple; and there were flashes of lightning, rumblings, peals of thunder, an earthquake, and heavy hail" (Rev. 11:19). John experiences some of the typical cosmic elements of a theophany: lightning, thunder, earthquake, and water (hail). This theophany was announced by seven angels with seven trumpet blasts. Thus, the blast of a trumpet serves as another element of a theophany that reveals the glory of the LORD and the glory of the Lord (Jesus).

9. Gilmour, "Revelation," 956.
10. Collins, "Revelation," 1006.
11. Ibid.

10

Smoke

WHILE IT MIGHT SEEM odd to treat the element of smoke before fire, that is how it is presented in the narrative description of "Mount Sinai . . . wrapped in smoke" (Exod 19:18), "the mountain smoking" (Exod 20:18), and "the thick darkness where God was" (Exod 20:21). Concerning these verses, Ryken states that the reader is moved to envisage a volcano.[1] However, the writer may be describing something like a dense fog or low cloud cover, a phenomenon that occurs frequently in mountains. The kind of smoke portrayed in the Exodus story is not like other references to smoke that is the result of fire. The description of Mount Sinai does include smoke going up like the smoke of a kiln (Exod 19:18), which would have been heated with fire. Schwartz notes that when the LORD descends upon Mount Sinai (Horeb), the Israelites perceive only "thunder and lightning, the mountain being conveniently covered by smoke."[2]

The prophet Isaiah employs this same kind of image when describing the glory of the new Jerusalem. "Then the LORD will create over the whole site of Mount Zion and over its places of assembly a cloud by day and smoke . . . " states the prophet (Isa 4:5). The conjunction of cloud and smoke echoes the description of Mount Sinai (Horeb) in the Book of Exodus as that found in the CB (NT) Book of Revelation: " . . . [T]he temple was filled with smoke from the glory of God and from his power" (Rev 15:8). As already noted above, this is not the smoke that results from fire as Isaiah portrays later (Isa 6:4). In other places, smoke is equated with God's anger,

---

1. Ryken, *Dictionary*, 287.
2. Schwartz, "Priestly Account," 125

as in Psalm 18: "Smoke went up from [God's] nostrils" (Ps 18:8a; cf. 2 Sam 22:9a). In Psalm 74 the psalmist asks God, "Why does your anger smoke against the sheep of your pasture?" (Ps 74:1b) Similarly, Isaiah declares that the name of the LORD comes "burning with his anger and in thick rising smoke" (Isa 30:27a). The author of the Book of Revelation in the CB (NT) loves the image of smoke. From the shaft of the bottomless pit rises smoke, "like the smoke of a great furnace" (Rev 9:2). Smoke comes out of the mouths of the horses (Rev. 9:17–18), and the smoke of torment is but one of many afflictions caused by God's wrath (Rev. 14:11).

Another aspect of smoke that deserves investigation as an element of a theophany is its ability to represent burnt offerings. After the Mount Horeb (Sinai) experience, a variety of laws stipulate what the Israelites are to offer to the LORD. For example, the HB (OT) Book of Exodus legislates that the fat of animals is to be turned into smoke on the altar (Exod 29:13); a whole ram is turned into smoke on the altar as a pleasing odor to the LORD (Exod 29:18); and various grain offerings are turned into smoke on the altar (Exod 29:25)—all this for the ordination of Aaron and his sons as priests. The concept or understanding is this: The invisible God who manifests himself in smoke cannot accept or receive material gifts. Therefore, they must be turned into almost invisible offerings. When they are burned with fire, another element of a theophany, they become invisible or barely visible as smoke which rises from the middle story of the earth to the top story of heaven where God lives.

The HB (OT) Book of Leviticus spends even more words describing animals from the herd or the flock—sheep, goats, birds—that are offered to the LORD; the whole animal is turned into smoke on the altar (Lev 1:9, 13, 15, 17). These burnt offerings are unique among those legislated, because all other sacrifices involved only a portion of the offering being turned into smoke; the remainder was given as food to the priests, the poor, or the donor. For example, only a handful of a grain offering is turned into smoke; the rest is given to Aaron and his sons (Lev 2:2–3). If the grain offering is baked, only a portion broken off is turned into smoke (Lev 2:8–9); likewise if it is a grain offering of first fruits, only a portion is turned into smoke (Lev 2:14). However, it is important to note that anything made with leaven (yeast) or honey, because they caused fermentation and are considered to be ritually unclean, is not turned into smoke (Lev 2:11). Only a portion of sacrifices of well-being is turned into smoke (Lev 3:5, 11, 16) as well as purification offerings (Lev 4:10, 19, 26, 31, 35; 5:12). There are even a set of supplementary instructions concerning the smoke (Lev 6:12, 15, 22; 7:5, 31).

Chapter 8 of the Book of Leviticus contains another account of the consecration of Aaron and his sons as priests; this chapter contains a number of references to the required offerings turned into smoke on the altar (Lev 8:16, 20, 21, 28). This chapter is followed by one that demonstrates Aaron fulfilling his duties as priest, that is, turning sacrifices into smoke (Lev 9:10, 13, 14, 17, 20). On the day of atonement, after performing the ritual with the two goats (Lev 16:15–22), Aaron makes a burnt offering and a sin offering and turns them into smoke on the altar (Lev 16:25). The HB (OT) Book of Numbers contains two references to turning offerings into smoke (Num 5:26; 18:17). All these references to turning offerings into smoke can be summarized with three verses from Psalm 66: "I will come into your house [, O God,] with burnt offerings; I will pay you my vows, those that my lips uttered and my mouth promised when I was in trouble. I will offer to you burnt offerings of fatlings, with the smoke of the sacrifice of rams; I will make an offering of bulls and goats" (Ps 66:13–15).

However, the CB (NT) Book of Revelation describes a scene with an angel holding a golden censer to whom great quantities of incense—often referred to as frankincense in the HB (OT)—"to offer with the prayers of all the saints on the golden altar that is before the throne" of God. "And the smoke of the incense, with the prayers of the saints, rose before God from the hand of the angel" (Rev 8:3–4). The author is echoing the prayer in Psalm 141: "Let my prayer be counted as incense before you," O LORD (Ps 141:2a).

Another characteristic of smoke closely associated with turning sacrifices into it is the fact that smoke vanishes in the air. This further adds to the understanding that once a sacrifice is burned and turned into smoke, it completely becomes invisible to the invisible God! Psalm 37 compares wicked people, God's enemies, to "the glory of the pastures; they vanish— like smoke they vanish away" (Ps 37:20). Psalm 68 begins with a prayer asking that God's enemies be scattered; then, it states, "As smoke is driven away, so drive them away" (Ps 68:2a). Psalm 102 compares the passing way of days like smoke (Ps 102:3), while the prophet Isaiah declares that "the heavens will vanish like smoke" (Isa 51:6b) and the OT (A) Book of Wisdom declares that "the breath in our nostrils is smoke" (Wis 2:2c) and the hope of the ungodly "is dispersed like smoke before the wind" (Wis 5:14c).

The prophet Hosea declares that those who make idols will vanish "like smoke from a window" (Hos 13:3).

Echoing the description of smoke on Mount Horeb (Sinai), mountains are said to smoke. Psalm 104 asks that the glory of the LORD, who touches the mountains and they smoke, endure forever (Ps 104:31–32). A portion of Psalm 144 turns the description of a theophany into a request, as the singer asks the LORD to bow the heavens into a bridge and come down to the earth in order to touch the mountains so that they smoke (Ps 144:5). There are also three biblical references to a column of smoke. Dentan says, "The column of smoke, it has often been noted, suggests the coming of Yahweh [the LORD] from Sinai (cf. Ps 18:8)."[3] The first use is found in the Book of Judges in a description of Israel's destruction of the Benjaminite city of Gibeah; a cloud, a column of smoke, rose from the city (Judg 20:40) to indicate that God was defeating the Benjaminites (Judg 20:35). In the Song of Songs, Solomon's retinue is like a column of smoke coming from the wilderness (Song 3:6). Biblical scholars think that Song 3:6–11 is a later insertion about a king who loved women (1 Kgs 11:1). However, it may be an allusion to the cloud that filled the temple that Solomon built (1 Kgs 8:10–11). The third reference is to the burning of wickedness which causes a swirling upward in a column of smoke (Isa 9:18). The prophet Isaiah uses the image of a brush fire to describe the LORD's anger. Like a brush fire burns briers, thorns, and forest thickets and the smoke swirls upward in a column of smoke, so does God's anger burn against the wickedness of his people (Isa 9:18–19). This is meant to echo the passages explored above concerning smoke likened to God's anger. Thus, while there are biblical references to smoke caused by fire, smoke like that of a cloud or fog is one of the elements of a theophany revealing the glory of the LORD.

---

3. Dentan, "Song," 326.

11

Fire

"Fire is an element in the theophanies," states McKenzie.[1] "Fire is a sign of the presence of Yahweh [the LORD], for fire is the element proper to deity," he adds.[2] The writer of the Mount Sinai (Horeb) experience records that "the LORD had descended upon [the mountain] in fire" (Exod 19:18). Later, he describes it this way: "The glory of the LORD settled on Mount Sinai. . . . Now the appearance of the glory of the LORD was like a devouring fire on the top of the mountain in the sight of the people of Israel" (Exod 24:17; cf. Deut 18:16). Schwartz refers to the manifestation of the glory of the LORD as "the divine firecloud."[3] He identifies it as the same fire that "has accompanied the Israelites from Egypt;" it "descends from the heavens to the mountain, remaining there in full view of the people while Moses meets with God."[4] Later, it will enter into the tabernacle and, ultimately, take up permanent residence in the temple. "This association of God with fire runs throughout the Bible," writes Ryken.[5]

After Aaron and his sons are ordained priests and make the appropriate sacrifices (Lev 8:1—9:24), the author of the HB (OT) Book of Leviticus states that "the glory of the LORD appeared to all the people. Fire came out from the LORD and consumed the burnt offering and the fat on the altar . . ." (Lev 9:23b–24a). Faley writes about this scene stating that the LORD's

---

1. McKenzie, *Dictionary*, 277.
2. Ibid.; cf. Gray, "Exodus," 47.
3. Schwartz, "Priestly Account," 125.
4. Ibid.
5. Ryken, *Dictionary*, 287.

glory "takes the form of fire issuing from the meeting tent and consuming the already burning offerings on the altar to the awe of the onlookers. The meaning of the theophany is clear: the ordination proceedings and the sacrifices of the priest are approved as sacred and acceptable to the Lord."[6] Milgrom explains that this fire "is an essential climax of the promised revelation and is to be understood as a supernatural flame which immediately consumed, i.e., totally reduced to ashes, the offering being slowly burned by the ordinary process."[7]

Indeed, fire is the primary element earlier in the Book of Exodus where the writer records Moses experience of "the angel of the LORD" appearing "to him in a flame of fire out of a bush" on Mount Horeb (Sinai) (Exod 3:2). According to the description, "the bush was blazing, yet it was not consumed" (Exod 3:2). When Moses' curiosity gets the best of him, he investigates why the bush was not burned, and he hears God calling to him out of the bush. Clifford states, "The bush that burns but is not consumed mediates the divine voice."[8] The experience of Gideon in the HB (OT) Book of Judges is similar to that of Moses. The angel of the LORD—a code phrase for God[9]—appears to him. Gideon makes an offering of a kid, unleavened cakes, and broth, placing the meat and cakes on a rock and pouring the broth over them. "Then," according to the narrative in Judges, "the angel of the LORD reached out the tip of the staff that was in his hand, and touched the meat and the unleavened cakes; and fire sprang up from the rock and consumed the meat and the unleavened cakes . . . " (Judg 6:21). In the CB (NT) fire is unique to John the Baptist's words in Q. In both Matthew's Gospel and Luke's Gospel, the Baptizer states that the one who is coming after him "will baptize . . . with the Holy Spirit and fire" (Matt 3:11; Luke 3:16). Kee notes that "the baptism with fire points to the judgment that is to fall on [human]kind, but there is no clear indication . . . of how the Holy Spirit is related to the fire."[10] The author of Luke's Gospel sees the Baptizer's words fulfilled in his description of "[d]ivided tongues, as of fire," appearing among Jesus' followers with a tongue resting on each one of them (Acts 2:3). Karris comments: "Jesus will use the superior purifying and refining agents of the Holy Spirit and fire. In Acts 2 Luke shows how

---

6. Faley, "Leviticus," 67.
7. Milgrom, "Leviticus," 74.
8. Clifford, "Exodus," 46.
9. Ibid., 55.
10. Kee, "Matthew," 612.

the fire of the Holy Spirit accomplishes its work in human beings."[11] Thus, the element of fire in a theophany of the LORD is applied to a theophany of the Holy Spirit. Fire reveals the glory of the LORD.

One of the more extensive uses of fire mentioned in biblical literature signifying a theophany is the pillar of fire by night which leads the Israelites in their exodus from Egypt. One of the pillar of fire's responsibilities is to provide light to the Israelites for their nighttime traveling (Exod 13:21; Neh 9:12; Pss 78:14, 105:39). It does not leave its place in front of the people (Exod 13:22; Neh 9:19) until Moses is ready to lead the people through the parted waters of the Red Sea when it throws the Egyptian army into panic (Exod 14:24). Fire is the Divine Presence, which the Israelites can see at each stage of their journey (Exod 40:38; Deut 1:33). As Moses recalls to the Israelites in the Book of Deuteronomy, "[T]he LORD spoke to you out of the fire. You heard the sound of words but saw no form" (Deut 4:12; cf. 4:15, 36; 5:4, 22–26; 9:10; 10:4).

In the HB (OT) Book of Numbers, the pillar of fire is equated with the LORD by Moses in a dialogue with God. First, Numbers says that the cloud covering the tabernacle had the appearance of fire by night (Num 9:15–16). Second, Moses says that the LORD is in the midst of the Israelites, that he is seen face to face, and that he goes before them as a pillar of fire at night (Num 14:14). God "provided a flaming pillar of fire as a guide for [his] people's unknown journey," states the OT (A) Book of Wisdom (Wis 18:3ab). Isaiah expresses a hope after the destruction of the temple that one day the LORD will create over the whole site of Mount Zion "the shining of a flaming fire by night" (Isa 4:5). Later, he declares that the LORD will visit Zion "with thunder and earthquake and great noise, with whirlwind and tempest, and the flame of a devouring fire" (Isa 29:6). Thunder, earthquake, wind, and fire are typical theophanic elements.

The psalms, when they refer to a theophany, mention God as fire in a number of ways. For example, Psalm 18 declares that a devouring fire comes from God's mouth (Ps 18:8). Likewise, glowing coals, coals of fire, flaming fire, flames of fire, or devouring fire indicate the divine presence (Pss 18:8, 12; 29:7; 50:3). Sometimes fire goes before him (Ps 97:3), and at other times he makes fire and flame his ministers (Ps 104:4). The prophet Isaiah announces that under the LORD's glory a burning will be kindled, like the burning of fire (Isa 10:16b), so that the Holy One is a flame (Isa 10:17). Later, Isaiah states the LORD will come in fire and in flames of fire

---

11. Karris, "Luke," 686.

(Isa 66:15). The prophet Zechariah records an angel saying that the LORD will be a wall of fire all around Jerusalem to protect it, echoing the pillar of fire above (Zech 2:5). Cody writes:

> The imagery of fire, common in descriptions of theophany because it expresses the danger of approaching too near to God, and the imagery of glory which expresses his earthly presence in the Temple, are used to show why the new Jerusalem will not need defending walls. God's own awesome presence in the city will suffice to ward off all earthly enemies.[12]

Following in the tradition of a fiery God in the HB (OT), the CB (NT) Gospel According to Luke uniquely portrays Jesus declaring that he "came to bring fire to the earth" (Luke 12:49), and the Letter to the Hebrews says it best: "... [I]ndeed our God is a consuming fire" (Heb 12:29). The author of Hebrews is borrowing from the Book of Deuteronomy: "[T]he LORD ... God is a devouring fire" (Deut 4:24; cf. 9:3).

Portraying God as a consuming fire and at the same time portraying him as the protective presence of Israel makes the LORD paradoxical. Fire consumes or destroys, and fire protects life by giving heat. This paradoxical characteristic is stated in the wisdom of Sirach: "The basic necessities of human life are water and fire" among others (Sir 39:26), yet "water extinguishes a blazing fire" (Sir 3:30). It is also found in the narrative of Elijah's experience on Mount Horeb (Sinai). The narrator of the story presumes that the reader knows about Moses' experience of fire on the same mountain. However, for Elijah on the mountain there is wind, earthquake, and after the earthquake a fire, but the LORD is not in the fire (1 Kgs 19:12). Elijah's theophany adds to the paradox that the LORD is both in fire and not in fire! Walsh names this an "enigmatic theophany in which traditional manifestations of divine presence (wind, earthquake, and fire) are reduced to mere precursors of a mysterious 'sound of fine silence.'"[13]

The consuming-fire characteristic of theophanies is best illustrated by the many biblical references to offerings by fire. Granted, there can be unholy fire when someone offers to God what he has not commanded to be offered (Lev 10:1; Num 3:4, 26:61); it results in a fire coming out "from the presence of the Lord" that consumes those making the offering (Lev 10:2; Num 16:35). Likewise, any type of blemished animal—blind, injured, maimed—is not acceptable (Lev 22:22). Offerings by fire refer to sacrifices

---

12. Cody, "Haggai, Zechariah, Malachi," 354.
13. Walsh, "1–2 Kings," 172.

that are burned, that are "wholly destroyed by fire."[14] Cattle, sheep, and birds are made invisible by fire so they can be accepted by the invisible LORD, Israel's God.[15] In a manner of speaking, God (fire) turns offerings into God (fire); the smoke that rises from the burning (see Smoke) illustrates the three-storied universe; on earth fire turns sacrifices into smoke which rises to the LORD's dwelling above the dome of the sky. Only those Israelites belonging to the tribe of Levi may share in the offering by fire made to the LORD God of Israel (Josh 13:14; 1 Sam 2:28). Basically, the directions stipulate that a whole animal or a part of one or grain offerings and frankincense are to be turned into smoke on the altar as burnt offerings with a pleasing odor to the LORD, "an offering by fire to the LORD" (Exod 29:18, 25, 41; 30:20; Lev 1:9, 13, 17; 2:2, 3, 9, 10, 11, 16; 3:5, 9, 11, 14, 16; 4:35; 5:12; 6:17, 18; 7:5, 25, 30, 35; 8:21, 28; 10:15; 22:27; 23:25, 27, 36, 37; 24:7, 9; Num 15:3, 10, 13, 14, 25; 18:17; 28:2, 3, 6, 8, 13, 19, 24; 29:6, 13, 36). Faley says that "the altar, which was a sign of the divine presence, brought about the victim's transition from the earthly sphere to the divine realm."[16] In order to keep the laws concerning burnt offerings, the Book of Leviticus states, "A perpetual fire shall be kept burning on the altar; it shall not go out" (Lev 6:13). Faley explains how this was accomplished: "[T]he continuation of the fire on the altar was the priests' responsibility. Each morning firewood was added prior to the early holocaust and the other offerings of the day. The perpetual fire, a characteristic trait of Persian cult, served as an uninterrupted prayer of the Hebrew community to the Lord."[17] Every burnt offering by fire and the perpetual fire burning on the altar is a theophany because God's fire, like that on Mount Horeb (Sinai), wraps the offering in fire and consumes it, making it invisible, while also representing the Divine Presence.

Before David brings the ark to Jerusalem, he builds an altar on the threshing floor of Ornan the Jebusite upon which he presents burnt offering and offerings of well-being to the LORD. David calls upon the LORD, and the LORD answers him with fire from heaven (1 Chr 21:26–28). The same phenomenon occurs after Solomon builds the first temple; he ends his prayers and fire comes down from heaven to consume the burnt offering and the sacrifices. The glory of the LORD fills the temple (2 Chr 7:1).

14. Faley, "Leviticus," 62.
15. Ibid.
16. Ibid.
17. Ibid., 65.

Like they did at Mount Sinai (Horeb), all the Israelites witness the fire and the LORD's glory (2 Chr 7:3). Job hears a messenger tell him, "The fire of God fell from heaven and burned up the sheep and the servants, and consumed them" (Job 1:16). This begins part of Job's tribulations that end up transforming him.

A patriarchal story involving the transfiguring property of fire is that of God's call to Abraham to take his son, Isaac, and make of him a burnt offering. After making a three-day journey, indicating that God is present, they find the place where God wants the sacrifice to take place. Abraham carries the fire, but Isaac notes the fire without a lamb for a burnt offering. Ultimately, just as Abraham is about to kill his son, the angel of the LORD—God—stops him. They find a ram and offer it as a burnt offering (Gen 22:1–14). Not to be missed in the story and the verses that follow it is the three occasions that God speaks to Abraham (Gen 22:1–2, 11–12; 15–18).

In a similar three-fold fire story, King Ahaziah of Samaria sends messengers to the god Baal to divine his fate after a fall. The messengers are intercepted by the prophet Elijah. In response, the king sends Elijah a captain with his fifty men; five indicates grace or a freely offered gift. The captain addresses the prophet as a man of God and tells him the king wants him to come and see him (2 Kgs 1:9) and tell him his fate. Elijah says, "If I am a man of God, let fire come down from heaven and consume you and your fifty" (2 Kgs 1:10). And fire comes down and consumes the captain and the fifty men! The same scenario is presented a second time (2 Kgs 1:11–12) and a third time (2 Kgs 1:13–14). However, the third time the angel of the LORD tells Elijah to go see the king and tell him that he will die as a result of an accident, and so he did (2 Kgs 1:15–17). The OT (A) Book of Sirach refers to Elijah as a prophet of fire (Sir 48:1), who three times brought down fire (Sir 48:3). Fire demonstrates the consuming Divine Presence, and the three sendings of fifty men each time further enhances the stamp of divinity on this story. It is topped with the angel of the LORD—God—sending Elijah to Ahaziah and informing him of his fate.

This story about Elijah is further enhanced by the fire of the LORD that fell from heaven and consumed the burnt offering of the bull, the wood, the stones, the dust, and the water that the prophet had offered on Mount Carmel (1 Kgs 18:38). And certainly it is echoed by the chariot of fire and horses of fire that separate Elisha from Elijah and takes the latter in a whirlwind to heaven (2 Kgs 2:11; cf. Sir 48:9) and the horses and chariots of fire all around Elisha (2 Kgs 6:17).

Divine anger or wrath is often equated with fire, illustrating the consuming aspect of the theophanic element and the punishment of the wicked. Psalm 11 declares that the LORD rains coals of fire on the wicked (Ps 11:6a). God's enemies will be swallowed in his wrath and consumed with fire (Ps 21:9; cf. Sir 45:19). "As wax melts before the fire, let the wicked perish before God" states Psalm 68 (Ps 68:2). The lengthy Psalm 78 describes the LORD's rage as kindled fire (Ps 78:21), and Psalms 79 and 89 describe his wrath burning like fire (Pss 79:5; 89:46). The prophet Isaiah states that the LORD burns with anger (Isa 30:27), with furious anger and a flame of devouring fire (Isa 30:30); his fire is in Zion and his furnace is in Jerusalem (Isa 31:9). It is a fire that burns all day long (Isa 65:5b). However, it is later in the prophetic book that Isaiah describes God's anger most succinctly: "For the LORD will come in fire, and his chariots like the whirlwind, to pay back his anger in fury, and his rebuke in flames of fire. For by fire will the LORD execute judgment . . . " (Isa 66:15–16a).

Jeremiah, too, compares God's wrath to fire (Jer 4:4, 21:12) and his anger to fire (Jer 15:14, 17:4). The HB (OT) Book of Lamentations states, "The LORD gave full vent to his wrath; he poured out his hot anger, and kindled a fire in Zion that consumed its foundations" (Lam 4:11). The prophet Ezekiel echoes this when he portrays the Lord GOD declaring: "I will pour out my indignation upon you, with the fire of my wrath I will blow upon you" (Ezek 21:31, 22:31). The prophet Nahum asks, "Who can stand before his indignation? Who can endure the heat of his anger? His wrath is poured out like fire . . . " (Nah 1:6). The prophet Zephaniah phrases God's words this way: " . . . [M]y decision is to gather nations, to assemble kingdoms, to pour out upon them my indignation, all the heat of my anger; for in the fire of my passion all the earth shall be consumed" (Zeph 3:8). Thus, God's flame burns the wicked (Ps 106:18).

This equation of God's anger and fire leads to the presupposition of punishment in eternal fire in the CB (NT). The author of Matthew's Gospel is its major proponent, but some of his material comes from Mark's Gospel in which Jesus speaks about Gehenna, often translated as *hell*, being a place of unquenchable fire (Mark 9:43, 45, 48). At one point in time, Gehenna was a place of child sacrifice, but by the time of Jesus "it was used as a garbage dump by the inhabitants of Jerusalem."[18] And in the garbage dump

---

18. Ryken, *Dictionary*, 376.

burned a fire that seldom, if ever, was extinguished. Matthew references the fire in the Jerusalem landfill seven times (Matt 5:22, 29; 10:28; 18:8, 9; 23:15, 33), Luke mentions it once (Luke 12:5), and the Letter of James mentions it once (Jas 3:6).

Besides the unquenchable fire in Gehenna that becomes a metaphor for God's punishment of the wicked, there is another biblical understanding that the world will be destroyed by fire. Stemming from the prophet Malachi, who writes about a coming day, "burning like an oven, when all the arrogant and all evildoers will be stubble," a "day that comes [to] burn them up" (Mal 4:1), Paul tells the Corinthians that there will come a day, "revealed with fire, and the fire will test what sort of work each has done" (1 Cor 3:13). Those who are saved are saved through fire (1 Cor 3:15). The author of the Second Letter of Peter also thinks that "the present heavens and earth have been reserved for fire, being kept until the day of judgment and destruction of the godless" (2 Pet 3:7); the elements will be dissolved with fire (2 Pet 3:10) and "the heavens will be set ablaze and dissolved, and the elements will melt with fire" (2 Pet 3:12).

The author of the Second Letter to the Thessalonians connects Jesus' return in glory to fire, writing that the Lord Jesus will be revealed from heaven with his mighty angels "in flaming fire, inflicting vengeance on those who do not know God and on those who do not obey the gospel of our Lord Jesus" (2 Thess 1:8). What had once been applied to God as judge is now applied to Jesus. And the best example of this in the CB (NT) is found in the Book of Revelation whose author loves fire! He mentions fire twenty-four times. He describes the Son of Man, Jesus, as having eyes that are like a flame of fire (Rev 1:14; 2:18; 19:12). As a heavenly traveler, John of Patmos watches fire thrown to the earth (Rev 8:5, 7, 8); he sees fire-breathing horses (Rev 9:17, 18), an angel with legs like pillars of fire (Rev 10:1), and two fire-producing olive trees and lampstands (Rev 11:5), which Gilmour thinks refers to Elijah's calling down of fire on the messengers of King Ahaziah and Moses bringing a plague of hail mixed with fire on the Egyptians.[19] On the earth John sees a behemoth-like creature which can make fire come down from heaven to earth (Rev 13:13); those who worship the beast are tormented with fire (Rev 14:10). John identifies an angel who comes out of the altar as one who has authority over fire (Rev 14:18). An angel pours one bowl of God's wrath on the sun, which scorches people with fire (Rev 16:8) while the whore (Babylon, Rome) will be burned with

19. Gilmour, "Revelation," 958.

fire (Rev 17:16; 18:8) and others will be consumed with fire (Rev 20:9) and thrown into a lake of fire (Rev 19:20; 20:10, 14, 15; 21:8). Thus, the theophanic element of fire permeates the last book of the CB (NT).

While the last book of the Bible is more concerned with fire's destructive characteristic, the HB (OT) Book of Daniel is more concerned with its protective characteristic. In this book that has several additions to it, fire is praised because it saves three men. The king of Babylon, Nebuchadnezzar, made a golden statue and decreed that everyone in his kingdom must worship it or "be thrown into a furnace of blazing fire" (Dan 3:6, 11, 15, 17, 20, 21, 23). However, the Jewish captives—Shadrach (Hannaniah), Meshach (Mishale), and Abednego (Azariah)—whom Daniel (Belteshazzar) has had appointed over the affairs of the province of Babylon (Dan 2:49) refuse to worship a false god. Nebuchadnezzar becomes enraged and orders "the furnace heated up seven times more than was customary" (Dan 3:19). Then, the three men were thrown into the furnace. When Nebuchadnezzar looked into the blazing fire, he saw "four men unbound, walking in the middle of the fire" (Dan 3:25), unhurt, and the fourth had the appearance of god (Dan 3:25). Nebuchadnezzar orders the three men to come out of the furnace, calling them servants of the Most High God (Dan 3:26). They emerge unhurt. Nebuchadnezzar blesses their God "who has sent his angel and delivered his servants who trusted in him" (Dan 3:28). The sacred number three—three men—indicates divine presence, as does the heating of the furnace seven times beyond its usual strength. Knight adds that the fiery furnace is "a fit symbol of the trial [the three men] were undergoing."[20] The fourth man, described as having the appearance of a god and an angel signals a saving theophany occurring on the earth (four) through protective fire.

In the sixty-eight verses of the OT (A) that are inserted between Daniel 3:23 and 3:24, more theophanic material is given. The reader is told that the three men walked around in the midst of the flames, singing hymns and blessing God (Sg Three 1:1 [Dan 3:24]). Meanwhile, the king's servants keep stoking the furnace, from which the flames pour out, even burning those standing around it (Sg Three 1:23–25 [Dan 3:46–48]). A fuller description of the angel of the Lord, who comes down into the furnace and drives the fiery flame out of it, is given (Sg Three 1:26–27 [Dan 3:49–50]). In a very lengthy hymn, the three men even call upon fire to bless the Lord (Sg Three 1:44 [Dan 3:66]), who, using one of the elements

---

20. Knight, "Daniel," 440.

of a theophany—fire—delivered them from "the midst of the burning fiery furnace; from the midst of the fire" he delivered them (Sg Three 1:66 [Dan 3:88b]). In other words, God has appeared as fire and saved three of his people. Knight comments: " . . . [T]he men have learned to praise God wholeheartedly only when they have met with adversity. Adversity is here represented as fire."[21]

Fire (along with columns of smoke), as an element of a theophany, also serves as a portent for the prophet Joel's day of the LORD (Joel 2:30). In one of Peter's speeches in the Acts of the Apostles, Peter explains that the fire of Pentecost is fulfillment of Joel's day of the Lord with its signs of fire and smoky mist (Acts 2:19). In other words, Pentecost is a theophanic experience of fire, which brings the presence of God (Spirit) to Jesus' followers in Jerusalem, just as it had done on Mount Horeb (Sinai), with the ark, and in the temple. Blenkinsopp, commenting on Moses' words about the blazing mountain (Deut 4:11), states: "The fire is symbolic of the numinous presence of the covenant God; the absence of a form is in keeping with the aniconic ideology of the book."[22]

---

21. Knight, "Prayer," 582.
22. Blenkinsopp, "Deuteronomy," 97.

12

Earthquake

ANOTHER LESS-USED BIBLICAL ELEMENT, but nevertheless a sign of a theophany, is earthquake. In the description of the Mount Sinai (Horeb) experience, the author states that "the whole mountain shook violently" (Exod 19:18). McKenzie writes that "earthquakes are caused by the footstep or the voice of Yahweh [the LORD], and they are a feature of the theophany."[1] Ryken adds that they "are often seen as manifestations of the direct action of God's power."[2] This can be seen in Psalm 18, which states: " . . . [T]he earth reeled and rocked; the foundations also of the mountains trembled and quaked because [the LORD] was angry" (Ps 18:7; 2 Sam 22:8). Psalm 77 recalls Moses' experience on Mount Sinai (Horeb) when "the earth trembled and shook" (Ps 77:18), while the CB (NT) author of the Letter to the Hebrews refers to the "voice [that] shook the earth" (Heb 12:26). In the prophet Habakkuk's description of the Sinai (Horeb) theophany, he states that the LORD "stopped and shook the earth" (Hab 3:6) as does the OT (A) Second Book of Esdras (2 Esd 3:18). Portraying the LORD enthroned, the author of Psalm 99 exhorts the earth to quake (Ps 99:1b). Ortlund explains that this is "a common reaction to theophany."[3] Psalm 114 references the exodus and exhorts the earth to tremble at the presence of the LORD, the God of Jacob (Ps 114:7). The trembling of the deep is an appropriate response to the LORD's presence (Pss 77:16; 97:4).

---

1. McKenzie, *Dictionary*, 209.
2. Ryken, *Dictionary*, 225.
3. Ortlund, "Intertextual Reading," 281.

Earthquake

The prophet Isaiah considers an earthquake a sign that the LORD is visiting his people (Isa 29:6), while the narrative about Elijah fleeing to Mount Horeb (Sinai) and encountering God on the mountain begins by mentioning that the LORD is not in the earthquake (1 Kgs 19:11). Thus, the Bible presents type and anti-type of this theophanic element.

Because "[e]arthquakes in Palestine have been frequent and violent throughout recorded history,"[4] two biblical authors allude to an earthquake during the reign of King Uzziah of Judah (783–742 BCE), also known as Azariah. The prophet Amos dates his book two years before the earthquake (Amos 1:1), and the prophet Zechariah tells his readers that they shall flee as they fled from the earthquake in the day of King Uzziah of Judah (Zech 14:5). Probably neither had read the OT (A) reflections of Sirach about a wooden beam firmly bonded into a building not loosened by an earthquake (Sir 22:16).

Knowing that an earthquake is an element of a theophany, the CB (NT) author of Matthew's Gospel uniquely uses the element to enhance the resurrection narrative he found in Mark's Gospel. Immediately after Jesus dies in Matthew's Gospel, "the earth shook" (Matt 27:51); the author uses the portent of an earthquake to spur the centurion and those who were watching over Jesus' dead body to declare that he is God's Son (Matt 27:54). A few verses later, he describes another great earthquake as an angel of the Lord descends from heaven and rolls away the stone from the entrance to Jesus' tomb to show that he has been raised from the dead (Matt 28:2). If that is not enough to illustrate Matthew's understanding that the resurrection of Jesus is a theophany, he adds the description of the angel's appearance as being like lightning with white clothing (Matt 27:3). Luz says that God is acting; he has used earthquakes to reveal himself throughout the Bible.[5] Luz sates that this is "a supernatural quake that upsets the entire natural world . . . and thus indicates that it is God himself who acts here."[6] With the first quake God verifies that Jesus is his Son, a confession made by the centurion and the soldiers.[7] With the second earthquake God demonstrates his power over death; according to Luz, "The evangelist . . . could not make it clearer that God on his own initiative is intervening in the story."[8]

---

4. McKenzie, *Dictionary*, 208.
5. Luz, *Matthew 21–28*, 566.
6. Ibid., 567.
7. Ibid., 570.
8. Ibid., 595.

Divine Presence

Another earthquake that represents a theophany is found in the CB (NT) Acts of the Apostles. Paul and Silas make their way to Philippi, where they encounter a slave-girl with a spirit of divination which brings her owners' great income by fortune-telling. Paul casts out the unclean spirit. With their economic livelihood cut, the slave's owners have Paul and Silas beaten with rods and thrown into jail where their feet are fastened in stocks (Acts 16:16–24). The story continues by describing the theophany: "About midnight Paul and Silas were praying and singing hymns to God, and the prisoners were listening to them. Suddenly there was an earthquake, so violent that the foundations of the prison were shaken; and immediately all the doors were opened and everyone's chains were unfastened" (Acts 16:25–26). Johnson refers to this event as "divine intervention."[9] Pervo calls it an epiphany—a sibling word for theophany that means the manifestation of the divine—that comes suddenly: "An earthquake of apocalyptic force causes the doors to fly open and the fetters to fall off."[10] Pervo adds: " . . . [T]he jailer knew an epiphany when he saw one. . . . "[11] Later, Pervo states, "The jailer treats the affair as a theoxeny."[12] A theoxeny is the hospitality shown towards a god who visits as a guest. In other words, the theophany, signaled by the earthquake, results in the jailer showing hospitality to Paul and Silas, who represent God, to whom they were singing hymns, in this account (Acts 16:24–40).

The author of the CB (NT) Book of Revelation loves earthquakes. He records the great earthquake that occurs when the sixth seal is opened (Rev 6:12), the earthquake that occurs when an angel throws a censer on the earth (Rev 8:5), a great earthquake that kills seven thousand people (Rev 11:13), and a violent earthquake that follows the seventh angel pouring his bowl into the air (Rev 16:18). However, the one that captures the elements of a theophany the best—including an earthquake—is found at 11:19: "Then God's temple in heaven was opened, and the ark of his covenant was seen within his temple, and there were flashes of lightning, rumblings, peals of thunder, an earthquake, and heavy hail." Ryken is right on target when the states that earthquakes remind people "that the only fixed ground is God himself. Not even the earth is ultimately stable."[13] An earthquake reveals the glory of the LORD.

---

9. Johnson, *Acts*, 300.
10. Pervo, *Acts*, 411.
11. Ibid.
12. Ibid., 412.
13. Ryken, *Dictionary*, 225.

13

Terms of the Event (Covenant)

THERE ARE TERMS THAT need to be established in a theophany; these terms, often referred to as covenant, are an important element in theophanies. Clifford explains that a covenant is "a sworn agreement between persons, ordinarily oral, to do something."[1] In biblical literature, the oral agreement evolves into a written document. In the Mount Sinai (Horeb) theophanic experience, God gives Moses what have come to be known as Ten Commandments (Exodus 20:1–17; cf. Deut 5:6–21). Clifford writes that such "[l]aw codes were expressions of the divine will."[2] These ten rules, written on stone tablets by God, specify the Israelites' obligations in relationship with the LORD. McKenzie states that "the covenant of Israel itself as a people was the covenant of Sinai" [Horeb].[3] Moses serves as God's regent or mediator. Clifford explains: "The Covenant Code is proclaimed at Israel's creation by God's regent, Moses. Like other codes, it does not aim for completeness; it offers a sample of the divine intention for Israel and establishes the mediating office of Moses."[4] Ryken explains that this was a change from previous covenants: "The primary change is that the covenant is no longer established with a series of patriarchs and their families but with an entire nation."[5] The terms of the theophany are not sealed in covenant between two equals. The Sinai (Horeb) covenant is one "between the greater

1. Clifford, "Exodus," 52.
2. Ibid., 53.
3. McKenzie, *Dictionary*, 155.
4. Clifford, "Exodus," 53.
5. Ryken, *Dictionary*, 177.

and the lesser; the greater imposes his will upon the lesser, but it is also an act of grace and liberality."[6] McKenzie explains this in detail:

> In the covenant Yahweh [the LORD] imposes certain duties upon Israel and in return promises to be their God, to assist them, and to deliver them. The Israelites accept the obligations, the most important of which is to worship no other god but Yahweh [the LORD], and to observe the standards of cult and conduct which he establishes. If they are unfaithful, Yahweh [the LORD] will withdraw his favor.[7]

The basic themes of covenant theology, according to McKenzie are "the sovereignty of Yahweh [the LORD], his saving deeds, Israel's unique position as the people of Yahweh [the LORD], and its unique obligations to him."[8]

Wright delves a little deeper into the understanding of covenant, which he defines as "a pact or treaty between two parties which is sealed by a vow."[9] He explains:

> This form of treaty was understood to portray the relationship between God and Israel, and the following were some of the results of the concept: (a) God is the world's sovereign and Israel became his special vassal, his servants having a service to perform for him. . . . (b) God's wondrous acts of goodness toward Israel were tied closely to the obligation which in gratitude to him she vowed to assume. The primary expression of these obligations was the Ten Commandments. . . . (c) The concept of treaty furnished a major element in worship; the recital of God's mighty acts was tied closely to covenant renewal. . . . (d) It also furnished the deuteronomic historian and the pre-exilic prophets their central theme—God's legal case or "controversy" with his people for their breach of the pact.[10]

As indicated above, before Sinai (Horeb) the LORD made covenants with individual patriarchs and their families. The terms of the theophany witnessed by Noah "is a covenant with the entire creation, including nature

---

6. McKenzie, *Dictionary*, 154.
7. Ibid.
8. McKenzie, "Aspects," 1298.
9. Wright, "Theological Study," 986.
10. Ibid.

Terms of the Event (Covenant)

as well as people."[11] God says to Noah, " . . . I am establishing my covenant with you and your descendants after you, and with every living creature that is with you. . . . I establish my covenant with you, that never again shall all flesh be cut off by the waters of a flood, and never again shall there be a flood to destroy the earth" (Gen 9:9–11). For Noah and his family the terms laid down by God are these: Noah may eat from anything on the earth except for "flesh with its life, that is, its blood" in it (Gen 9:4). Furthermore, there is to be no homicide, because God requires a life for a life taken (Gen 9:5–6).

In the HB (OT) Book of Genesis, God enters into agreement with Abram. The first time this occurs the LORD tells the patriarch to go to the land that he will show him. If he goes, God will make of him a great nation and make his name great. God also promises to bless those who bless Abram and curse those who curse him. Abram goes and receives the promise of land from the LORD (Gen 12:1–9). The second time this occurs follows the covenant-making ceremony involving three, three-year-old animals (Gen 15:9–21). Before this event, God promises Abram that his descendants will be as countless as the stars and they will possess the land of Canaan (Gen 15:1–8). The third time God enters into covenant with Abram, he changes his name to Abraham and, again, promises him numerous descendants and land. The terms of this covenant involve Abraham walking blamelessly with God (Gen 17:1) and circumcision (Gen 17:10–14).

The fourth experience of covenant-making between God and Abraham occurs when three men visit Abraham in the heat of the day. The sacred number three immediately signals a theophany. While the three visitors wait under a tree, Abraham and Sarah prepare a feast—another element of a theophany—for them. Then, after eating one of the men promises that by the following year Abraham and Sarah will have a son (Gen 18:1–15). The narrative of the fifth experience of covenant-making between God and Abraham is more like a bargaining session. It immediately follows the story about Abraham and Sarah having a son, while Abraham remains standing before the LORD (Gen 18:22). In a succession of bargaining sessions for the lives of the people of Sodom, Abraham asks the LORD if fifty—representing grace—people are found in the city, will God spare it. The LORD says he will. Then, this same type of dialogue goes on as Abraham decreases the number in increments of five to forty-five, forty, thirty, twenty, and ten

---

11. Ryken, *Dictionary*, 177.

(Gen 18:22–33). However, not even ten righteous people can be found in the city, and so the LORD destroys it.

In the HB (OT) Book of Judges there is the five-chapter story of Samson (Judg 13:1—16:31). Manoah's unnamed wife, who is barren, is the recipient of a theophany. The angel of the LORD—God—appears to her and announces that she will conceive and bear a son (Judg 15:1–3). The terms of the theophany involve the woman not drinking wine, not eating anything unclean, and not cutting her son's hair (Judg 15:4–5, 7, 14). After the woman tells her husband about her experience, he prays to the LORD, asking him to send the angel (also called "the man of God") back, and the LORD answers his request by sending the angel to the woman again. She leaves the angel and fetches Manoah, to whom the angel delivers the same message as before (Judg 13:8–14). Manoah offers to prepare a feast—an element of a theophany—for the angel, who tells him to prepare a burnt offering and offer it to the LORD (Judg 13:15–16). Manoah prepares a kid and a grain offering and offers them on a rock (altar)—another element of a theophany—to God. "When the flame went up toward heaven from the altar, the angel of the LORD ascended in the flame of the altar while Manoah and his wife looked on" (Judg 13:20). The element of fire makes Manoah and wife aware that they have seen God (Judg 13:21–23). The woman bears a son, Samson, and follows the terms of the theophany.

Earlier in the same book Gideon has a similar experience after preparing a kid, unleavened cakes and broth. He places the items on a rock, and the angel of LORD reaches out the tip of his staff and touches them; and fire springs up from the rock and consumes everything. And the angel of the LORD vanishes from Gideon's sight after which he realizes that he has seen God (Judg 6:19–23). The terms of Gideon's theophany involve leading the Israelites to defeat the Midianites among many other things (Judg 6:25—8:35).

The narrator of the call narrative of Samuel begins by stating that the word of the LORD was rare in those days, and visions were not widespread (1 Sam 3:1b). However, that quickly changes as God calls Samuel three times (1 Sam 3:4, 6, 8), but he did not yet know the LORD. Finally, with the fourth call, when the LORD came and stood before him, Samuel answers (1 Sam 13:10). Then, after experiencing this theophany, God gives Samuel the terms, namely, he is going to punish Eli's sons with death for their abuses of profaning sacrifices and replace Eli and his sons with Samuel (1 Sam

Terms of the Event (Covenant)

2:27–36; 3:12–14); Eli and his sons have been serving as priests before the ark at Shiloh.

The term of the theophany Elijah witnesses is the death of the four hundred fifty prophets of Baal. After Elijah instructs that they be seized, he brings them to a dry stream bed and kills them (1 Kgs 18:40). Before this, the people who had witnessed the theophany "fell on their faces and said, 'The LORD indeed is God; the LORD indeed is God'" (1 Kgs 18:39).

In the call narratives of the major prophets—Isaiah, Jeremiah, and Ezekiel—after the experience of a theophany, each is given a mission. Isaiah is told to tell the people that their land will be ruined because they have rejected God's words sent to them by Isaiah (Isa 6:9–13). Jeremiah, who experiences a theophany and then pleads with the Lord GOD not to send him, receives the terms of experience of the Divine. He is to be a prophet to the nations and deliver God's words to them (Jer 1:9–10). Ezekiel, who is in Babylon with the exiles, receives the terms of the theophany he has experienced (Ezek 1:4–28). God tells him that he is sending him "to the people of Israel, to a nation of rebels who have rebelled against [him]" (Ezek 2:3). Ezekiel is commissioned to speak God's words to the captives, even though God tells him they will not listen (Ezek 2:1–7).

In the CB (NT), in a dream theophany, the angel of the LORD appears to Joseph to explain that the child that his fiancée is carrying comes from the Holy Spirit (Matt 1:20–21). He is also told what name to give the child when he is born (Matt 1:22–23). The narrator of the gospel informs the reader that "he did as the angel of the Lord commanded him" (Matt1:24). In a similar way, the angel Gabriel is sent by God to Mary in Luke's Gospel. He announces that God is favoring her with the conception of a son through the overshadowing of the Most High and the coming of the Holy Spirit to her (Luke 1:26–37). She agrees to be God's servant, letting his word be fulfilled in her (Luke 1:38). In other words, like many before her, she accepted the terms of the theophanic event as an element of God's manifestation of his glory.

Refusing to accept the terms of the theophany can result in muteness. The author of Luke's Gospel tells the unique story of the priest Zechariah ministering in the temple and entering the sanctuary to offer incense. In the cloud—an element of a theophany—Zechariah sees an angel of the Lord—God—standing at the right side of the altar of incense. The angel tells him that he and his wife, Elizabeth, who is barren, will conceive a son, whom they are to name John the Baptist. Zechariah, who knows that old people do not conceive children, questions the angel, who reveals his name as Gabriel. Because Zechariah doubts the angel's words, Zechariah is struck mute until the words are fulfilled (Luke 1:5–20). In other words, because Zechariah did not accept or believe the terms of the theophany, he becomes mute. However, once the child is born and named, his muteness is removed (Luke 1:64). Thus, there are terms that are established in a theophany; these terms, often referred to as covenant—of which they are more than three hundred fifty mentions in the Bible—are an element in theophanies.

14

Sign

THE TERMS OF THE event or covenant are often accompanied by a sign of some kind in biblical theophanies. It is not that enough signs of the Divine Presence have not been given; it means that some sign that seals or ratifies the deal is presented. At Sinai (Horeb), while the text says that "Moses wrote down all the words of the LORD" (Exod 24:4a), the primary sign is "the tablets of stone with the law and the commandment" which the LORD writes for the Israelites' instruction (Exod 24:12). Even though Moses breaks the tablets later in the narrative, he remakes them and places them in the ark of the covenant, "the visible symbol of Yahweh's [the LORD's] presence in Israel."[1] Thus, the two stone tablets of the law in the ark represent the terms of the covenant. The sign of acceptance of the terms of the covenant is the blood of oxen divided into two equal portions; one portion is dashed against the altar, and the other portion is dashed on the people. The blood of the covenant is the secondary sign that seals the agreement (Exod 24:1–8). This blood-sign is meant to echo the blood that was put on the lintel and the doorposts of the Israelites' homes, saving them from death (Exod 12:13, 21–27). The CB (NT) applies the sign of blood to Jesus, whose "sprinkled blood . . . speaks a better word" (Heb 12:24).

In the account of Moses first encounter with the LORD on Mount Horeb (Sinai), God gives him the sign that he is sending Moses to Pharaoh. God says, "[T]his shall be the sign for you that it is I who sent you: when you have brought the people out of Egypt, you shall worship God on this mountain" (Exod 3:12). Of course, Moses wants more signs, and

---

1. McKenzie, *Dictionary*, 155.

God gives them to him. The first sign is the staff that turns into a snake, the second is Moses' leprous hand, and the third—indicating the presence of the LORD—is pouring water from the Nile River on dry ground and watching it turn into blood (Exod 4:1–9). Clifford indicates that these three signs are "demonstrations of the divine power that Moses can count on in the future."[2] He adds, "The rod-turned-snake and the Nile-turned-bloody anticipate the first plague . . . , and his leprous hand looks forward to Moses' vindication as leader in Num[bers] 12."[3] God also gives the sign of the flies, one of the plagues, that the Israelites are his people (Exod 8:22–24). Boadt states: "Signs are evidence of God's power at work; thus, the exodus is accomplished in great 'signs and wonders' (Deut 4:34; Ps 105:27)."[4]

Similarly, the sign of the terms of the covenant between God and Noah is a rainbow. God tells the patriarch that he sets his bow in the clouds to be a sign of the covenant between him and the earth. When he brings clouds over the earth and he sees the bow, he will remember his covenant with Noah and every living thing (Gen 9:12–16). The rainbow serves two purposes in theophanies. It functions as a bridge from the top story of the world to the middle story. In a manner of speaking, God walks over the bridge to get from heaven to earth. It also functions as a bow, which God uses to shoot his lightning arrows, as already seen in the chapter on lightning.

Joshua sets up twelve stones in the Jordan River as a sign that the waters of the river stopped so that the Israelites could cross over (Josh 4:6); this is a sign of the re-enactment of the crossing of the Red Sea. In the HB (OT) Book of Judges, Gideon witnesses the theophany as a sign that the LORD is truly speaking to him and sending him on a mission to rescue his people from the Midianites (Judg 6:14–23); in this regard Gideon is like Moses who wanted to be sure that it was the LORD speaking to him and calling him.

For Abraham the sign of the terms of the covenant is the circumcision of every male. "You shall circumcise the flesh of your foreskins, and it shall be a sign of the covenant between me and you," God tells Abraham (Gen 17:11). This sign begins with Abraham and extends to all his offspring. In the CB (NT) Paul refers to this "sign of circumcision as a seal of the

---

2. Clifford, "Exodus," 47.
3. Ibid.
4. Boadt, "Ezekiel," 316; cf. Clifford, "Exodus," 48.

righteousness that [Abraham] had by faith while he was still uncircumcised" (Rom 4:11).

The HB (OT) Second Book of Kings records a sign given to King Hezekiah who becomes sick to the point of death. Isaiah is sent to him to inform him that he will live. The king asks for a sign: "What shall be the sign that the LORD will heal me, and that I shall go up to the house of the LORD on the third day?" (2 Kgs 20:8) Isaiah tells him, "This is the sign to you from the LORD, that the LORD will do the thing that he has promised: the shadow has now advanced ten intervals; shall it retreat ten intervals?" (2 Kgs 20:9) Isaiah is referring to the sundial that marks the passing of the daylight. Thus, another element of a theophany has been introduced: light and darkness. Hezekiah knows that it is normal for the shadow of the sun to pass ten—totality—intervals on the sundial. However, the narrator of the story writes: "The prophet Isaiah cried to the LORD; and he brought the shadow back the ten intervals, by which the sun had declined on the dial of Ahaz" (2 Kgs 20:11; cf. 2 Chr 32:24). Ultimately, the king gets better, and the sign proves that this was a theophany.

In the CB (NT), Jesus is portrayed in the Synoptic Gospels as echoing the blood of the covenant that signs the agreement at Sinai (Horeb). On the night before his death, while eating the Passover meal, Jesus takes a cup of wine and declares it to be his "blood of the covenant" (Mark 14:24; Matt 26:28). The author of Luke's Gospel records him declaring it to be "the new covenant in [his] blood" (Luke 22:20). McKenzie notes that just "as the blood of the old covenant united the partners in one relationship, so the blood of Jesus is now the bond of union between the covenant parties...."[5]

The author of John's Gospel in the CB (NT) structured a part of his book around seven signs to indicate that Jesus is the fullness of God's sign and is the LORD's incarnate presence in the world. Perkins states that "[f]or John, Jesus is the reality of all the great religious symbols of Israel."[6] The first sign Jesus gives is in Cana of Galilee where six stone water jars—an incomplete sacred number—are filled with water and become wine (John 2:1–10). The fact that this sign occurs "on the third day" (John 2:1) is enough to indicate that it is a theophany, but just to be sure that the reader recognizes that, the narrator adds that Jesus "revealed his glory" (John 2:11). The second sign in John's Gospel is Jesus' healing of the son of a royal

5. McKenzie, *Dictionary*, 156.
6. Perkins, "John," 954.

official (John 4:46–54). Jesus' third theophanic sign occurs near water, itself an element of a theophany. The sign involves the healing of man who had been ill for thirty-eight years; because he is two years away from forty, his time of suffering is not to end in death, but he will be cured. And so Jesus cures him on a sabbath, trumping the law that forbad work on that holy day of the week (John 5:2–17). The theophanic character is noted by the narrator, who writes that Jesus was calling God his Father, "thereby making himself equal to God" (John 5:18).

While Jesus' fourth sign (John 6:1–15) is also found in the Synoptic Gospels (Mark 6:30–44; Matt 14:13–21; Luke 9:10–17), it is only the author of John's Gospel that uses the narrative in a significant manner. The first element of a theophany is the mountain upon which Jesus sits (John 6:3). The second element is the feast or the meal that he is going to provide for the five thousand people present (John 6:10); five thousand intensifies the grace that is present. This latter element is further enhanced by the fact that the feast of Passover was near (John 6:4), thus connecting this account to that of the theophany events that preceded the Hebrews' escape from Egypt. Jesus discovers from his disciple Andrew that there is a boy present in the crowd who has five barley loaves and two fish—added together they make seven, signifying fullness (John 6:9). Another sacred number is employed after everyone has eaten; twelve baskets of fragments are gathered (John 6:13), representing God's people Israel and the new Israel, Jesus' twelve disciples—although in John's Gospel there is no narrative of Jesus choosing twelve apostles. The result of this sign of Jesus feeding twelve thousand people is that they proclaim him to be the prophet who was coming into the world, that is, the one God announced to Moses before his death (Deut 18:15, 18; Acts 3:22, 7:37).

The Johannine Jesus' fifth sign, the walking on water (John 6:16–21), is also found in Mark's Gospel (6:45–52) and in Matthew's Gospel (14:22–27); however, only in John does it function as a sign. The first theophanic element that is present is water, mentioned as the sea four—another element of a theophany—times in the short narrative. Water signifies chaos, over which only God presides or orders, as seen in the first creation account and the great flood narrative, as well as elsewhere. Thus, when the sea becomes rough and other theophanic elements are added—wind, rowing three (the number for the Divine) or four miles—Jesus comes to his disciples in a boat walking on the water. That alone is enough to identify him as God! To be sure that the reader understands, the writer records Jesus telling them, "It is I; do not be afraid" (John 6:20). Literally, the Greek states, "I am," which, of course, is nothing other than the name God gave to Moses (Exod 3:14). This theophany ends with Jesus in the boat reaching shore immediately.

Chapter 9 of John's Gospel contains the sixth sign, namely the cure of the man born blind, which unfolds in eight—perfection—scenes (John 9:1–5, 6–7, 8–12, 13–17, 18–23, 24–34, 35–39, 40–40–41. The purpose of the account, as stated by Jesus, is that "God's works might be revealed in him" (John 9:3). Light and darkness are presented as an element of this theophany (John 9:4–5, 41). As he did in the fifth sign, Jesus acts like God in the sixth sign. He spits on the ground and makes mud, which he spreads on the blind man's eyes; in other words, Jesus acts like God at creation, ordering the chaos of blindness into sight. The next element of a theophany present in this account is water (John 9:7–8); the man is sent to wash away the mud and see. Of course, Jesus does this work on a sabbath (John 9:14), which as seen above in the second sign, indicates that Jesus trumps the Torah's prohibition against work on the last day of the week; in a manner of speaking, God (Jesus) changes God's (the LORD's) law. While the light and darkness element, in terms of sight and blindness, permeate the story, it reaches its first crescendo with the former blind man's words: "Never since the world began has it been heard that anyone opened the eyes of a person born blind. If this man were not from God, he could do nothing" (John 9:32–33); the formerly blind man refers to the order of creation and identifies Jesus as God. The second crescendo follows, when Jesus tells the formerly blind man: "You have seen [the Son of Man], and the one speaking with you is he" (John 9:37). The blind man then calls him "Lord" (John 9:38). The formerly blind man identifies his healing as a theophany.

The last or seventh sign that Jesus gives in John's Gospel is commonly called the raising of Lazarus. The character named Lazarus, whose name means *God has helped*, is suddenly introduced in the first verse of chapter 11 of John's Gospel; he is the brother of Mary and Martha, two others characters who are suddenly introduced. A message is send to Jesus that Lazarus is ill. Jesus tells an unidentified audience (or he speaks to himself), "This illness does not lead to death; rather it is for God's glory, so that the Son of God may be glorified through it" (John 11:4). Later, he employs the light and darkness element of a theophany (John 11:9–10) before deciding to go visit Lazarus, whom the reader discovers has been in the tomb for four days; here four serves two purposes: it represents the earthen cave into which Lazarus has been placed and it indicates that the man is truly dead;

Jewish belief was that after three days a person was finally dead. Stating that Lazarus was dead for four days indicates that he is most dead! Before Jesus gets to the tomb, Martha greets him and she and Jesus enter into a dialogue about life, death, and resurrection (John 11:20–27). Then, he repeats the dialogue with Mary (John 11:28–32). Finally, Jesus goes to the tomb and instructs that the stone covering the entrance to the cave be rolled away (John 11:33–39). The Johannine Jesus repeats what he had said at the beginning of the story about seeing the glory of God (John 11:40). After praying, Jesus commands Lazarus to emerge from the tomb, and he does (John 11:41–44). Thus, the most dead Lazarus is raised to life; a theophany marks this last of seven signs that Jesus performs in John's Gospel just as it does for the previous six.

According to John's Gospel, Jesus is the incarnate theophany (John 1:14). Moloney writes that "signs can lead the believer beyond the sign to a recognition that Jesus Christ is the Son of God" in John's Gospel.[7] He adds, "John demands that believers 'look upon' Jesus the unique revealer of God to see the revelation of the Father."[8] Brown, after noting that the Johannine Jesus often refers to his signs as works, states that this "shows that the miracles are an integral part of the work given to Jesus by the Father, and indeed a continuation of the 'works' of God in the OT, like creation and the exodus."[9] The Johannine author's use of elements common to theophanies indicates Jesus is the incarnate theophany. And the Johannine theophanies demonstrate the glory of God and seal the terms flowing from the event.

---

7. Moloney, "Johannine Theology," 1426.
8. Ibid.
9. Brown, "Aspects," 1372.

15

Transformation

THE RESULT ON THE part of those who witness a theophany is transformation. In the narrative of the Mount Sinai (Horeb) theophany, God tells Moses that he has already witnessed the LORD's theophanies in Egypt. "Now therefore, if you obey my voice and keep my covenant, you shall be my treasured possession out of all the peoples," says the LORD (Exod 19:5). The Israelites are to be "a priestly kingdom and a holy nation" (Exod 19:6). They have been transformed by the voice from heaven (Exod 20:22). There will be further transformation when more theophanies occur, such as the angel who will go before the people to guard them and bring them to the place God has prepared for them (Exod 23:20–24). Finally, after relaying all the words and ordinances of the LORD to the Israelites, they demonstrate their transformation by declaring, "All the words the LORD has spoken we will do" (Exod 24:3b). Ryken notes that "[t]he archetypal pattern of transformation in the Bible signals an important part of the biblical message. . . . [T]he motif captures the dynamic nature of human life, in which things never stay the same, but always change into something better or worse, or at least different."[1] Bergmann prefers to refer to this as transfiguration. He explains that "transfiguration describes the spiritual dimension within, not above or beyond, evolution."[2] He continues: " . . . [A]ll life is given and in the process of becoming. The transfiguration of the cosmos draws created life closer to God. . . . Creation is . . . on its way to God with God. . . . "[3]

---

1. Ryken, *Dictionary*, 883.
2. Bergmann, *Religion*, 204.
3. Ibid., 205.

He says, " . . . [C]hange is a creation of a transfiguration."[4] Savran, too, emphasizes the element of transformation in theophanies: "The theophany narrative describes a movement from the human world to the divine and back again, from public to private, reflecting the dynamic of a temporary meeting between the two separate spheres of existence."[5]

Moses undergoes many transformations as a result of theophanies. Before he witnesses the burning bush he is a shepherd with a speech impediment; afterward he is Pharaoh's opponent with a magic staff and his brother Aaron as his spokesperson (Exod 3:1—4:31). Moses and Aaron transform Pharaoh's stubbornness through God's plagues on the land of Egypt (Exod 5:1—13:22). At God's command Moses transforms the sea into dry land, and those who witness this are transformed into believers in the LORD and in his servant Moses (Exod 14:1–31). The author of the HB (OT) Book of Exodus explains a transformation that occurs to Moses, to whom the LORD used to speak face to face, as one speaks to a friend (Exod 33:11; cf. Deut 34:10). After he comes down the mountain with the two new tablets of the covenant in his hand, Moses does not know that the skin of his face shines because he has been talking with God (Exod 34:29). What was most likely a sunburn from spending time on Mount Horeb (Sinai), Moses shining face scares the Israelites so much that they are afraid to come near him (Exod 34:30). Schwartz writes that when Moses "comes into sight, unaware that the residual radiation of the divine reflection still shines from his face, he creates quite a stir, causing the people to flee."[6] What the biblical author is attempting to describe using the metaphor of a shining face is the transformation that has occurred in Moses. Matthews reminds the reader that "Moses has had the singular honor of speaking with YHWH (the LORD) face to face."[7] However, no person can "withstand the full radiance of God's glory, [which] has been held in check during [God's and Moses'] previous meetings."[8] Now, "Moses' face has acquired a measure of the deity's glory."[9] After Moses delivers the LORD's commandments to the people, he puts a veil over his face; he removes the veil when he speaks to God (Exod 29:33–34). When the Israelites could see Moses' shining face,

---

4. Ibid., 216.
5. Savran, "Theophany," 134.
6. Schwartz, "Priestly Account," 115.
7. Matthews, "Theophanies," 311.
8. Ibid.
9. Ibid.

he would drop the veil over it (Exod 29:35). The cloud on the mountain veils the LORD's fiery radiance; Moses, who by speaking face to face with God has been transformed by some of the fiery radiance, must shield the Israelites from it. Schwartz refers to this as "the radiation emanating from Moses' face."[10]

In the CB (NT), Paul explains how life-giving Spirit has outshone the radiation glory of the Mosaic covenant which was so great "that the people of Israel could not gaze at Moses' face because of the glory of his face" (2 Cor 3:7). Paul thinks that that glory has been surpassed by the new covenant, which is "not like Moses, who put a veil over his face to keep the people of Israel from gazing at the end of the glory that was being set aside" (2 Cor 3:13). According to Paul, everyone can see the glory of the Lord as they "are being transformed into the same image from one degree of glory to another" by the Spirit (2 Cor 3:18). Thus, according to Paul, God's glory transforms everyone who is moved by the Spirit.

Noah and his family are transformed before, during, and after the great flood. They were changed by their acceptance of God's word, by the time they spent on the ark with the animals, and afterward when they become the new primogenitors of the human race. Both Abraham and his son, Isaac, are transformed through the theophany on a mountain in the land of Moriah. Just as he is ready to slaughter his son, the angel of the LORD—God—appears to stop him (Gen 22:1–14). Not only has Abraham been transformed by previous theophanic experiences, but his trust of the LORD is firmly sealed by this one. Furthermore, Isaac, who is good as dead, is transformed into life and given a share in the promise of "offspring as numerous as the stars of heaven and as the sand that is on the seashore" (Gen 22:17). Isaac's son, Jacob, is transformed through his dream of "a ladder set up on the earth, the top of it reaching to heaven; and the angels of God . . . ascending and descending on it" (Gen 28:12). The LORD stands beside Jacob and repeats the terms of the covenant made with Abraham (Gen 28:13–15). When he awakes from his theophanic dream, the patriarch declares, "Surely the LORD is in this place—and I did not know it!" (Gen 28:16) He memorializes the experience with a stone (Gen 28:18–19). Then, he proceeds to seek wives so that God's promise of countless descendants can be realized through him.

In the First Book of Samuel, barren Hannah and her husband Elkanah are not only transformed by the conception and birth of their son Samuel,

---

10. Schwartz, "Priestly Account," 121.

but also through the experience of offering him in service to the LORD along with a three-year-old bull (1 Sam 1:1–11). After the cloud fills the temple Solomon built, the king is transformed by the glory of the LORD as seen in the prayers he makes and the blessings he bestows on the Israelites (1 Kgs 8:1–66). God's second appearance to him confirms his transformation (1 Kgs 9:1–9).

One of the HB's (OT's) best narratives of transformation as a result of a theophany is that of Naaman and Elisha (2 Kgs 5:1–19). Naaman, a Syrian army commander, has leprosy, which in itself has transformed him. Elisha is a prophet and successor to Elijah. A young Jewish girl, who had been captured in a raid by the Syrians on Israel, serves Naaman's unnamed wife. The girl suggests that Naaman go to Elisha in the hope of getting a cure for his leprosy. In other words, Israel's enemy is going to go to Israel's prophet to seek a cure! Once Naaman arrives in front of Elisha's house, the prophet sends him a message: "Go, wash in the Jordan seven times, and your flesh shall be restored and you shall be clean" (2 Kgs 5:10). The reader will note that the prophet instructs his enemy to bathe a fullness of times in the Jordan River and become clean and disease free. Naaman becomes angry because he wants Elisha to do some magic by calling upon the name of the LORD and waving his hand over the commander's leprosy. Furthermore, he reasons that the rivers in Syria are cleaner than the Jordan, and so it would make more sense for him to go bathe in one of them. However, Elisha, who had accompanied Elijah when he parted the Jordan to cross it and parted it himself after Elijah went to heaven into a fiery chariot, knows the power of the water, an element of a theophany. The little girl urges Naaman to do as the prophet says. So, Naaman went to the river "and immersed himself seven times in the Jordan, according to the word of the man of God; his flesh was restored like the flesh of a young boy, and he was clean" (2 Kgs 5:14). In other words, Naaman experiences a theophany that transforms him. His response is to return to Elisha and offer gifts to him, but Elisha refuses because he knows that it is the LORD who has cured Naaman, who declares, "Now I know that there is no God in all the earth except in Israel" (2 Kgs 5:15). After Elisha refuses Naaman's gifts, Naaman asks the prophet if he can take two mule-loads of earth with him to Syria so he can worship Israel's God on Israel's soil!

In the CB (NT) it is the author of Luke's Gospel who begins his narrative with the story of the transformation of Zechariah, a priest, who, when offering incense (see Smoke), has the theophanic experience of "an angel

TRANSFORMATION

of the Lord, standing at the right side of the altar of incense" (Luke 1:11). Because he fails to believe the message that he and his wife, Elizabeth, will have a son in their golden years, he becomes mute, unable to speak, until the child is born and named (Luke 1:19-25; 57-64). Then, not only is he transformed by receiving back his ability to speak, but he is "filled with the Holy Spirit," another way to write about transformation, and speaks a prophecy (Luke 1:67).

As seen above in the chapter on signs, Jesus gives seven signs that transform those who witness them. After changing six stone jars of water (an element of a theophany) into wine, the narrator states that Jesus revealed his glory and his disciples believed in him (John 2:11). In other words, his disciples were transformed from unbelievers to believers. After Jesus assures the royal officer that his son will live, the man believes the word that Jesus speaks to him (John 4:50); in other words, the royal official and his whole household come to believe (John 4:53b). After Jesus heals the ill man lying by the pool, the transformed man picks up his mat and walks (John 5:9) and then proclaims to the Jews that it was Jesus who made him well (John 5:15). John's narration of Jesus' fourth sign—the feeding in Galilee—leads those who have been transformed by eating bread and fish to declare that Jesus is the prophet who was predestined to succeed Moses (John 6:14-15). When Jesus comes walking on the sea toward his disciples in a boat, they are transformed from brave fishermen to terrified followers (John 6:19) until he calms them and they decide to take him into the boat (John 6:21). The curing of the man born blind—Jesus' sixth Johannine sign—transforms the blind man to one who can see (John (9:6-7) while it also transforms those who can see into the blind (John 9:18-23, 40-41). And the last sign, the raising of Lazarus, transforms Lazarus from the dead to alive (John 11:43-44); it transforms the man's sister, Martha, from a supposed believer into an unbeliever (John 11:21-22; 39); it transforms the dead man's sister, Mary, into a believer (John 11:32); and it transforms some in the crowd of mourners into believers (John 11:45).

Most likely the greatest transformation that results from a theophany is that recorded in the CB (NT): Jesus' transfiguration (see Sacred Numbers), which appears in the gospels of Mark (9:2-8), Matthew (17:1-8), and Luke (9:28-36a). Presuming that Matthew's Gospel and Luke's Gospel are derived from Mark's Gospel, in Mark there are two transformations; Jesus is transfigured (Mark 9:2) and Peter didn't know what to say, and he, James, and John were terrified (Mark 9:6). The sign of Jesus' transformation—dazzling white clothes (Mark 9:3)—is contrasted with that of the three disciples whose response is to say nothing to anyone (Mark 9:9–10). Matthew's Gospel states that Jesus' face shone like the sun in addition to his clothes becoming dazzling white (Matt 17:2) to indicate his transformation. According to Viviano, in Matthew's Gospel "Jesus becomes a being of light; his nature becomes luminous, transparent to the disciples' gaze."[11] As in Mark, the disciples are "overcome by fear" in Matthew (Matt 17:6). Furthermore, while Mark says that at the end of the event the disciples saw "only Jesus" (Mark 9:8), Matthew writes that they see "no one except Jesus himself alone" (Matt 17:8). Viviano states that "Moses and Elijah have withdrawn, i.e., diminished in significance before the fuller revelation in Jesus."[12] After the theophany is over, Mark portrays Jesus telling his disciples "to tell no one about what they had seen, until after the Son of Man had risen from the dead" (Mark 9:9). However, Matthew writes that Jesus told them to tell "no one about the vision until the Son of Man has been raised from the dead" (Matt 17:9). Matthew has introduced another element of a theophany here—dream or vision—because he understands Mark's transfiguration narrative as a type of metamorphosis, which will not be complete and proven until Jesus appears after his crucifixion, death, and resurrection. The original ending of Mark's Gospel has no post-resurrection appearance stories, but Matthew adds two (Matt 28:9–10; 16–20). Matthew's post-resurrection appearance stories are meant to commission the disciples to begin a mission to all the nations. Since the Matthean Jesus demonstrates that he has been raised through two post-resurrection appearances, retrospectively the transfiguration account in Matthew gives an advanced viewing of the risen Christ in a dream or vision (see Dream) whereas in Mark it was the viewing of the risen, transfigured or transformed, Christ.

The author of Luke's Gospel portrays Jesus "as bodying forth God's glory in his kingdom ministry."[13] Thus, he turns Mark's transfiguration event into a theophany, using "symbols of the transcendent"[14] which he found in the Mount Sinai (Horeb) narrative. The Lukan Jesus' disciples go up the mountain to pray (Luke 9:28), and that it is while they are praying that Jesus' face changes and his clothes become dazzling white (Luke 9:29). Moses and Elijah appear in glory—the glory of the LORD—and they

11. Viviano, "Matthew," 660.
12. Ibid.
13. Karris, "Luke," 700.
14. Ibid.

speak to Jesus about the next phase of his ministry, which he will accomplish in Jerusalem (Luke 9:31); they speak about his exodus which he will accomplish through death, resurrection, and ascension to the glory of the LORD. Luke notes that even though Peter, James, and John are sleepy, "they saw [Jesus'] glory and the two men who stood with him" (Luke 9:32).

As a result of the experience, Peter wants to erect three dwellings, but he and his companions are terrified (Luke 9:34). Luke interprets this theophanic event "in the light of the harvest festival of Tabernacles, the abundance of which came to symbolize God's consummation of history."[15] Just as in Mark, the voice of the LORD is heard from the cloud, indicating that Jesus is his chosen one (Luke 9:35). The disciples are told to listen to him (Luke 9:35b), just as in Mark (9:7b). However, in Luke this command to be attentive is focused on "this new phase of God's revelation of who the Son is: one who returns to God via the cross"[16] and resurrection and ascension. Then, after the voice all returns to as it was before: "Jesus was found alone" (Luke 9:36a). Moses and Elijah have been superseded by the Lukan Jesus; that is, the Lukan Jesus has been transformed into the glory of the LORD. The Lukan disciples, like Moses and Elijah before them, get to see the glory and live; they, too, have been transfigured. In Luke's second volume, the Acts of the Apostles, they will bear witness to what they have seen, to how they have been transformed, as they travel to the end of the earth. Thus, transformation becomes an element in theophanies revealing the glory of the LORD and the glory of the Lord (Jesus).

---

15. Ibid.
16. Ibid.

16

Altar

While an altar, "a sign of the divine presence,"[1] could be considered under the element of sign, it is important enough in theophanies to be named as a separate element in them and occupy its own entry. Following God's giving of the Ten Commandments to Moses, the LORD instructs Moses to make him "an altar of earth" (Exod 20:24) upon which to sacrifice a variety of offerings. If Moses chooses to make "an altar of stone," it may not be built "of hewn stones" because a chisel profanes the stones (Exod 20:25). McKenzie notes that the altar described as one of earth "is doubtless the oldest form of Israelite altar, and more primitive in general; it is to be made of earth heaped up, or in a heap of unhewn stones."[2] Gray agrees, stating: "The altar of earth was probably made of compacted clay or crude brick, which would have the added advantage of absorbing the blood of the sacrifice."[3] Castelot says that altars were "built of earth or unbaked brick or of uncut stone."[4] The prohibition against using a chisel to shape the stones, rendering them profane, means that they have been changed from the state in which they came from God.[5] Gray adds other possibilities to this understanding: "The motive for prohibiting stone dressed with an edged tool probably combine the desire to avoid materials contaminated by man and the early superstitious fear of iron as a trade secret of an alien smith

 1. Castelot, "Religious Institutions," 1267.
 2. McKenzie, *Dictionary*, 23.
 3. Gray, "Exodus," 55.
 4. Castelot, "Religious Institutions," 1266.
 5. McKenzie, *Dictionary*, 23; cf. Castelot, "Religious Institutions," 1267.

caste."[6] Moses follows God's directives. After rising early in the morning, he builds an altar at the foot of Mount Sinai (Horeb) by setting up twelve pillars, one for each of the twelve tribes of Israel (Exod 24:4). Taking half of the blood of sacrificed oxen, he dashes it against the altar, representing the presence of God, and taking the other half of the blood, he dashes it on the Israelites as the parties of the covenant (Exod 24:5–8).[7] Castelot notes that "the victim's blood, the most sacred element, was brought into direct contact with [the altar]. In every sacrifice, the blood was poured out at the base of the altar."[8] Through his ritual, God and the Israelites became blood brothers and sisters.

Reminiscent of this theophany is the one experienced by the prophet Elijah on Mount Carmel. In this dueling-prophets narrative, Elijah summons the Israelites and then repairs "the altar of the LORD that had been thrown down" (1 Kgs 18:30). Again, just like Moses (Josh 5:13–15), he takes "twelve stones, according to the number of the tribes of the sons of Jacob" and "with the stones he [builds] an altar in the name of the LORD" (1 Kgs 18:31–32). After several other preparations, he places the sacrificed bull on top of wood on the altar, has water poured over it, prays, and stands back to watch the theophany occur. God's fire consumes it all; there can be no doubt that the LORD is God, and the altar represents his all-consuming presence.

Before these two important HB (OT) theophanies, there are others which mention the building of an altar. For example, after the flood theophany, Noah builds an altar to the LORD and offers burnt offerings which smell pleasing to God (Gen 8:20–21). Likewise, Abram builds altars after experiencing the LORD appear and speak to him (Gen 12:7, 8, 13:4, 18). Of course, the more famous altar that Abraham built is the one upon which he was going to sacrifice Isaac until the LORD stopped him (Gen 22:9). Following in the footsteps of his father, Isaac built an altar after the LORD appeared to him (Gen 26:25). Isaac's son, Jacob, built an altar in Bethel to commemorate God's multiple appearances to him there (Gen 28:10–22; 35:1–15).

Once the Mount Sinai (Horeb) experience is concluded and the Israelites begin their journey to the promised land, portable altars are made so the people can take the Mount Sinai (Horeb) experience of the LORD's

---

6. Gray, "Exodus," 55.
7. Ibid., 59.
8. Castelot, "Religious Institutions," 1272.

presence with them (Exod 27:1–2; 30:1–3). One altar is used for burnt offerings of various kinds, and the other one is used for burning incense, that is, re-creating the cloud of the divine presence. Schwartz says that "the theophany happened to occur at Sinai [Horeb]; it could have occurred anywhere, and its residue, the divine Presence, is portable."[9] He writes: "The mountain recedes into the distance long before the Israelites depart from it. Once the [cloud] enters the divine abode [that is, the tent with the ark of the covenant in it and the altars before it] the mountain disappears, having served only as a temporary resting-place."[10] Schwartz also clarifies that the tent is "the portable abode of the deity, replacing not the mountain on which he temporarily rested during his descent to earth, but rather his heavenly palace and throne-room."[11] The Book of Exodus makes clear that the altar for burnt offerings, covered in bronze, is most holy, and that whatever touches the altar—blood, animals, grain, etc.—becomes holy (Exod 28:37). Likewise, the altar upon which incense is burned, covered in gold, stands before the ark of the covenant (Exod 40:5); incense creates a cloud of smoke that indicates the presence of God. The HB (OT) Books of Leviticus and Numbers contain minute details concerning what is offered and how it is to be offered to the LORD.

Joshua, Moses' successor, is depicted as doing what Moses did. Thus, Joshua, after crossing the Jordan and capturing Jericho and Ai, builds "on Mount Ebal an altar to the LORD, the God of Israel, just as Moses the servant of the LORD had commanded the Israelites, as it is written in the book of the law of Moses, 'an altar of unhewn stones, on which no iron tool has been used'; and they offered on it burnt offerings to the LORD, and sacrificed offerings of well-being" (Josh 8:31). He also wrote a copy of the law on stones (Josh 8:32).

An altar is an element of the narrative concerning Gideon in the HB (OT) Book of Judges. Once he experiences his offering consumed by the fire of the angel of the Lord, Gideon builds an altar there to the LORD (Judg 6:24) and proceeds to tear down Baal's altar (Judg 6:25–32). In the same book, Manoah and his wife experience several theophanies and respond by making offerings on an altar (Judg 13:20). Likewise, the last chapter (24) of the Second Book of Samuel contains the narrative of David experiencing the theophany of the LORD's plague of pestilence, after which he buys

---

9. Schwartz, "Priestly Account," 133.
10. Ibid.
11. Ibid., 124.

a threshing floor and builds an altar to the LORD in order to avert the plague. He offers burnt offerings and offerings of well-being upon it (2 Sam 24:1–25; cf. 1 Chr 21:14—22:1).

David's son, Solomon, builds the first temple in Jerusalem "with stone finished at the quarry, so that neither hammer nor ax nor any tool of iron was heard in the temple while it was being built" (1 Kgs 6:7). Then, the ark of the covenant is brought from the tent into which David had placed it, and a theophany occurs (1 Kgs 8:10–13; cf. 2 Chr 5:14). Before the ark stands the altar of incense made of cedar and overlaid with gold (1 Kgs 6:20, 22). Now, the portable presence of the LORD from Mount Horeb (Sinai) to an ark in a tent has found a permanent home (1 Kgs 8:21). Outside the holy of holies, is found the altar for burnt offerings, before which Solomon prays (1 Kgs 8:22–53) and upon which he offers sacrifices (1 Kgs 8:62–64). The Second Book of Chronicles states: "When Solomon had ended his prayer, fire came down from heaven and consumed the burnt offering and the sacrifices; and the glory of the LORD filled the temple" (2 Chr 7:1). The First Book of Kings also indicates the three times a year Solomon offered burnt offerings and sacrifices on the altar, and he also offered incense before the LORD (1 Kgs 9:25).

After the Babylonians destroy Jerusalem and its temple and Ezra and Nehemiah oversee its rebuilding as the second temple, Antiochus Epiphanes profanes it in 167 BCE "by superimposing on it an altar to Olympian Zeus."[12] Once the Maccabees drive out their Greek overlords and establish self-rule for a short amount of time, Judas Maccabeus chooses Jewish priests who cleanse the sanctuary and remove "the defiled stones to an unclean place" (1 Macc 4:43). The narrator of the OT (A) First Book of Maccabees tells the rest of the story:

> They deliberated what to do about the altar of burnt offering, which had been profaned. And they thought it best to tear it down, so that it would not be a lasting shame to them that the Gentiles had defiled it. So they tore down the altar, and stored the stones in a convenient place on the temple hill until a prophet should come to tell what to do with them. Then they took unhewn stones, as the law directs, and built a new altar like the former one. (1 Macc 4:44–47; cf 2 Macc 10:2–3)

The prophet Isaiah mentions the altar in his narrative about his theophanic experience (Isa 6:6). There can be no doubt that the altar

---

12. Castelot, "Religious Institutions," 1267.

represents God, because the prophet hears the voice of the LORD asking him to be his messenger (Isa 6:8). Likewise, in one of his many theophanic visions, the prophet Ezekiel receives directions from God about how to build the altar (Ezek 43:13–27). Once the second temple and the altars are destroyed by the Romans in 70 CE, the altar, for all practical purposes, disappears from biblical literature. The Matthean Jesus references it (Matt 5:23–24; 23:18–20), and the Lukan narrator mentions the altar of incense (Luke 1:11).

In the Acts of the Apostles, the Lukan Paul is standing in front of the Areopagus in Athens and addressing the people, who, it seems, have many altars dedicated to the appearances of their gods. Paul says,

> Athenians, I see how extremely religious you are in every way. For as I went through the city and looked carefully at the objects of your worship, I found among them an altar with the inscription, "To an unknown god." What therefore you worship as unknown, this I proclaim to you. The God who made the world and everything in it, he who is Lord of heaven and earth, does not live in shrines made by human hands, nor is he served by human hands, as though he needed anything, since he himself gives to all mortals life and breath and all things. From one ancestor he made all nations to inhabit the whole earth, and he allotted the times of their existence and the boundaries of the places where they would live, so that they would search for God and perhaps grope for him and find him—through indeed he is not far from each one of us. For "In him we live and move and have our being"; as some of your poets have said, "For we too are his offspring." Since we are God's offspring, we ought not to think that the deity is like gold, or silver, or stone, an image formed by the art and imagination of mortals. (Acts 17:22–29)

The CB (NT) Letter to the Hebrews mentions the golden altar of incense before the ark of the covenant (Heb 9:4), but it is the Book of Revelation that exploits the theophanic element of the altar of incense. The author mentions an angel that is given incense to offer with the prayers of the saints before God's throne while standing at the altar (Rev 8:3), an angel that takes fire from the altar and throws it on the earth (Rev 8:5), a voice that comes from the four horns of the golden altar (Rev 9:13), and the response of the altar after the third bowl of God's wrath is poured on the earth: "Yes, O Lord God, the Almighty, your judgments are true and just!" (Rev 16:7) In other places, the author mentions the souls of those who had been slaughtered for the word of God under the altar (Rev 6:9), the measurements of the altar (Rev 11:1), and an angel that comes out from the altar (Rev 14:18).

Thus, while God is invisible, an altar makes him visible. Faley states that "the altar . . . was a sign of the divine presence."[13] McKenzie puts it this way:

> The altar symbolized the deity in the sacrificial ritual, and the victim was presented to the deity by contact with the altar. In earlier times it does not appear that the altar was employed for burning the victim or the portions given to the deity; the offering was made by applying the blood of the victim, which symbolized its life, to the altar.[14]

Once, sacrificial offerings were burned on an altar, it was the altar which "brought about the victim's transition from the earthly sphere to the divine realm."[15] The fire (see Fire) that is always kept burning on the altar, that is, always going upward to heaven, is how the food offered to God, that is, his meal, got to him.[16] This makes the altar an element of a theophany that reveals the glory of the LORD.

---

13. Faley, "Leviticus," 62.
14. McKenzie, *Dictionary*, 23.
15. Faley, "Leviticus," 62.
16. Castelot, "Religious Institutions," 1267–8.

17

Feast (Meal)

ANOTHER ELEMENT OF A theophany is feasting; some type of sacred meal involving eating and drinking is present. In the Mount Sinai (Horeb) narrative, Moses, Aaron, Aaron's two sons—Nadab and Abihu—and seventy elders of Israel go up the mountain where they behold God, and they eat and drink (Exod 24:11). "The fact that this unique occurrence comes upon the reader as a bolt from the blue highlights its narrative significance," states Robinson.[1] Clifford states that "[o]n this momentous occasion . . . the invited leaders are protected [from seeing God's face] by the rules of hospitality; they share a meal with their divine host."[2] God, as royal host, gives food and drink to his human guests; this is a manifestation of divine hospitality.[3] Ryken notes that feasts, not parties, are "celebrations of God's goodness toward his people"; they are "celebrations of the faithfulness of God's provision."[4]

Before Moses and the others ascend the mountain, God tells Moses about the festivals that he wants observed (Exod 23:12–19); all these involve feasting. Ryken notes that God establishes these feasts "to commemorate and to celebrate [the] blessed relationship" he has with his people.[5] In addition to unity engendered between God and the Israelites, the feasts also bring the Israelites into close fellowship with each other. Each feast,

1. Robinson, "Theophany and Meal," 160.
2. Cliffort, "Exodus," 55.
3. Robinson, "Theophany and Meal," 165.
4. Ryken, *Dictionary*, 278.
5. Ibid.

according to Ryken, "was celebrated by refraining from the usual work of the day, by assembling together in fellowship, and by eating a festive meal of meat, grain (i.e., bread), and wine that had been ritually offered to God."[6] In the Mount Sinai (Horeb) narrative, Moses and the others who ascend the mountain represent all the Israelites feasting with God.[7] Eating the feast on the mountain "highlights God's desire to dwell with his people in joyful assembly."[8]

Gray calls this and other meals a celebration of "a communion meal."[9] He prefers to refer to peace offerings as "'communion offerings,' in which the blood, fat, and vital organs were burned on the altar to God and the rest was eaten by the worshipers, who thus effected solidarity with one another and with God."[10] Castelot refers to this as a "communion sacrifice." He writes: "A union between God and the donor was effected by a thanksgiving offering."[11] Castelot notes three different kinds of communion sacrifices or meals: sacrifices of praise, freewill sacrifices made out of pure devotion, and votive offerings made in fulfillment of a vow.[12] No matter what form the sacrifice took, it indicated that the person making the offering was symbolically surrendering to God, and God, by accepting the offering, bound himself in some way to the person making the offering.[13] Thus, "it is with the people that the covenant is made."[14] Furthermore, "[o]nly those sprinkled with the sacrificial blood can enjoy communion with the Deity."[15]

Before the Mount Horeb (Sinai) feast, there is the meal inaugurating Passover. A lamb is chosen from the flock and kept for a few days before it is slaughtered and roasted over a fire after its blood is drained from it and given to God (Exod 12:1–13). The LORD instructs Moses: "This day shall be a day of remembrance for you. You shall celebrate it as a festival to the LORD; throughout your generations you shall observe it as a perpetual ordinance" (Exod 12:14). Coupled with the eating of the lamb is the eating

6. Ibid., 279.
7. Robinson, "Theophany and Meal," 170.
8. Ryken, *Dictionary*, 279.
9. Gray, "Exodus," 59.
10. Ibid., 55.
11. Castelot, "Religious Institutions," 1268.
12. Ibid.
13. Ibid., 1272.
14. Robinson, "Theophany and Meal," 172.
15. Ibid.

of unleavened bread for a week; leaven was considered to be a corrupting agent in the ancient world, and no corruption could be present when marking a feast in honor of the LORD. The festival of unleavened bread lasts for seven days to commemorate the fact that God brought the Israelites out of Egypt (Exod 12:14–20).

Other biblical records of feasting as an element of theophanies include that of Abraham welcoming three visitors to his tent in the heat of the day. The patriarch tells his wife, Sarah, to take flour, knead it, and make cakes. He takes a calf from the herd and gives it to one of his servants to slaughter, dress, and cook. Then, taking curds and milk, Abraham sets the bread and meat before his visitors (Gen 18:1–8). He doesn't know that they are a theophanic experience of God, who announces that the elderly couple will conceive a child within the next year (Gen 18:9).

Feasting is a part of the narrative describing King David bringing the ark of God from Baale-judah to Jerusalem in the HB (OT) Second Book of Samuel (2 Sam 6:1–2). After placing the ark on a new cart, David and his entourage begin the procession to Jerusalem. However, one man reaches out to stabilize the ark when the oxen pulling the cart shake it; that man receives God's anger and is struck dead because he touched the ark (2 Sam 6:3–7). Because of this theophanic event, David changes his plan and has the ark brought to the house of Obed-edom where it remained for three—divine—months (2 Sam 6:8–11). Finally, David brings the ark to Jerusalem (2 Sam 6:12–15), and it is housed in a tent (2 Sam 6:17–18) just like it was after Moses made it and the tent under which it travelled with the Israelites. As the text makes clear, on this solemn occasion, David "distributed food among all the people, the whole multitude of Israel, both men and women, to each a cake of bread, a portion of meat, and a cake of raisins" (2 Sam 6:19a).

After Solomon, David's son, inherits his father's throne, he experiences a theophanic dream in which Solomon asks the LORD for the gift of wisdom to govern the Israelites (1 Kgs 3:9). God is please with Solomon's request and tells him that he will give him a discerning mind. When Solomon awakens from this theophanic dream, he provides a feast for all his servants (1 Kgs 3:15). Likewise, after having built the temple in Jerusalem and housed the ark of the LORD in it, Solomon experiences a theophany (1 Kgs 8:9–13; cf. 2 Chr 7:1–3); after the dedication of the temple is complete, he holds a festival before the LORD for seven days (1 Kgs 8:65; cf. 2 Chr 7:8–10).

Feast (Meal)

Before his contest with the prophets of Baal on Mount Carmel, Elijah visits the widow of Zarephath. Because there is severe drought, she is gathering a few sticks to use in making a fire in order to bake into bread the last bit of flour she has. As the instrument of the theophany, Elijah informs her: "The jar of meal will not be emptied and the jug of oil will not fail until the day that the LORD sends rain on the earth" (1 Kgs 17:14). According to the narrator of the theophany, "The jar of meal was not emptied, neither did the jug of oil fail, according to the word of the LORD that he spoke by Elijah" (1 Kgs 17:16). For many days she and her whole household enjoyed the feast.

In the midst of chaos in Jerusalem on Mount Zion, the prophet Isaiah presents words of hope to the suffering inhabitants: "On this mountain the LORD of hosts will make for all peoples a feast of rich food, a feast of well-aged wines, of rich food filled with marrow, of well-aged wines strained clear" (Isa 25:6). Roberts says that the "banquet on the mountain is presumably a covenant-type banquet on Yahweh's [the LORD's] sacred dwelling place in which the peoples participate to acknowledge Yahweh's [the LORD's] rule over them."[16] Isaiah's description of the festival echoes the meal served by God on Mount Horeb (Sinai). Roberts adds that "it is a sumptuous banquet befitting the king of the world."[17]

The prophet Ezekiel reverses Isaiah's imagery of the banquet on Mount Zion. God tells the prophet to summon birds and wild animals "to the sacrificial feast that [he is] preparing..., a great sacrificial feast on the mountains of Israel, [where they] shall eat flesh and drink blood" (Ezek 39:17). The birds and wild animals will be able to eat fat until they are filled and drink blood until they are drunk at the sacrificial feast that the Lord GOD prepares for them (Ezek 39:19). Boadt writes that in this great sacrificial feast "the enemy is the victim and God's creatures the sacrificers who give glory to God by their banquet."[18] According to Ezekiel, this is a way that God displays his glory among the nations so that they know that he is the LORD (Ezek 39:21–23); he lets the nations know "that the house of Israel went into captivity for their iniquity" (Ezek 39:23).

In the CB (NT) the multiplication of the loaves and fish by Jesus not only echoes the feast that God provided through Elijah to the widow of Zarephath, but it, too, is a theophanic event. Mark's Gospel contains two accounts of this theophany (Mark 6:30–44; 8:1–9). In the first story, Jesus

---

16. Roberts, *First Isaiah*, 322.
17. Ibid.
18. Boadt, "Ezekiel," 326.

takes five loaves and two fish and feeds a minimum of five thousand men; in the second story, he takes seven loaves and a few small fish and feeds four thousand people. There can be no doubt that this is the same story told two different ways—probably preserved in oral tradition in multiple versions—and that this is a theophany—signaled by the use of the number seven in both accounts. When Matthew copies Mark's Gospel, he keeps both versions of the story (Matt 14:13–21; 15:32–39). However, when Luke copies Mark's Gospel, he recognizes that both editions are the same story told in two different ways and keeps only the first one (Luke 9:10–17). Another account of the multiplication of the loaves and fish, similar to the first one in Mark and Matthew and the one in Luke, is found in John's Gospel, in which it functions as one of the seven major signs (see Signs) worked by the Johannine Jesus (John 6:14). While this story is usually referred to as a miracle, it is more properly named a theophany, a feast, a celebration of the faithfulness of God's provision.

Another story of a feast that is unique to John's Gospel is found in the last chapter, commonly labeled the appendix or epilogue. It is obvious that the gospel ends at John 20:31; however, at some point in its transmission it picked up a second ending (John 21:1–25). There is no doubt that this post-resurrection experience is a theophany. Jesus presents himself to his disciples—seven of them (John 21:2)—by water—the Sea of Tiberias (John 21:1). The author mentions daybreak, the element of light and darkness (John 21:4). The disciples, who are fishing and have caught nothing, do not recognize Jesus standing on the shore. He tells them where to lower the net. They do as he says and haul up a huge catch of fish. At this moment, one of the disciples shouts, "It is the Lord!" (John 21:7) The theophany causes Peter to jump into the water and swim to shore, while the rest bring the boat and the fish. When they all get to shore, they see that Jesus has prepared a charcoal fire with fish on it and bread to eat (John 21:9). In other words, he has prepared a breakfast feast for his disciples. He tells them to bring some of the fish they caught. Then, the narrator states: "Now none of the disciples dared to ask him, 'Who are you?' because they knew it was the Lord" (John 21:12b). And to be sure that the reader recognizes this story as a theophany, he adds that this was the third time—the number referring to God—that Jesus appeared to his disciples after he was raised from the dead (John 21:14). Thus, feasting is, indeed, an element of a theophany that reveals the glory of the LORD and the glory of the Lord (Jesus).

18

Wind

THE ELEMENT OF WIND does not occur in the narrative of the making of the covenant on Mount Sinai (Horeb). However, it is an element in the opening theophany in the HB (OT) Book of Genesis in which the narrator states that "a wind from God swept over the face of the waters" (Gen 1:2) just as God was getting ready to create order out of the chaos. Hiebert notes that wind "is identified in Gen[esis] 1:2 not as a created substance but as an aspect of the divine being."[1] He adds, "[A]s the first aspect of the world so described, [it is] the first sacred thing. [It is] an aspect of God's own presence in creation."[2] Job alludes to this poetically when he says that "by his wind the heavens were made fair" (Job 26:13) and "when he gave to the wind its weight, and apportioned out the waters by measure" (Job 28:25). Similarly, after the chaos of the great flood, "God made a wind blow over the earth, and the waters subsided" (Gen 8:1) so that he could begin to order creation again. The author of Ecclesiastes declares, "No one has power over the wind to restrain the wind" (Eccl 8:8). Yet, Psalm 135 declares that the LORD "brings out the wind from his storehouses" (Ps 135:7c; cf. Jer 10:13; 51:16) and "makes his wind blow" (Ps 147:18). The prophet Amos merely states that the LORD "creates the wind" (Amos 4:13).

Wind it also present in other theophanies. When Moses stretches out his staff over the land of Egypt, "the LORD [brings] an east wind upon the land all that day and all that night; when morning came, the east wind had brought the locusts" (Exod 10:13). After Pharaoh acknowledges his sin to

---

1. Hiebert, "Air," 15.
2. Ibid.

Moses, he asks him to request that God remove the locusts. "The LORD changed the wind into a very strong west wind, which lifted the locusts and drove them into the Red Sea" (Exod 10:19a).

If that were not enough to identify wind as an element of theophanies, the narrative about the parting of the water of the Red Sea will do so. After Moses stretches out his hand over the sea, "The LORD [drives] the sea back by a strong east wind all night, and [turns] the sea into dry land; and the waters [are] divided" (Exod 14:21). After all the Israelites have crossed through the sea with Pharaoh's army in pursuit, Moses follows God's command and stretches out his hand over the sea again to reverse the previous action. The water returns to its normal depth, drowning Pharaoh's army (Exod 14:26–29). In his song of triumph, Moses and the Israelites declare to the LORD, "You blew with your wind, the sea covered them; they sank like lead in the mighty waters" (Exod 15:10). Hiebert uses this last verse to show the "close connection between storm wind and deity, widespread in the Bible."[3] He explains:

> ... [B]iblical Israel's preoccupation with the winds of the thunderstorm is directly related to its agrarian economy of dry farming, which was dependent upon ... seasonal rains. This fact lies behind Israel's association between ... storm winds and God. Upon the regular return of the westerly blowing winds each winter and the moisture they bore, rested the success of Israel's annual harvests and the survival of its people. Thus, this particular atmospheric phenomenon was an especially obvious medium of the divine presence and activity, which ensured the lives of God's people in their land. ...[4]

While the Bible contains references to "the four winds of the earth" (Jer 49:36; Dan 7:2, 8:8, 11:4; Zech 2:6, 6:5; Mark 13:27; Matt 24:31; Rev 7:1)—four representing the earth—of these different winds—north (Prov 25:23; Eccl 1:6; Song 4:16; Sir 43:17b, 20; Acts 27:14), south (Job 37:17; Eccl 1:6; Song 4:16;; Sir 43:16; Luke 12:55; Acts 27:13, 28:13), west (Exod 10:19), and east (Gen 41:6, 23, 27; Job 15:2, 27:21, 38:24; Pss 48:7, 78:26; Isa 27:8; Jer 18:17; Ezek 17:10, 19:12; 27:26; Hos 12:1, 13:15; Jonah 4:8)—it is the east wind that "most often blows a dry, scorching wind from the desert," states Ryken.[5] Furthermore, as seen in the narrative of the Red Sea cross-

---

3. Ibid., 14.
4. Ibid.
5. Ryken, *Dictionary*, 952.

ing, the wind presents "God's supremacy, his authority over his creation, his judgment on that creation, and the very Spirit that breathes new life into a human soul."[6]

As a theophanic element, the wind is often personified as a winged being. In a psalm in the Second Book of Samuel, the writer states that the LORD "rode on a cherub, and flew; he was seen upon the wings of the wind" (2 Sam 22:11). A cherub, a mythical, griffin-like creature, is the LORD's transport supported by the wind. Psalm 18 declares that "he came swiftly upon the wings of the wind" (Ps 18:10), while Psalm 104 makes the clouds his chariot which rides "on the wings of the wind" (Ps 104:3b). In the CB (NT) Letter to the Hebrews, the author says, "He makes his angels winds" (Heb 1:7).

Wind that goes out from the LORD brings quails from the sea to feed the Israelites (Num 11:31). According to the author of Ecclesiastes, most of life is "a chasing after wind" (Eccl 1:14, 17, 2:11, 17, 26, 4:4, 6, 16; 6:9), "toiling for the wind" (Eccl 5:16), or pursuing the wind (Sir 34:2). Psalm 103 compares mortals to a flower of a field over which the wind passes and is gone (Ps 103:16), while the Book of Proverbs says that controlling a contentious wife is like trying to restrain the wind (Prov 27:16). A theophanic wind can be described as great (Job 1:19), raging (Ps 55:8), stormy (Pss 107:25, 148:8; Ezek 1:4, 13:11, 13), mighty (Wis 5:23), whistling (Wis 17:18; Dan 3:50), scorching (Sir 34:19; Isa 11:15), hot (Jer 4:11), destructive (Jer 51:1), and violent (Wis 4:4); it can scatter straw (Job 21:18) and chaff (Pss 1:4, 35:5, 83:13; Isa 17:13, 49:10; Jer 13:24). And it can be the vehicle for scattering, as in Ezekiel's phrase "scatter to the wind" (Ezek 5:2, 10, 12, 12:14, 17:21).

In the CB (NT) Jesus emphasizes this point in the unique Johannine dialogue between Nicodemus and himself. He tells the Pharisaic leader of the Jews (John 3:1): "The wind blows where it chooses, and you hear the sound of it, but you do not know where it comes from or where it goes. So it is with everyone who is born of the Spirit" (John 3:8). Perkins identifies this verse as "a short proverb about the 'wind,' the same word as 'Spirit' in both Hebrew (*ruah*) and Greek (*pneuma*), to explain the mysterious activity of the Spirit."[7]

The story in the gospels about Jesus calming the wind demonstrates that he is like God in the Book of Exodus. In Mark's Gospel, he demonstrates

---

6. Ibid., 951.
7. Perkins, "John," 955.

his ability to calm a great windstorm on an unnamed body of water. All he has to say is, "Peace! Be still!" (Mark 4:39a) The narrator then states, "Then the wind ceased, and there was a dead calm" (Mark 4:39b). Matthew, who records Jesus concluding his sermon on the mount with a wisdom saying about building a house on rock so that it can withstand the winds (Matt 7:24–27), basically follows Mark's version of the story (Matt 8:23–26), while Luke writes that a windstorm sweeps down on the lake they are crossing, and Jesus rebukes the wind (Luke 8:22–24). The response of Jesus' disciples is great awe toward the one whom the wind obeys (Mark 4:41; Matt 8:27; Luke 8:25).

In another story featuring an adverse wind, Jesus walks on the sea. When he gets to his disciples in a boat, he goes onboard, the wind ceases, and they are utterly astounded by his ability to calm the wind (Mark 6:47–52; Matt 14:22–27; John 6:16–21). It is the "sound like the rush of a violent wind" (Acts 2:2) that announces Pentecost in the Acts of the Apostles. It is meant to echo the loud sounds of God's presence at Mount Sinai (Horeb) even though the wind is not mentioned in that account. Because the Hebrew word for wind (*ruah*) can also mean breath and spirit, its use in the Acts of the Apostles represents one of its possibly three meanings. McKenzie states, "The wind is be the breath of Yahweh [the LORD], and thus spirit becomes an agent of power."[8]

Sometimes the wind is identified as a whirlwind, a column of air rotating rapidly around a core of low pressure. In the fourth speech of Elihu, a figure who appears suddenly only at the beginning of chapter 32 of the HB (OT) Book of Job, declares that "from its chamber comes the whirlwind" (Job 37:9). The Book of Proverbs emphasizes the suddenness of a whirlwind, comparing calamity to it (Prov 1:27). Sirach states that it is at God's will that the whirlwind blows (Sir 43:17b). As part of Israel's punishment, the prophet Hosea declares that the people will "sow the wind, and they shall reap the whirlwind" (Hos 8:7a). The prophet Nahum says that the LORD's "way is in whirlwind and storm" (Nah 1:3c). Wahl explains: "Yahweh [the LORD] appears in the sirocco, the desert windstorm frequent during the change of seasons. The sirocco imagery is characteristic of hymns to Yahweh's [the LORD's] kingship. The east wind of the sirocco, symbolizing Yahweh's [the LORD's] rebuke, dries up everything before it."[9] In other words, any type

---

8. McKenzie, *Dictionary*, 840.
9. Wahl, "Zephania, Nahum, Habakkuk," 259.

of luxuriant growth will be withered with the LORD's theophanic advance for judgment.[10]

The biblical person most associated with the whirlwind is the prophet Elijah. The narrator of the HB (OT) Second Book of Kings prepares the reader for the prophet's heavenly journey. He writes: " . . . [W]hen the LORD was about to take Elijah up to heaven by a whirlwind, Elijah and Elisha were on their way" together (2 Kgs 2:1). While they are walking and talking, the theophany occurs. " . . . [A] chariot of fire and horses of fire separated the two of them, and Elijah ascended in a whirlwind into heaven" (2 Kgs 2:11). The author of the OT (A) Book of Sirach addresses Elijah, saying: "You were taken up by a whirlwind of fire, in a chariot with horses of fire" (Sir 48:9). Then, he writes that "Elijah was enveloped in the whirlwind" (Sir 48:12). Isaiah understands that the LORD of hosts visits his people "with whirlwind" (Isa 29:6), and both he and Jeremiah write about how the LORD's "chariots [are] like the whirlwind (Isa 66:15; Jer 4:13). The prophet Nahum says it best: The LORD's "way is in whirlwind" (Nah 1:3). And the Book of Job declares two times that "the LORD answered Job out of the whirlwind" (Job 38:1, 40:6). MacKenzie explains that "[t]he theophany, the encounter with God, is Job's real experience. . . . "[11] The whirlwind or storm is a traditional setting for a theophany.[12]

While the First Book of Kings does not record the theophany experienced by Elijah on Mount Horeb (Sinai) as using the element of wind—"there was a great wind, so strong that it was splitting mountains and breaking rocks in pieces before the LORD, but the LORD was not in the wind" (1 Kgs 19:11)—the prophet Ezekiel finds the element of wind in his theophanic vision of dry bones that come back to life in the middle of a valley (Ezek 37:1–6). The dry bones represent the whole house of Israel in Babylonian captivity (Ezek 37:11–14). As the theophany begins, the bones come together and are covered with sinews, flesh, and skin, "but there was no breath in them" (Ezek 37:8). The LORD tells Ezekiel: "Prophesy to the breath, prophesy, mortal, and say to the breath: Thus says the Lord GOD: Come from the four winds, O breath, and breathe upon these slain, that they may live" (Ezek 37:9). The prophet does as he is told, and the dry bones live. Zimmerli states that the breath that enters the slain is "to be regarded as something which pervades the whole world, which now blows

10. Toombs, "Psalms," 264.
11. MacKenzie, "Job," 486.
12. Ibid.

upon the human corpses like a wind in order to transform them into living creatures."[13] He states that the wind usually blows from only one direction at a time, as noted above, but "the irruption of the breath of life into the dead bodies is represented as an event which happens from all four points of the compass simultaneously. . . . "[14] Keeping in mind that the word in Hebrew for wind is the same word for spirit, it is not too hard to understand that at God's command the dead, who have returned to the clay from which they were created (Gen 3:19), have been re-created with breath, wind, or spirit (Gen 2:7). Hiebert confirms this, writing:

> . . . "[A]ir" is summoned from the entire atmosphere (the four winds) to enter these human beings as breath and bring them to life. Every time the term is used, its double meaning as "atmosphere/breath" is prominent in the listener's mind. The language of the Hebrew Scriptures thus captures a fundamental self-understanding: human life is always and everywhere dependent upon . . . "air," the canopy of air that it inhabits and which it breathes.[15]

Thus, wind is an element of a theophany; it reveals the glory of the LORD.

---

13. Zimmerli, *Ezekiel* 2, 261.
14. Ibid.
15. Hiebert, "Air," 12.

19

Light and Darkness

ANOTHER ELEMENT THAT APPEARS in many theophanies but not in the one about Mount Sinai (Horeb) is light and darkness. The ninth plague in Egypt best illustrates this element. Moses stretches out his hand towards heaven and darkness covers the land of Egypt, "a darkness that can be felt" (Exod 10:21). The narrator of the Book of Exodus states that it was a "dense darkness in all the land of Egypt for three days. People could not see one another, and for three days they could not move from where they were; but all the Israelites had light where they lived" (Exod 10:22–23). Since this is a plague, it is also a theophany. Any doubts are removed by the number for God mentioned two times: three days. Because "light is the element proper to deity" and "it is a feature of the theophany,"[1] God's chosen people enjoy the light, while the Egyptians are immersed in total darkness; light and darkness exist together. Gray says that the darkness portends the ultimate disaster, "the reign of chaos in Egyptian mythology, where the inveterate enemy of the sun god Re, of whom Pharaoh was thought to be the incarnation, was Apophis, the serpent of chaotic darkness."[2]

The author of the OT (A) Book of Wisdom reflects upon this same event in chapter 17. He writes that "no power of fire was able to give light" to the Egyptians (Wis 17:5); yet, for the Hebrews "the whole world was illumined with brilliant light, . . . while over those people alone heavy night was spread, an image of the darkness that was destined to receive them; but still heavier than darkness were they to themselves" (Wis 17:20–21).

---

1. McKenzie, *Dictionary*, 511.
2. Gray, "Exodus," 44.

Chapter 18 continues the author's reflection on this paradox: For God's "holy ones there was very great light. Their enemies heard their voices but did not see their forms" (Wis 18:1). Then, a few verses later, the author writes that the Egyptian "enemies deserved to be deprived of light and imprisoned in darkness" because they had kept God's "children imprisoned, through whom the imperishable light of the law was to be given to the world" (Wis 18:4). The interplay of darkness for the Egyptians and light for the Hebrews in the same geographical area creates a space for God to act.

While it is true that light, associated with good and God, usually triumphs darkness, associated with bad and evil, is present in much of biblical literature, in theophanies, as indicated above, it is the dialogue, interchange, and paradox that is present with light and darkness. In the HB (OT) Book of Deuteronomy, Moses expresses this idea when he reminds the Israelites that they "heard the voice out of the darkness, while the mountain was burning with fire" (Deut 5:23), referring to their Mount Sinai (Horeb) experience. This paradox is expressed quite frequently in the HB (OT) Book of Job. For example, once Job begins to bemoan the day he was born, he begs God to leave him alone that he might find a little comfort before he goes "to the land of gloom and deep darkness, the land of gloom and chaos where light is like darkness" (Job 10:21–22). Later he says that God "uncovers the deeps out of darkness, and brings deep darkness to light" (Job 12:22). Job states that the righteous "make night into day; 'the light,' they say, 'is near to the darkness'" (Job 17:12). Job's best expression of the paradox of light and darkness is found in his reflections in chapter 30: " ... [W]hen I looked for good, evil came; and when I waited for light, darkness came" (Job 30:26).

Psalm 18 also presents this paradox in its description of a theophany. The LORD, who lights up darkness (Ps 18:28) bows the heavens and comes to earth with "thick darkness ... under his feet" (Ps 18:9b' cf. 2 Sam 22:10). "He made darkness his covering around him, his canopy thick clouds dark with water" while "[o]ut of the brightness before him there broke through his clouds hailstones and coals of fire" (Ps 18:11–12; cf. 2 Sam 22:12–13). Echoing Psalm 18:11, Psalm 97 proclaims that "[c]louds and thick darkness are all around him" (Ps 97:2a). And the author of Psalm 139 addresses the LORD directly, singing: "If I say, 'Surely the darkness shall cover me, and the light around me become night,' even the darkness is not dark to you; the night is as bright as the day, for darkness is as light to you" (Ps 139:11–12).

King Solomon presents the paradox of light and darkness during the dedication of the temple. He says, "The LORD has said that he would dwell in thick darkness" (1 Kgs 8:12). The God who is usually considered to be all light has chosen to "reside in thick darkness" (2 Chr 6:1). The prophet Isaiah echoes Solomon's words when he tells Cyrus that the LORD is giving him "the treasures of darkness" (Isa 45:3a).

The interplay of light and darkness is also found in the CB (NT) gospels. Using material they found in Q (*Quelle*, meaning a source shared by Matthew and Luke) Jesus tells his disciples, "What I say to you in the dark, tell in the light" (Matt 10:27a). Luz says: "The disciples should already act in the present in a way that is appropriate to the final revelation that takes place in the last judgment."[3] In Luke's Gospel, Jesus tells them, " . . . [W]hatever you have said in the dark will be heard in the light" (Luke 12:3a). Bovon, grasping the paradox of the saying, states: "[I]t refers to the interior and suggests a witnessing that is almost secret."[4] In another Q passage, the Matthean Jesus states, "If then the light in you is darkness, how great is the darkness!" (Matt 6:23b) Luz says that this is an oxymoron: "Its meaning is: if your actions, your obedience, your generosity are not in order, the darkness is complete."[5] Betz says that the cause of evil is the inner light, "if it has been turned into darkness."[6] Luke records Jesus saying, " . . . [C]onsider whether the light in you is not darkness" (Luke 11:35). Bovon explains: "A light that is darkness is a paradoxical and suggestive expression. It rules out any assured possession of the light. Light can get lost, go out. All the more reason to watch out, to 'take care' that things do not turn out that way."[7]

The same paradox is found in the Book of Revelation. The fourth angel blows his trumpet and a third of the sun, the moon, and the stars have their light darkened; "a third of the day was kept from shining, and likewise the night" (Rev 8:12).

The paradox is found in the biblical authors' repeated use of the phrase "a pillar of cloud by day and a pillar of fire by night" (Exod 13:21, 14:20). The pillar of cloud (see Cloud) leads the Israelites along the way, while the pillar of fire (see Fire) gives them light so they can travel by night as well as by day. This dialogue between light and darkness is also found in the HB (OT) Book of Nehemiah (9:12, 19) and the Book of Psalms (78:14; 105:39).

---

3. Luz, *Matthew 8–20*, 101.
4. Bovon, *Luke 2*, 178.
5. Luz, *Matthew 1–7*, 334.
6. Betz, *Sermon*, 453.
7. Bovon, *Luke 2*, 150.

Divine Presence

The interplay of light and darkness begins with the second verse of the HB (OT) Book of Genesis. It records that "darkness covered the face of the deep" (Gen 1:2). The first thing God does in this theophany of creation is to say, "'Let there be light'; and there was light" (Gen 1:3). God sees that the light is good and God separates the light from the darkness (Gen 1:4), calling the light Day and the darkness Night (Gen 1:5). It is not until the fourth day of creation—referring to the earth—that God creates the greater light of the sun to rule the day and the lesser light of the moon to rule the night (Gen 1:16) and once again to separate light and darkness (Gen 1:18). Darkness represents chaos, and light represents order, just as water represents chaos, and land represents order (see Water). God has created a boundary between light and darkness, but one cannot exist without the other.

Job refers to the "boundary between light and darkness" established by God (Job 26:10) as does God, when he asks Job: "Where is the way to the dwelling of light, and where is the place of darkness?" (Job 38:19) Isaiah echoes Job when he portrays the LORD declaring, "I form light and create darkness" (Isa 45:7a). Furthermore, Isaiah states that it is God who turns darkness into light (Isa 42:16); it is God who orders the dark chaos with bright light, that is, he establishes a boundary between them as an element of a theophany. Isaiah also writes about light rising in the darkness (Isa 58:10), as does the prophet Jeremiah, who declares that God brings deep darkness while people look for light (Jer 13:16).

The prophet Daniel returns the reader to the paradox of light and darkness, when he calls upon light and darkness to bless the Lord (Sg Three 1:48 [Dan 3:72]). The prophet Amos declares that the LORD of hosts makes the morning darkness (Amos 4:13); he "turns deep darkness into the morning, and darkens the day into night" (Amos 5:8). The prophet Zechariah does the same, writing that "there shall be continuous day (it is known to the LORD), not day and not night, for at evening time there shall be light" (Zech 14:7).

In the First Book of Samuel, Saul, the first king of Israel, while on campaign against the Philistines, tells his forces: "Let us go down after the Philistines by night and despoil them until the morning light" (1 Sam 14:36). While the people tell Saul to do what he thinks is good, the unnamed priest suggests that he consult God. So, a form of divination is used which determines that the people are in the light and Saul and his son, Jonathan, are in the darkness. The result is that the Philistines are no longer pursued (1 Sam 14:36–46). Using the light and darkness element, the OT (A) Book of Tobit

Light and Darkness

portrays the book's namesake and his future daughter-in-law praying for solutions to their respective problems. Tobit, who is blind, prays for death, while Sarah prays to be released from a wicked Persian demon, which kills her husbands on their wedding night! The Book of Tobit states:

> At that very moment, the prayers of both of them were heard in the glorious presence of God. So Raphael was sent to heal both of them: Tobit, by removing the white films from his eyes, so that he might see God's light with his eyes; and Sarah, daughter of Raguel, by giving her in marriage to Tobias, son of Tobit, and by setting her free from the wicked demon Asmodeus. (Tob 3:16–17a)

The theophany here is the sending of Raphael, whose name means *God heals*. Tobit's literal darkness and Sarah's demonic darkness are removed, and both bask in God's healing light.

In his prophesy against the shepherds of Israel, the prophet Ezekiel declares that the Lord GOD will rescue his sheep, bringing them into his light "on a day of clouds and thick darkness" (Ezek 34:12). In the CB (NT) the author of Luke's Gospel sees this prophecy fulfilled when the shepherds "keeping watch over their flock by night" experience the appearance of an angel of the Lord, and "the glory of the Lord [shines] around them" (Luke 2:8–9). They tell the shepherds that a Savior has been born; he is the Messiah, the Lord (Luke 2:11). Bovon comments on this text, stating: "The time of night affirms both the unexpected event and the dark predicament of the people of Israel. . . . After this signal of a divine intervention"—the appearance of the angel of the Lord—"Luke adds an unusual motif: the glory of God appears and surrounds the shepherds. The juxtaposition of night and light is composed as elegantly as in the messianic text of Isaiah (9:2)."[8] Isaiah 9:2 states: "The people who walked in darkness have seen a great light; those who lived in a land of deep darkness—on them light has shined."

In the CB (NT), the paradox of light and darkness is turned into the opposition of light and darkness in much of Johannine literature. Jesus is presented as the light of God shining in the darkness. The author of John's Gospel understands him to be the light of all people. "The light shines in the darkness," states the Johannine author, "and the darkness did not overcome it" (John 1:5). Using the *I AM* name God gave to Moses when he encountered the burning bush, the Johannine Jesus declares, "I am the light of the world" (John 8:12). "As long as I am in the world, I am the light of the world," he states (John 9:5). Later in the gospel, he declares:

---

8. Bovon, *Luke 1*, 87.

"The light is with you for a little longer. Walk while you have the light, so that the darkness may not overtake you. If you walk in the darkness, you do not know where you are going. While you have the light, believe in the light, so that you may become children of light" (John 12:35–36). As if none of those statements make the point firmly enough, Jesus declares: "I have come as light into the world, so that everyone who believes in me should not remain in the darkness." (John 12:46). The Johannine Jesus is an incarnate theophany who speaks about himself as light, one of the elements of a theophanic experience; he reveals the glory of the LORD, but he removes the darkness that keeps the paradox of light and darkness.

Other Johannine literature strengthens this understanding with this statement: " . . . God is light and in him there is no darkness at all" (1 John 1:5). Ryken notes that light occupies a place of primacy in the interpretation of biblical literature and "is signaled in the Bible by the fact that God's creation of light is the first recorded event."[9] He adds, "With the conflict between light and darkness as a context, light has the properties of rulership over the universe, with an accompanying sense of awe. . . . "[10] Shepherd explains the origin of the opposition of light and darkness: "Greek philosophers used the imagery of light to describe the goodness and truth of ultimate reality. The religion of Zoroaster, stemming from Persia and increasingly influential in the Roman world, divided all reality into a mighty conflict of two opposing realms of light and darkness."[11] In other words, light alone replaces the light-darkness paradox to signal a theophany.

This is also true in the theophanies narrated in the Acts of the Apostles. Saul (Paul) experiences a light from heaven flashing around him (Acts 9:3, 22:6, 22:9, 11, 13). In his Second Letter to the Corinthians, his experience leads Paul to ask: " . . . [W]hat fellowship is there between light and darkness?" (2 Cor 6:14) Likewise, Peter experiences an angel of the Lord appearing as light (Acts 12:7).

However, while much of the CB (NT) places light as opposite to darkness, the narratives of Jesus' death and resurrection in the Synoptic Gospels attempt to keep the paradox. The Markan narrator states, "When it was noon, darkness came over the whole land until three in the afternoon" (Mark 15:33). However, "very early on the first day of the week, when the sun had risen" (Mark 16:2), the women go to the tomb where Jesus was

9. Ryken, *Dictionary*, 509.
10. Ibid.
11. Shepherd, "First Letter of John," 936.

buried and hear the message that he has been raised (Mark 16:6). Using his Markan source, Matthew merely states that "[f]rom noon on, darkness came over the whole and until three in the afternoon" (Matt 27:45) and completes the paradox with "the first day of the week . . . dawning" (Matt 28:1), adding his own unique element of earthquake (see Earthquake). Using his Markan source, Luke makes clear that "[i]t was . . . about noon, and darkness came over the whole and until three in the afternoon" (Luke 23:44) and finishes the paradox with the women bringing spices to the tomb "on the first day of the week, at early dawn" (Luke 24:1), adding his own unique element of "two men in dazzling clothes" (Luke 24:4) (see Sacred Numbers and Transformation). Those in dazzling clothes (Luke 9:29) are clothed in lightening, another element of a theophany. In his second volume, the Acts of the Apostles, Luke brings back the "two men in white robes" (Acts 1:10) to accompany the theophanic ascension of Jesus into heaven, another unique Lukan account (Luke 24:50–51; Acts 1:9–11).

Commenting on Mark's account of the three-hour darkness, which is the source for Matthew's and Luke's account, Miller states that there may be a "theological or symbolic interpretation of the darkness."[12] It may be an allusion to the three days of darkness in the land of Egypt; the number three indicates its divine origin. As noted above, in the HB (OT) Book of Exodus, the Hebrews are not affected by the darkness, whereas in Mark's Gospel Jesus' final words seem to indicate that he is. Miller states that "darkness is related to the advent of God in judgment on the world."[13] Mark's Gospel highlights "the role of God in bringing about darkness over the land," although the reader is not told "who is the agent or the cause of the darkness."[14] According to Miller, "Darkness descends upon the land aligning the natural world with the suffering of Jesus. During this period of three hours no human voice is heard."[15] As soon as Jesus dies, the darkness comes to an end, preparing for the light of the first day of the week a few verses later. Miller writes: "The descent of darkness is a disruptive action because human beings and the natural world depend upon a cycle of light and darkness in order to sustain life. When this cycle is broken, there can be no growth of plants or harvests of crops. The darkness over the land reminds humans of their powerlessness in the face of disruptions in the

---

12. Miller, "Descent of Darkness," 123.
13. Ibid., 124.
14. Ibid.
15. Ibid., 125.

natural world and its cycles."[16] Furthermore, darkness, associated with the force of chaos at the crucifixion, is held in paradox with the light, associated with the force of order at the resurrection in Matthew, Luke, and John. "In Mark, however, the darkness ends with Jesus' death. That light returns when Jesus dies indicates that the normal cycle of light and darkness has resumed."[17]

Bringing the reader back to the theophany of the separation of light and darkness at the beginning of the HB (OT) Book of Genesis, Miller writes: "Without the boundaries of light and darkness, the land cannot bear fruit. In Mark the descent of darkness indicat[es] a return to the state of chaos and darkness before God brings an ordered environment into existence."[18] Once Jesus dies, the light returns along with the early light on the first day of the week, when the sun had risen in Mark and the light of post-resurrection appearances in Matthew, Luke, and John. Thus, the light and darkness paradox serves as an element of theophanies.

---

16. Ibid., 127.
17. Ibid., 128.
18. Ibid.

20

Jewels (Precious Stones)

IN THE NARRATIVE ABOUT Moses on Mount Sinai, when Moses, Aaron, Aaron's two sons, and seventy elders of Israel climb the mountain, they see the God of Israel (Exod 24:10a). The narrator states: "Under his feet there was something like a pavement of sapphire stone, like the very heaven for clearness" (Exod 24:10b). Clifford states the men see God "from below, as through transparent sky-blue tiles."[1] Gray agrees, stating, "Sapphire probably refers to the blue sky."[2] Sapphire is a brilliant, deep-blue mineral. It is being used to describe the dome of the sky, which, of course, appears bright blue on a humid-free, desert day. The biblical author presupposes a three-storied universe in which God dwells above the dome of the sky. That is why the pavement, the sky under his feet, is like sapphire. Jewels and precious stones, like sapphire, are an element of some theophanies.

Robinson thinks the "pavement of sapphire stone" is better translated as "pavement of lapis lazuli."[3] He says that it is a work of art; "this pavement is an artistic marvel."[4] As indicated above, the human visitors see God from below through the pavement, which is nothing other than the dome of the sky under which people stand to view the God who lives above it. Robinson adds: "Lapis lazuli is a rock of varying composition, sometimes opaque, sometimes translucent; probably the latter is envisaged here. . . . [This] means that the pavement was so bright that it dazzled [those sharing

---

1. Clifford, "Exodus," 55.
2. Gray, "Exodus," 59.
3. Robinson, "Theophany and Meal," 161.
4. Ibid., 162.

the meal], making their sight of the Deity even more indirect."[5] In other words, "Israelite leaders on the mountain side are granted sight of their God in heaven above through a dazzling azure pavement...."[6]

The prophet Ezekiel begins his narrative of the departure of the glory of the LORD from the Jerusalem temple by describing what he sees in his theophanic vision: "... [A]bove the dome ... there appeared ... something like a sapphire, in form resembling a throne" (Ezek 10:1). Here, the prophet echoes what he had previously written in 1:26a—"above the dome ... there was something like a throne, in appearance like sapphire"—however, now the throne is empty. As indicated above, the human visitor sees the empty throne from below, that is, through the dome of the sky under which people stand on the earth to view the God who lives above the dome.

In the description of the priest's breastpiece is found the mention of twelve jewels or precious stones set in four rows of three each: "carnelian, chrysolite, and emerald ... [in] the first row; and the second row a turquoise, a sapphire, and a moonstone; and the third row a jacinth, an agate, and an amethyst; and the fourth row a beryl, an onyx, and a jasper" (Exod 28:17–20; cf. 39:10–13). Ryken notes: "The effect is a dazzling profusion of beauty, splendor, and value, symbolic of the holiness of worship."[7] Not only are the jewels and previous stones arranged according to the sacred numbers four and three, but the twelve stones—another sacred number—represent the names of the sons of Israel (Jacob) (Exod 28:21). This priestly garment serves as a vehicle for a theophany. "The high priest stood at the boundary between the divine and human realms," states Ryken, "moving in both as he ministered in the Holy of Holies, and the [breastpiece] inset with twelve precious stones engraved with the twelve tribes of Israel hinted at his more-than-human status."[8] Messages and guidance for the Israelites came through the priest clothed with the breastpiece of judgment. It was a type of pouch for the Urim and Thummin, light and dark stones used to determine the deity's will in a given situation. Thus, they are "on Aaron's heart when he goes in before the LORD;" Aaron bears "the judgment of the Israelites on his heart before the LORD continually" (Exod 28:30).

The prophet Ezekiel employs jewels and precious stones other than sapphire (Ezek 1:26a; 10:1) to describe his visionary theophany. Appearances of various objects are "like the gleaming of beryl" (Ezek 1:16,

5. Ibid., 163.
6. Ibid.
7. Ryken, *Dictionary*, 452.
8. Ibid.

Jewels (Precious Stones)

10:9), "shining like crystal" (Ezek 1:22), and "like gleaming amber" (Ezek 1:27)—all help to describe "the appearance of the likeness of the glory of the LORD" (Ezek 1:28). Later in the book, the prophet describes the king of Tyre as being covered with every precious stone: "carnelian, chrysolite, and moonstone, beryl, onyx, and jasper, sapphire, turquoise, and emerald" (Ezek 28:13bc). Nine of the same stones in the breastplate are named here; omitted are agate, jacinth, and amethyst.

The author of the CB (NT) Book of Revelation borrowed the sapphire from the Exodus narrative explained above (Rev 9:17), Ezekiel's jewels and previous stones as elements of his theophanic experience, and most likely the OT (A) Book of Tobit's description of a rebuilt Jerusalem: "The gates of Jerusalem will be built with sapphire and emerald, and all your walls with precious stones. The towers of Jerusalem will be built with gold, and their battlements with pure gold. The streets of Jerusalem will be paved with ruby and with stone of Ophir" (Tobit 13:16cde). The pseudonymous author of Revelation describes the new Jerusalem in this way: "it has the glory of God and a radiance like a very rare jewel, like jasper, clear as crystal" (Rev 21:11). Later, he adds: "The wall is built of jasper, while the city is pure gold, clear as glass" (Rev 21:18). Then, matching almost exactly the jewels and precious stones found on the breastpiece noted above,[9] he writes:

> The foundations of the wall of the city are adorned with every jewel; the first was jasper, the second sapphire, the third agate, the fourth emerald, the fifth onyx, the sixth carnelian, the seventh chrysolite, the eighth beryl, the ninth topaz, the tenth chrysoprase, the eleventh jacinth, the twelfth amethyst. And the twelve gates are twelve pearls, each of the gates is a single pearl, and the street of the city is pure gold, transparent as glass. (Rev 19:19–21)

Turquoise and moonstone in the breastplate are replaced with topaz and chrysoprase in the wall.

Emerald, a green stone, is mentioned by the author of the Book of Revelation when he describes the one seated on a throne he sees in heaven in his theophanic vision. He describes the one of the throne as looking "like jasper and carnelian, and around the throne is a rainbow that looks like an emerald" (Rev 4:3). All of the jewels and precious stones point to the richness of the city, and they are associated with the twelve signs of the zodiac. Thus, jewels and precious stones are an element in some theophanies, and they reveal the glory of the LORD.

---

9. Collins, "Apocalypse," 1015.

21

Dream

WHILE A DREAM IS not an element in the Mount Horeb (Sinai) theophany, it does appear as such in some other biblical stories about the manifestation of God. One well-known dreamers is Jacob, who, as indicated above (see Mountain) dreamed about a ladder set on the earth and reaching into the heaven with God's angels ascending and descending upon it (Gen 28:12). Later, in the HB (OT) Book of Genesis he explains how God told him in a dream how to increase the size of his flock (Gen 31:10–13).

The best-known dreamer, however, is Jacob's son, Joseph. He not only followed in his father's footsteps as a dreamer, but he became an interpreter of dreams. In the HB (OT) Book of Genesis, there are three—indicating the presence of the divine—sequences of two dreams each. All three stories presume that the dreams enable the dreamer to know the future as part of God's plan. In the first sequence, Joseph narrates his dream about his brothers' sheaves bowing down to his sheaf (Gen 37:5–8) and his dream about the sun, the moon, and eleven stars bowing down to him (Gen 37:9–11). While there is "neither God nor an angel [that] appears or speaks in them," and "[n]o one in the story takes Joseph's dreams to be divine revelations,"[1] nevertheless the dreams serve to place Joseph within the HB (OT) theophanic dream tradition as an instrument of God's providence.

The second sequence occurs in Egypt where Joseph meets the Pharaoh's cupbearer and baker in prison. Each has a dream, whose interpretation belongs to God (Gen 40:8).[2] First, Joseph hears the cupbearer's

1. Marks, "Genesis," 26.
2. Clifford, "Genesis," 37

dream and interprets the three branches on the vine as three days before the cupbearer will be restored to Pharaoh's service (Gen 40:9–13). In other words, the Divine Presence, signified by the number three, is at work here. Then, Joseph hears the baker's dream about three cake baskets with birds eating from the topmost vessel. Joseph explains that the three cake baskets represent three days before the baker's head is removed from his body (Gen 40:16–19). While no reason is given for the cupbearer being restored to his position and the baker being hanged (Gen 40:20–22), they are a part of God's plan revealed to Joseph; "God's providence, which is a basic premise to the entire story, is made known in human terms which must be interpreted. . . ."[3] Clifford notes: "Dreams and their interpretation are important in the ancient Near East, especially when they are royal, because they suggest a particular relationship with the divine."[4]

The third and final sequence of two dreams are those of Pharaoh, who tells Joseph that he saw seven fat cows and seven lean cows grazing along the Nile River as the seven lean cows ate the seven fat ones. This dream is followed by seven plump ears of grain on a stalk followed by seven blighted ears of grain on a stalk; as in the previous dream, the seven blighted ears ate the seven plump ears (Gen 41:1–7). Before Joseph begins to interpret Pharaoh's dreams he makes it very clear that it is not he, but God, who interprets dreams (Gen 41:16). Marks states: "Dreams were thought in ancient times to be divine communications, and their interpretation was considered [to be] a science. Joseph is not trained in its techniques; rather he believes that God-given dreams must be interpreted through God-given inspiration, of which he himself may be the recipient."[5] After Pharaoh re-tells the two dreams (Gen 41:17–24), Joseph states that "God has revealed to Pharaoh what he is about to do" (Gen 41:25, 28), namely, there will be seven years of plenty and seven years of famine (Gen 41:26–31). Joseph concludes his dream interpretation, stating, "[T]he doubling of Pharaoh's dream means that the thing is fixed by God, and God will shortly bring it about" (Gen 41:32).

It is not by accident that the author of Matthew's Gospel in the CB (NT) presents his Joseph character, son of Jacob (Matt 1:16), as a dreamer modeled after the HB (OT) Joseph. Viviano says, "Dreams in Matthew

---

3. Marks "Genesis," 26.
4. Clifford, "Genesis," 38.
5. Marks, "Genesis," 28.

furnish divine guidance."[6] Just as Matthew's Joseph is prepared to divorce his fiancée because she is pregnant, "an angel of the Lord [appears] to him in a dream" (Matt 1:20), telling him not to do so. This "is the first of a series of dreams, revealing each a divine warning or counsel," states Kee.[7] The angel of the Lord appears to Joseph again in a dream and directs him to flee to Egypt with Mary and Jesus (Matt 2:13). And to make sure that the reader understands that this is part of God's plan, the angel of the Lord appears a third, divine time in a dream to Joseph in Egypt and directs him to return to Israel (Matt 2:19–20), but he is warned in a dream about Archelaus, son of Herod, and goes to Galilee instead (Matt 2:22). The fourth dream theophany, which does not mention the angel of the Lord, indicates that this one is for the whole world while the first three awaken the reader to God's plan.

In addition to those dreams attributed to Joseph, the unique magi are warned in a dream not to return to Herod (Matt 2:12), and Pilate's unnamed wife, who makes a cameo appearance in Matthew's Gospel, tells him about a dream she had about Jesus (Matt 27:19). Kee notes that the dream "is presented as a divine warning that Jesus is innocent."[8]

Solomon experiences the LORD in a dream after offering sacrifices on an altar (see Altar) in Gibeon (1 Kgs 3:5–15a). Then, he goes to Jerusalem, where he stands before the ark of the covenant of the LORD and offers burnt offerings and offerings of well being and provides a feast (see Feast [Meal]) for his servants (1 Kgs 3:15bc). Like Solomon, the prophet Daniel experiences the LORD in dreams. The author of the Book of Daniel states that God gave him "insight into all visions and dreams" (Dan 1:17; cf. 2:25; 5:11–12). Like Joseph before him, Daniel explains that "there is a God in heaven who reveals mysteries, and he has disclosed . . . what will happen at the end of days" (Dan 2:28); in context, these are the end of the days of King Nebuchadnezzar of Babylon who "has a dream that no one but Daniel can interpret."[9] Hartman draws out the comparison between Daniel and Joseph: "Just as Joseph was raised to a high position in the government by Pharaoh as a reward for interpreting his dream, so Daniel is similarly made a sort of prime minister by Nebuchadnezzar, while his three companions

---

6. Viviano, "Matthew," 671–2.
7. Kee, "Matthew," 611.
8. Ibid., 641.
9. Hartman, "Daniel," 413.

Dream

are appointed local governors."[10] Hartman also mentions that it is "Daniel's ability, with God's help, to divine and interpret Nebuchadnezzar's dream."[11]

Throughout the Book of Daniel, the prophet is about interpreting dreams that are elements of theophanies. Knight explains how the Jews

> shared with [their] Near Eastern neighbors the belief that dreams were vehicles for divine communication to men. . . . The interpretation of dreams was a profession involving considerable lore, as borne out by instruction books discovered in both Egypt and Mesopotamia. Persons skilled in this art were maintained as members of royal courts for frequent consultation.[12]

Closely associated with dreams are visions. The psalmist leaves no doubt in one's mind when he writes that the LORD "spoke in a vision" (Ps 89:19), referring to the prophet Nathan's words to David (2 Sam 7:4–17; cf. 1 Chr 17:3–15). The Book of Daniel refers to such a dream as "a vision of the night" (Dan 2:19, 7:2) as do Job (20:8; 33:15) and Isaiah (29:7). He also narrates other visions (Dan 8:1–2), often hearing a holy one or an angel speak to him (Dan 8:13, 15–17; 9:21–23; 10:7–8, 16), which causes him to fall into a trance (Dan 8:18; 10:9). Concerning Daniel's visions, Knight notes:

> Though most of what they purport to predict has already happened, their emphasis is on the divine action that is soon to occur. They declare that just as God has been faithful in the past, so is he to be relied on now and in the unknown days to come. No matter how strong the forces of evil may become, they cannot prevent the living God from bringing his plans for [human]kind to fruition.[13]

The visions which result in a trance or a deep sleep—falling from the LORD upon people (1 Sam 26:12)—begin in the HB (OT) Book of Genesis. The LORD comes to Abram in a vision (Gen 15:1) which results in the patriarch falling into a deep sleep (Gen 15:12), which itself is modeled on the second story of creation in which God causes a deep sleep to fall upon the man before he removes a rib and creates a woman (Gen 2:21). In the HB (OT) Book of Numbers, Balaam experiences the spirit of the God coming upon him and he "sees the vision of the Almighty," falling down, "but

---

10. Ibid., 411.
11. Ibid., 410.
12. Knight, "Daniel," 439.
13. Ibid., 444.

with eyes uncovered" (Num 24:4, 16). The prophet Ezekiel describes being lifted up in spirit between earth and heaven as God brought him in visions to Jerusalem where he experiences the glory of the God of Israel (Ezek 8:3–4), only later to be brought in a vision by the spirit of God into Chaldea (Babylon) (Ezek 11:24). Before this, it took all but the first three verses of chapter 1 to describe the vision of the glory of the LORD (Ezek 1:4–28), upon which the author of the OT (A) Book of Sirach comments (Sir 49:8). Vision is also the topic of Isaiah (1:1), Obadiah (1:1), and Nahum (1:1), yet the Book of Lamentations declares that the prophets "obtain no vision from the LORD" as Jerusalem lay in ruins (Lam 2:9c). The author of the OT (A) Book of Sirach urges his readers to pay no attention to divinations, omens, and dreams "unless they are sent by intervention from the Most High" (Sir 34:6). In other words, one must allow for God-given dreams.[14]

In the CB (NT), Jesus refers to his transfiguration as a vision (Matt 17:9). Luke reports a vision of angels who announce Jesus' resurrection (Luke 24:23), and the Book of Revelation, which, being a book of vision, specifically identifies one vision about horses (Rev 9:17). There are multiple visions and trances associated with Saul (Paul) (Acts 9:10–19; 16:9–10; 18:9–10; 22:17–21; 26:19) and Peter (Acts 10:3–23; 11:5–18; 12:9). As in the dream theophanies above, these visions and trances presume that the dreams enable the dreamer to know the future as part of God's plan. Only in the Book of Job in Elihu's first speech are dreams, visions, and trances mentioned together in one verse. Elihu says that God speaks "[i]n a dream, in a vision of the night, when deep sleep falls on mortals, while they slumber on their beds" (Job 33:15). Earlier, Job had stated that God scared him "with dreams" and terrified him "with visions" (Job 7:13). Elihu's statement makes Job aware that God has been speaking to him all along; Job has not been listening. Thus, a dream, a vision, or a trance can be an element of a theophany in some biblical narratives.

---

14. Beavin, "Ecclesiasticus," 568.

22

Hermeneutic

FINDING THE QUESTION

Now that the elements of a theophany have been explored, it is time to examine what people might do with them today. Since, according to Hiebert, "God is associated with atmospheric conditions," that is, "the Middle Eastern thunderstorm,"[1] with what might people associate God today? Hiebert states: "The thunderstorm is in fact a characteristic setting for the theophany—the direct appearance of God—in the Hebrew Scriptures. The best-known example is the thunderstorm over Mount Sinai [Horeb] in which God speaks to the people in thunder and gives them the law."[2] Because the writers of the CB (NT) were familiar with the HB (OT) paradigm, they employed some of the elements of the thunderstorm in their compositions as well.

The question about with what people might associate God today requires a hermeneutic, that is, an interpretation of biblical texts. The word *interpretation* here does mean translation from one language to another; it implies metaphorical bridge-building from cultural texts embedded with cultural metaphors two thousand to four thousand years old. In other words, what do texts depicting God's presence as a thunderstorm say to modern scientific readers? How might readers of English biblical texts—translated from Aramaic, Hebrew, and Greek—interpret those texts using

---

1. Hiebert, "Air," 13.
2. Ibid., 13–14.

modern scientific paradigms while keeping in mind Bergmann's words: "If man [and woman] is separated from nature, then God, the Creator, is separated from the world"?[3] Hiebert seems to update one element of the ancient thunderstorm paradigm by equating "the breath of God's creatures with God's own breath and the dependence of all life on the divine."[4] As far as he is concerned, this concept of wind "undermines the notion that humans are of a totally different order than the rest of nature."[5] Hiebert adds: "In fact, [breath, wind] not only signifies that humans and the rest of nature are inseparable; it also claims that the atmosphere and respiration are really aspects of God's own being and therefore sacred."[6] If Hiebert is correct, then the foundational role that nature plays in biblical thought can be bridged with a regard for natural elements today as part of human existence in understanding past theophanies and recognizing modern ones.

Furthermore, if Bergmann is correct about "the central function of religion [being to] provide the skill of making oneself at home within the cosmos,"[7] how might this be done? How might the sage's words in the OT (A) Book of Wisdom—"the spirit of the Lord has filled the world, and that which holds all things together" (Wis 1:7) and the Lord's "immortal spirit is in all things" (Wis 12:1)—help in this hermeneutic? As Turner states, "The sage's statement encourages us to expect a consistent theology of God's presence that encompasses the whole of creation."[8] Marlow notes that "natural phenomena reveal something of the name (and therefore the character of YHWH" (the LORD).[9] As Clifford notes, "Yahweh [the LORD] . . . is surely a form of the verb 'to be' and probably the causative form, 'came to be, create.'"[10] Thus, the same question arises in different words: How can modern religion—specifically Judaism and Christianity—interpret biblical theophanic texts for its adherents today in order to make them aware of the presence of the God who causes all to be that displays the glory of the LORD?

---

3. Bergmann, *Religion*, 206.
4. Hiebert, "Air," 16.
5. Ibid.
6. Ibid., 17.
7. Bergmann, *Religion*, 283.
8. Turner, "Spirit of Wisdom," 113.
9. Marlow, "Other Prophet," 81.
10. Clifford, "Exodus," 47.

Hermeneutic

Batchelder approaches the question from a catechetical and mystagogical point of view. He explains that the work of "catechesis [is] teaching the why of what we say and do, and [the work of] mystagogy [is] reflecting upon the meaning of what we say and do."[11] It is important to note that Batchelder is writing about liturgy, but his words are more than appropriate for the task of hermeneutics. Batchelder states that "catechesis is only part of the task;"[12] his application to theophanies is evident: Reading the biblical text and understanding it in its context is only part of the task. "What must happen," states Batchelder, is meaning-filled liturgy and the experience of reflecting upon this experience."[13] What must happen with theophanies is meaning-filled reading and the experience of reflecting on and re-appropriating the biblical text within a scientific culture today. "Without the opportunity for such mystagogy, the conversion of the assembly which the liturgy always intends will be primarily an experience that is head-first rather than an experience of both head-and-heart."[14] Applying Batchelder's words to the theophanic task, mystagogy—a fuller and more effective understanding of biblical theophanic texts through intense reflection that is the basis for preaching—will not occur without intense study that connects ancient texts to modern scientific-minded people. In other words, merely reading the text and proclaiming it to be the word of God is not enough; everyone knows that lightning is not God shooting arrows with a rainbow! Once the text is understood in the head, how is it re-appropriated in the heart?

Cupitt notes: "Today history is secular, and it is hard to think of any supernatural claim that has recently been taken seriously—or could nowadays ever be taken seriously."[15] Raynal, in an editorial, attempts to articulate the question by noting the "inconvenient fact that people still cling to ancient patterns of imagination and insist that the old stories aren't mythic, but historical reportage."[16] He continues: "That way of thinking is at odds with the way people engage the everyday realities of living in a world shaped and formed by democratic politics and the results of scientific and technological thinking. Such make-believe thinking is receding and will continue to

---

11. Batchelder, "Holy God," 296.
12. Ibid., 297.
13. Ibid.
14. Ibid.
15. Cupitt, "Eschatology," 15.
16. Raynal, "Time," 2.

fade."[17] After noting the popularity of such modern stories as *Harry Potter* and *Star Wars*, which Raynal calls "works that excite and delight audiences across the globe," he writes: "What these stories demonstrate is the great hunger for imaginative worlds that engage and connect us with the realities of life—growing up, facing death, discovering one's gifts and friendships, embracing causes greater than ourselves, etc.—in ways that make life rich and meaningful."[18] If "good imagining is the gift that helps humans discover wholeness in living and being,"[19] then "we could use a new master story that brims with imaginative possibilities of a future founded in wisdom, established in justice, love, and peace, and infused with hope."[20] In other words, biblical theophanic narratives need to be imaginatively updated for a modern world.

Camile helps in this hermeneutical process. "While everything in the Bible is true," she writes, "not all of it actually happened. There's a difference between literary truth and historical fact."[21] She explains: "In history, things happen once and are therefore 'true in the past.' In storytelling, a thing may never have factually occurred in the past, but it's still 'true about human being or true for all time.' One could argue that literary truth is a higher form of truth, since it's universally and eternally true."[22] The task given to hermeneutics is to discover the literary truths of biblical theophanies and present their universal and eternal truth again today.

Nature's experienced occurrences—mountains, clouds, water, thunder, lightning, smoke, fire, earthquake, wind, light and darkness, etc.—are interpreted by biblical authors as theophanies that display the glory of the LORD. Because a theophany is usually an ordering of chaos which humankind cannot control, God is portraying as ordering such phenomena after creating them from the Book of Genesis to the Book of Revelation. This makes the LORD all-powerful in ancient eyes and experience, while it also gives security and safety to humans. In other words, what is beyond human control is predicated of Divine control. This common collection of what is today known as natural occurrences, which are interpreted by biblical authors as manifestations of God, are easily explained by scientists. For

17. Ibid.
18. Ibid.
19. Ibid.
20. Ibid.
21. Camile, "God's Great Collaborator," 47.
22. Ibid.

Hermeneutic

example, when a cloud appears in the sky, one does not conclude that it is a manifestation of the glory of the LORD. One does conclude that it is a mass of water that began as warm moisture rising from the earth. Such a water mass may meet cold air which condenses the water particles so that they result in rain falling back on the earth. Likewise, one does not conclude that thunder—a loud rumbling noise caused by the rapid expansion of air suddenly heated by lightning—is God speaking to people. So, what are modern scientific people to do with biblical narratives of theophanies?

In the pages that follow, a feeble attempt is made to answer that question. Through a process of title, text, reflection, meditation, and prayer, a fragile start is given to answer the question. The following entries are not intended to be exhaustive, but present possibilities to be explored. They are like yeast hidden in dough that keeps the potential bread rising and expanding. A five-part exercise is offered for every one of the twenty-one elements of theophanies presented in this book.

1. The name of the theophanic element indicates the focus of the entry. The number before the element is the same as the chapter that explored the element in its biblical contexts.

2. A few verses or sentences from a biblical text are provided. The text may be from the Hebrew Bible (Old Testament), Old Testament (Apocrypha), or Christian Bible (New Testament).

3. A reflective exploration follows the text. The reflection attempts to surface a possible meaning of the text for today. The exploration is not to be understood as exhaustive of the theophanic element; it is to be understood as an attempt to build a hermeneutic bridge over three thousand years of biblical texts to the modern world.

4. The reflection is followed by a question for journaling and/or personal meditation. The question functions as a guide for personal appropriation of the exploration, thus leading the reader into journaling and/or personal prayer. The journal/meditation question is designed to foster a process of actively applying the exploration to one's life and further development of it. The question gets one started; where the journal/meditation goes cannot be predetermined. It may be a single statement or an idea with which one lingers for a few minutes, a few hours, or a few days. It may surface a hermeneutical bridge that has not been explored in this book. The process has no end; the reader

decides when he or she has finished exploring the topic because he or she needs to attend to other things.

5. A prayer concludes the exercise and summarizes the original theme announced in the title, which was explored in the reflection and which served as the foundation for the meditation.

1 MOUNTAIN

Scripture: " . . . [T]he mountains may depart and the hills be removed, but [the LORD's] steadfast love shall not depart from [Israel], and [his] covenant of peace shall not be removed, says the LORD, who has compassion on [Israel]." (Isa 54:10)

Reflection: While few people literally climb mountains, there are some who relish standing at thirteen or fourteen thousand feet or even higher, knowing that they got there on their own two feet. Once a person has climbed a mountain or even hiked near one, he or she realizes how permanent it and its surrounding foot hills are; this is why the prophet Isaiah states that the LORD's steadfast love is even more permanent than a mountain! Climbing a specific mountain or hiking a trail, such as the Appalachian or Continental Divide, gets a person into the high country, where he or she can reflect upon the steadfastness of the rocks that form a mountain. The thrill of standing at heights that few people attain on foot can be compared to the excitement of a flight in an airplane. As either the small or the large aircraft lumbers down the runway, those inside are bombarded by the feeling of powerful engines that propel the winged creature into flight. Those parked on top of rockets that launch them into boundary-free space must experience the same powerful, inner silence that a mountaineer comes to appreciate deeply. Taking the stairs to ascend the floors of a sky scraper instead of the elevator may also give the stepper the same feeling as that experienced by a mountain climber. Maybe a roller coaster ride in an amusement park supplies the same experience. Thus, the theophanic element of mountain may find a modern equivalent in air and space travel, sky scraper steps, and roller coaster rides.

Journal/Meditation: For you, what might be an experience equivalent to mountain climbing? Did you experience the Divine Presence in it?

Prayer: O Lord, the mountains may depart and the hills be removed, but your steadfast love will not depart from me, and your covenant of peace will not be removed. I trust in your compassion and mercy now and forever. Amen.

2 SACRED NUMBERS

Scripture: "Thus says the LORD: For three transgressions of Judah, and for four, I will not revoke the punishment.... For three transgressions of Israel, and for four, I will not revoke the punishment...." (Amos 2:4a, 6a)

Reflection: The prophet Amos uses the sacred number three, indicating the realm of the divine, and the sacred number four, indicating the realm of the earth, to draw attention to Judah's and Israel's failure to keep the covenant. The same refrain is repeated over and over again (1:3, 6, 9, 11, 13; 2:1) in the prophet's oracles. The poetic device—"for three transgressions . . . , and for four"—merely means several. However, the sacred numbers indicate that the transgressions affect both heaven and earth. Unless it occurs in Christian doctrine, where it means three persons in one God, the number three may unconsciously serve as a paradigm to structure jokes, paragraphs in an essay, or items in an artistic display. Likewise, the number four serves to structure the seasons and the cardinal directions. Cultural sacred numbers consist of sixteen, the age when one can get a driver's license; twenty-one, the age when one can purchase and drink alcoholic beverages; forty, when one is over the hill; and sixty-five, the age of retirement. The Divine Presence is not signaled by any of these latter, non-biblical numbers, but the Christian doctrine of their being three persons in one God may still signal an experience of the Holy One.

Journal/Meditation: What numbers are sacred to you? Do any of them signal the Divine Presence? Explain how they do this.

Prayer: LORD God, through your prophet Amos you announce punishment on those who refuse to acknowledge your presence in and rule over all the worlds. Make me aware of your company when I encounter the numbers that you deem worthy to be signals of your presence now and forever and ever. Amen.

3 GOD'S VOICE

Scripture: Moses reminded the Israelites about what they said at Mount Sinai (Horeb): "Look, the LORD our God has shown us his glory and greatness, and we have heard his voice out of the fire. Today we have seen that God may speak to someone and the person may still live. So now why should we die? For this great fire will consume us; if we hear the voice of the LORD our God any longer, we shall die." (Deut 5:24-25)

Reflection: In old films, like *The Ten Commandments* (1956) and *Moses* (1975), the voice of God is the same as that of Moses, specifically Charlton Heston and Burt Lancaster, respectively. There is no booming voice from nowhere, because the directors of those films decided that Moses did not hear an audible divine voice, but, rather, the one in his own head. Today, this is referred to as conscience awareness. The metaphor is usually phrased as hearing the voice in one's own head. One intuitively knows what to say or what steps to take after hearing the inaudible voice. Thus, silence may be the best environment in which to place one to hear God's voice speaking in one's own brain. However, divine words can be heard in the Scriptures, and not just the Hebrew Bible (Old Testament) and the Christian Bible (New Testament), but in religions' many and different sacred writings, such as *The Quran*, *The Book of Mormon*, *The Rig Veda*, and *The Dhammapada*, to name only a few. In the gentle breeze that shakes the leaves on the oak tree, that dances the leaves on the aspen tree, and that rustles the fallen leaves of the maple tree, the divine voice may be heard. And the wind that whispers through the pine, the spruce, and the fir may also be God's voice. Even the voice the reader hears in his or her own head may be God's voice.

Journal/Meditation: What place is most conducive for you to hear God's voice? What means (the voice in your head, the silence, the printed word) is most conducive for you to hear God's voice? How do you separate other voices from God's voice?

Prayer: LORD, my God, I have heard your voice in my conscience, in the stillness of the world, and in the noise that surrounds me. Grant me the grace carefully to hear every word you speak that I may live in your Divine Presence all the days of my life now and in the life to come forever. Amen.

4 PEOPLE'S (PERSON'S) RESPONSE

Scripture: Jesus said, "Let your word be 'Yes, Yes' or 'No, No'; anything more than this comes from the evil one." (Matt 5:37)

Reflection: Today's world is one in which people tell what they know the other wants to hear. While it may not be an outright lie, the words are far from the factual truth. Students tell their teachers how much time they study, how much time they spent writing an essay, how much they enjoy a class not because those declarations are one hundred percent true, but in order to get a good grade in a class. Likewise, teenagers learn quickly how to tell their parents what they know they want to hear about using the car, going on a date, or hanging out with friends. Even adults tell those who have some kind of authority over them, such as managers, bankers, and clergy, what they know the boss likes to hear, the banker loves to hear, and the clergy get excited in hearing. It takes a lot of self-discipline and personal integrity always to tell the truth. It may be easy to say yes to help others, to volunteer in service to organizations that help others, and to donate to others' causes. It may be difficult to say no when asked to do something because a person needs time for himself or herself, it may be better to teach others to help themselves, or one has an obligation to minister to others in another venue. Likewise, one's response to God needs to be Yes, Yes, or No, No; any answer in between indicates neither integrity nor authenticity. As such, this element of a theophany presents a difficult hermeneutic to construct in a culture in which people tell others what they know they want to hear.

Journal/Meditation: Identify one specific instance when you authentically said Yes to God. What were the results? Identify one specific instance when you authentically said No to God. What were the results?

Prayer: Almighty God, your word to your people always has been "Yes, Yes" or "No, No." Grant that my response to you always will be Yes or No. Strengthen me in integrity of life and authenticity of purpose. You are LORD forever and ever. Amen.

5 CLOUD

Scripture: "Whatever the LORD pleases he does.... He it is who makes the clouds rise at the end of the earth; he makes lightning for the rain and brings out the wind from his storehouses." (Ps 135:6a, 7)

Reflection: Modern people see a cloud in the sky and recognize it as a visible mass of water or ice particles in the atmosphere from which rain and other forms of precipitation fall upon the earth. The clouds are formed by evaporation; warm air causes water on the earth to turn into a gas and rise, forming a cloud. When a mass of cold air comes in contact with the cloud, it cools it and causes it to drip its contents as rain, snow, or ice upon the earth. Airplanes, which often fly through clouds, display trails of moisture on their windows or shiny streaks of ice on their wings to those in the plane. From the earth, a contrail—a vapor trail—appears tracing the path of the plane through the sky. Dark clouds herald an approaching thunderstorm. Twisting clouds connecting heaven and earth announce a tornado, hurricane, cyclone, or typhoon. Wisps of cloud rise from atomic reactors in power plants, while fogs settle in the valleys below mountain peaks and hills and cover the earth like a blanket. The strongest cloud today is that of the mushroom which once settled over Hiroshima and Nagasaki—and in deserts—destroying all life for miles around and poisoning the earth with radioactivity. While some people may still enjoy lying in a hammock or sitting in a chase lounge and picking out figures in clouds, most do not immediately recognize the Divine Presence. Maybe the power of the atomic bomb and its ensuing mushroom cloud, while being a paradox when compared to biblical literature, nevertheless illustrates the presence of God today.

Another possible hermeneutic is cloud computing, a type of Internet-based computing that provides shared computer processing resources and data to computers and other devices on demand. It offers various capabilities to store and process data in third-party centers. It has been compared to the electricity grid over a network. While the cloud names an invisible entity, it also manifests a network of connectivity. In this latter regard, it illustrates the glory of the LORD, who is invisible and yet present as the source of all networks.

Journal/Meditation: When you see a cloud of any kind, what conclusion do you consciously or unconsciously reach? What does a cloud represent for you? Do you think the mushroom cloud is an appropriate sign of the Divine Presence? Explain. Do you think the computer cloud is an appropriate sign of the Divine Presence? Explain.

Prayer: LORD of heaven and earth, you are pleased to make the clouds rise at the end of the earth and from them to bring rain, snow, and ice to the earth. Grant that I may recognize your glory in all the clouds that surround me and praise you for your watchful presence now and forever. Amen.

6 WATER

Scripture: "[The LORD] opened the rock, and water gushed out; it flowed through the desert like a river." (Ps 105:41)

Reflection: The Israelites, finding water in a barren and rocky place, attributed their discovery to the LORD, their God. Not too long ago and in some places still now, some people attributed the discovery of potential wells to water witches or dowsers. These people carried forked twigs of peach or willow, a length of grape vine, or a mental rod that would bounce in their hands when an underground water source was present. A water witch was called before one began to dig a well to insure that water would be found. Also known as diviners, water witches supposedly located one of the elements of a theophany in a variety of environmental settings. Since most people are not familiar with them, the thrill of seeing the ocean for the first time may serve as the equivalent today. Listening to waves roll in and out and watching them paw the sand on the shore may evoke the same experience as observing a tree branch point to an underground water source. Sitting on a beach while listening to the waves roll in can be enhanced by a fiery sunrise or sunset; the streaks glide over and through the water forming a golden highway for light and directly connecting the earth to the sun on the horizon. Another aspect of water, namely, the flood, poses a different issue; no one says that God is destroying the earth. Those in flood-prone areas are advised to move to higher ground to protect themselves from the rising waters. Some selected experiences of water, like swimming in the sea, may elicit an awareness of the Divine Presence, but others, like a flood, do not serve that purpose today.

Journal/Meditation: When you experience water on a daily basis—shower, toilet, washing clothes, washing dishes, rivers, streams, ocean, sea, etc.—do your encounters trigger a theophany? What kind of water experiences make you aware of the Divine Presence? Which do not?

Prayer: You, LORD, opened the rock for your people, and water gushed out, flowing through the desert like a river. When I use any of the indoor plumbing in my home, make me aware of your presence. Make flow in me your grace now and forever. Amen.

7 THUNDER

Scripture: "Coming from the throne [of God] are flashes of lightning, and rumblings and peals of thunder, and in front of the throne burn seven flaming torches, which are the seven spirits of God." (Rev 4:5)

Reflection: As John of Patmos begins his heavenly travels, a door or portal in heaven opens and he sees the throne of God. He does not conclude that the rumbling and peals of thunder are caused by the rapid expansion of air heated by lightning, itself caused when there is a discharge of atmospheric electricity in the clouds or between clouds and the earth. Nor does the heavenly traveler conclude that angels are bowling, the explanation that some parents used in the not too distant past to comfort their children's fear during thunderstorms! John's experience leads him to recognize a theophany when he hears one, but such is not the case today. While there is a lot to be said to a sound over which one has no control—indeed one which upon occasion rattles the china in the cabinet and the pictures hanging on the wall—the best hermeneutical bridge might be the Japanese *taiko*, a large drum positioned on a stand and beat with *bachi*, drumsticks, in some Shumei religious services. The drumbeat is designed to open hearts to receive spiritual energy in this daughter of Shinto which is devoted to the happiness and well-being of individuals and a more harmonious and sustainable world community. The drumsticks represent a spiritual link between the body and the sky. The tympani in a symphony orchestra may be the closest experience most people come to hearing the rumbling and thunderous beats of the drum, which can raise awareness of the Divine Presence. For others, the ringing of bells or the sound of chimes, although less thunderous, may serve the same purpose.

Journal/Meditation: What type of rumbling or thunder serves to awaken you to the presence of God? What is the source of the rumbling or thunder?

Prayer: Coming from your throne, LORD God, your servant John heard rumblings and peals of thunder that awakened him to your presence. Grant that the rumblings and thunderous noises of my day may make me aware of your proximity now and in the future. Amen.

8 LIGHTNING

Scripture: "Bless the Lord, lightnings and clouds; sing praise to him and highly exalt him forever." (Sg Three 1:51 [Dan 3:73])

Reflection: Lightning, once thought to be God's biblical arrows shot to the earth with his rainbow, is caused by a discharge of atmospheric electricity in clouds or between clouds and the earth. When such a discharge occurs, a flash of light appears across the sky or between the sky and the earth. While it is not uncommon to see lightning on a hot summer evening, it usually occurs during a thunderstorm. A lightning strike to the earth can turn a tall tree into toothpicks. It can start a forest or prairie fire. A tall structure of any kind can be demolished by a lightning strike, and animals near one can be killed. With such power, it comes as no surprise that it is an element of theophanic narratives. However, while it still remains destructive and uncontrolled today, it no longer has the fear of the LORD attached to it. One possible hermeneutic bridge may be the sword, which is featured in multiple television shows and movies; a sword strike can elicit fear in those witnessing it lop off another person's head, hand, or foot or pierce one's heart. Even a more modern bridge may be the gun, the bomb, or the missile with a nuclear warhead. Certainly, the firing of a gun, the detonation of a bomb, or the explosion of a missile's warhead leaves only a flash of light. The destruction left by any and all of these devices mirrors the destruction of a lightning strike in theophanic narratives.

Journal/Meditation: In your experience, what has the force of lightning? How does that force help you to experience the Divine Presence?

Prayer: Mighty God, the lightning blesses your name and sings praise to you. When I see your flashes light up the sky, give me the courage to highly exalt you forever and ever. Amen.

Divine Presence

9 TRUMPET BLAST

Scripture: "God has gone up with a shout, the LORD with the sound of a trumpet." (Ps 47:5)

Reflection: The psalmist envisions God as a king being enthroned in the temple. He goes to his throne on an elevated platform while trumpets blare. Most people's familiarity with trumpets stems from hearing and seeing them in marching bands and orchestras. However, most of the time they are used to announce royalty, even though there may be little of even that left in the world. Thus, this brass musical instrument, either straight or coiled, with three valves and flared bell, is most likely out of the range of most people. Thus, the best hermeneutic might be the ever-present and well-known guitar. While duly acknowledging that mixing brass and strings is not good, the specialness of the trumpet in the Bible is best understood in the commonality of the guitar in the twenty-first century. An alternative to the guitar may be the harp. All three instruments produce pleasing musical sounds and are found in bands and orchestras today. While the queen or king of England may not be heralded with a guitar or harp, God might enjoy the alternative music as he approaches his chair!

Journal/Meditation: What musical instrument best reminds you of the Divine Presence? What is it about the instrument that triggers your awareness of God?

Prayer: LORD God, you ascend your heavenly throne to the accompaniment of the sound of the trumpet. Grant that I may recognize your presence in the sound of any musical instrument that praises your glory now and forever and ever. Amen.

10 SMOKE

Scripture: "May the glory of the LORD endure forever; may the LORD rejoice in his works—who looks on the earth and it trembles, who touches the mountains and they smoke." (Ps 104:31–32)

Reflection: There are various kinds of smoke. The psalmist understands God's touching of the earth resulting in smoke. He has in mind either a mountain lightning strike, a mountain forest fire caused by lightning, or a volcanic eruption. No matter which, the result is smoke, which rises from fire. A summer haze, caused by high humidity, can also function like smoke, especially when it hangs over the hills. Low rain and snow clouds can give the impression of smoke, especially when they drop down below mountain peaks and leave wisps of smoke in the sky. Some people see smoke rising from the fireplace through the chimney in their home, or they stand outside and watch it curl into and gradually disappear in the sky. Likewise, those who use such outdoor fireplaces as chimineas, fire pits, or fire rings enjoy seeing the smoke curling upward. The rising smoke, which disappears into the air, connects the earth to the heavens. While smoke signals fire to most people—and fire causes immediate panic—smoke detectors with their trumpet-like blares may be the next best thing to announcing the Divine Presence.

Journal/Meditation: What does smoke signal to you? What today do you consider equivalent to biblical smoke? Explain.

Prayer: When you touch the mountains, O LORD, they smoke. When you touch my life, O LORD, I tremble. Make me ever aware of your presence in all of my experiences of smoke. May your glory endure forever, and may you rejoice in your works forever. Amen.

11 FIRE

Scripture: "And in an instant, suddenly, you will be visited by the LORD of hosts with thunder and earthquake and great noise, with whirlwind and tempest, and the flame of a devouring fire." (Isa 29:5b–6)

Reflection: The devouring fire—along with the thunder, earthquake, whirlwind, and tempest—is typical theophanic language in praise of the LORD as a divine warrior set to save his people from their enemies, whom he will devour like fire devours whatever it touches. Fire is found in one's home in the fireplace (either wood or gas longs), in the furnace, in the hot water heater (gas or electric), in a light bulb, in a heater (gas or electric), in a kitchen range (gas or electric), etc. Outside the home, fire is found in a bonfire, in a shooting gun, in a meteorite, in a fire ring or fire pit, in a raging forest fire, in a house fire, etc. The paradoxes of fire are that it both draws people around it and it repels people from it; while it gives warmth necessary for life, it kills and consumes what once was alive! That is why it is predicated of the LORD; he devours his people's enemies while he makes his presence known with divine fire; he draws people to himself while also repelling those whom he considers enemies. The focus in today's world may be on fire departments that extinguish fire and fire crews that put out forest fires, but these may diminish the paradox. Fire in any paradoxical form is an element of a theophany and can be easily recognized today.

Journal/Meditation: What roles does fire play in your life? Make a list of them. Which of those have the ability to raise your awareness of the Divine Presence?

Prayer: LORD, in an instant, suddenly, you visit me with the flame of a devouring fire. As you draw me closer to your burning light, purify me and make me acceptable in your sight. Make me burn with your glory now and forever. Amen.

12 EARTHQUAKE

Scripture: "[The LORD] stopped and shook the earth; he looked and made the nations tremble. The eternal mountains were shattered; along his ancient pathways the everlasting hills sank low." (Hab 3:6)

Reflection: Long before geologists discovered tectonic plates ancient people conceived of the world as a flat, plate-like surface supported by columns. They mythically explained an earthquake by attributing it to God shaking the columns, thus manifesting one of the elements of a theophany. No one could be greater than the LORD, who shook the earth. However, modern people do not reach the same conclusion when an earthquake occurs and is measured on the Richter scale. The earth is not a plate; it is a sphere. It does not sit on columns; its surface floats on magma, which from time to time pushes its way through the crust and spews into what is called a volcano. Tectonic plates, segments of the earth's crust that move relative to other plates, produce seismic activity around their margins. Plates can rub against each other; one can slide under another; they can pull apart from each other. Such faults cause earthquakes. Some shifts in plates can be caused randomly by nature or by humankind when it engages in fracking, the process of drilling into the earth before a high-pressure water mixture is directed at rock to release the gas inside; water, sand, and chemicals, injected as high pressure, allows the gas to flow to the head of the well. While the structure of an earthquake is understood and the force can be measured, one cannot be predicted with any accuracy. That is why ancient people attributed them to God. Today, while they cannot be controlled, people no longer think that the Divine Presence is shaking the pillars of the earth to cause glass bottles of liquid and paper boxes of dry goods to fall off store shelves onto the floor. In areas of the world hit with earthquakes that destroy whole towns, no one concludes that God is stopping to shake the earth. Because of the destruction caused by such natural happenings and the negativity associated with them, it may be impossible to bridge this element of theophanies unless it is an auto accident, an airplane crash, a train crash, or some other earth shaking experience. It is important to keep in mind that such violent images that shock warm, fuzzy-feeling people today may be equivalent to the effect a biblical earthquake had on ancient people.

Journal/Meditation: What is your most earth-shaking experience? How was God present in it? Was it a destructive or a life-giving presence? Explain.

Prayer: LORD, mighty God, you stopped and shook the earth; you looked and made the nations tremble. The eternal mountains were shattered; along your ancient faults the everlasting hills sank low. In all the earth-shaking experiences of my life, help me to know your saving presence. You are God forever and ever. Amen.

13 TERMS OF THE EVENT (COVENANT)

Scripture: "The days are surely coming, says the LORD, when I will make a new covenant with the house of Israel and the house of Judah." (Jer 31:31)

Reflection: In most democracies chaos is ordered through law-making by elected officials. For the Hebrews—later known as the Israelites and Jews—the crafting of law codes was the responsibility of the LORD, Israel's God. Collectively, the codes are called the Torah; it consists of six hundred thirteen precepts: There are two hundred forty-eight commandments stipulating what is to be done and three hundred sixty-five prohibitions explaining what is to be avoided. The Torah, consisting of the first five books of the Bible—Genesis, Exodus, Leviticus, Numbers, and Deuteronomy—is designed as a guide through the chaos of life. It legislates how to live in relationship with the LORD, with others, and with all things. Thus, accompanying most theophanies are terms of the event or covenant. The prophet Jeremiah's declaration that God will make a new covenant with the Jews so that they and he can live in fidelity is rather shocking. It implies that the previous covenant had defects and that the fresh one will be a new and improved version. The Torah, written on tablets of stone, will be written on people's hearts. The principle difficulty with the previous covenant written exteriorly is that it permitted insincere obedience. God's new move is to plant his law within the interior intentionality of his people; thus, obedience will come naturally. The new covenant will be like a spiritual injection that makes its way through each person and corporately through the whole people. The LORD promises again to be their God, and they will be his people intentionally motivated from within. While most people are law-abiding citizens, democracies tend to foster extreme individuality with an attitude that no one will dictate what another can and cannot do. With the focus on individual identity, it is difficult to recover a sense of corporate recognition. Indeed, it seems that individual recognition is a prerequisite to forming any type of covenant community today. Individual biblical characters accept the terms of a theophany for the benefit of others and not for their own glorification. That fact sharply contrasts with today's individual who would accept the terms of a theophany for his or her aggrandizement. Furthermore, the interior motivation specified by Jeremiah may be lacking in those who obey the law so that they will not be punished or obey it only so they will not get caught disobeying it. For some people, an action is not wrong—no matter what the law may say—until they get caught breaking the law.

Journal/Meditation: What laws do you readily accept because they are for the common good? What laws do you readily accept because they benefit you? What laws do you reject because they do not benefit the common good? What laws do you reject because they do not benefit you? Is God manifest in the law? If so, why? If not, why not?

Prayer: The days are surely coming, you say, O LORD, when you will make a new covenant with all people. You declare that you will write it interiorly within them so that they will be your people, and you will be their God. Grant me the grace to live in fidelity to you that I may truly know you now and forever and ever. Amen.

14 SIGN

Scripture: "God said to Abraham, 'You shall circumcise the flesh of your foreskin, and it shall be a sign of the covenant between me and you.'" (Gen 17:9, 11)

Reflection: A sign is a thing that points to another thing. The most obvious sign is a stop sign, a metal octagon with the word *STOP* printed in bold, white, capital letters on a red background mounted on a pole. The sign indicates that an operator of a vehicle needs to bring the vehicle to a complete halt. For Abraham, the sign of his covenant with God was physical circumcision. Every time he looked upon his reproductive organ he would see that his foreskin was cut away and remember that he was in agreement with God. In a patriarchal culture, Abraham would have concluded that just as he transferred life from himself to his wife, Sarah, using the sign of the covenant—his circumcised penis—God had given him life through the promise of descendants. Such ancient signs, most of which are not intelligible to modern people, can be understood by reflecting on those that surround people today. The rose-and-purple streaked clouds in the sky of a sunrise or sunset can be a sign of God's fidelity. While every morning and evening does not feature the splendor of the orange-yellow disk peeking over the horizon or disappearing over the same, the daily rhythm remains the same. Night's darkness is conquered by morning's light; morning's light is chased by night's darkness. Steeples on churches, minarets on mosques, and towers on synagogues or temples are signs of sacred places. However, National Parks, too, serve as signs, identifying secular sacred places. And cemeteries are often filled with monuments—signs—disclosing some details about those who are buried under them. The sign of stone tablets gave way to the sign of scrolls, which gave way to the sign of a printed Bible. Such biblical signs of blood (donating blood at a blood bank), staff (walking stick or cane), rainbow (color or paint wheel), and twelve stones (family tree) need reinterpretation. Signs, demonstrations of God's power, change as quickly as cultures change.

Journal/Meditation: Today, what signs serve the same purpose—demonstrations of God's power—as these biblical ones: tablets of stone, blood, staff, rainbow, twelve stones, circumcision?

Prayer: Almighty LORD, you gave Noah the sign of a rainbow, Abraham the sign of circumcision, and Moses the sign of the tablets of stone as demonstrations of your power. Help me to recognize your strength in the signs that surround me today, tomorrow, and forever. Amen.

15 TRANSFORMATION

Scripture: "The LORD said to Moses, 'I will do the very thing that you have asked; for you have found favor in my sight, and I know you by name.' Moses said, 'Show me your glory, I pray.' And he said, 'I will make all my goodness pass before you, and will proclaim before you the name, 'The LORD'; and I will be gracious to whom I will be gracious, and will show mercy on whom I will show mercy. 'But,' he said, 'you cannot see my face; for no one shall see me and live.' And the LORD continued, 'See, there is a place by me where you shall stand on the rock; and while my glory passes by I will put you into a cleft of the rock, and I will cover you with my hand until I have passed by; then I will take away my hand, and you shall see my back; but my face shall not be seen.'" (Exod 33:17–23)

Reflection: The Bible is paradoxical in that it says that no one can see God's face and live, yet there are people who see God's face and live! Setting aside the paradoxical quality of biblical writers, it is the transformation that occurs in those who see God's face and those who do not see his face. Religion, a response to the circumstances in which one finds himself of herself, should foster transformation or realignment, the root meaning of the word *religion*. Ongoing transformation in the midst of those who prefer that no change be introduced can either empower people or paralyze them. That is why it is so important that people, like Moses, discern a particular calling and then engage in it in order to nurture even more realignment. Today's concern is not centered on seeing the face of an invisible God or anthropomorphically having him hold his hand over people in protection from himself. However, most folks have had some experiences that lifted them beyond themselves, lifted them beyond everydayness to see the bigger picture, the broader world, the unlimited universe. Those types of experiences, while harder to articulate, provoke change—radical change—that sparks new behaviors in terms of personal habits, like alcohol consumption, tobacco, caffeine, relationships, etc. Moses' willingness to be transformed by the back of the Divine Presence should prompt modern people to be transformed by the front of the Divine Presence, which can be seen in every person and everything.

Journal/Meditation: In whom or what do you see the face of God? How do those experiences transform you?

Prayer: If I have found favor in your sight, LORD, grant me a peek of your glory that I may experience all your goodness and graciousness passing before me. Do not hide me in the cleft of the rock, but transform me with your grace that I may name you in everyone and everything that passes by me all the days of my life. Amen.

16 ALTAR

Scripture: "When these [seven] days [of making atonement for the altar, cleansing it, and consecrating it] are over, then from the eighth day onward the priests shall offer upon the altar your burnt offerings and your offerings of well-being; and I will accept you, says the Lord GOD." (Ezek 43:27)

Reflection: The altar is both a place of sacrifice and a table for feasting. Ezekiel, functioning as another Moses, is the prophet delegated by God to inaugurate a new sacrificial cult. The altar itself must be purified in order for God to accept the offerings placed upon it. Ezekiel, like Moses before him, is given detailed instructions concerning the building and consecration of the altar in order to give pleasure to God. Without the proper seven-day consecration the sacrifices placed on the altar will not be acceptable, and if the sacrifices are not acceptable, then neither will the people encounter the pleasure of their God. The sacrifices are burned in whole or in part; the fire transforms them into smoke which rises to God, who enjoys the feast. While an altar may not be present in some places of worship, it may be represented by a table which serves a similar purpose but without the sacrificial aspect. Since most homes have tables of some kind, maybe even elaborate dining room tables, the hermeneutic can be found in the placement of the sacrificed and cooked animal (beef, pork, chicken, etc.) on the table and the eating that follows by those gathered around it. In churches that do have altars, they are the places for the non-bloody sacrifice and feast, usually consisting of bread and wine. Many shrines present altars for the burning of incense and the offering of flowers and other foodstuffs, thus preserving the dual character of the altar-table. While they may not be called altars, other eating places in the home—such as coffee tables, bars, and counters—may function in exactly the same way.

Journal/Meditation: Is the table in your home also an altar? What is sacrificed upon it? What feasts are celebrated around it? How has God been encountered through those gathered around it?

Prayer: Lord GOD, you take great pleasure in altars consecrated for the sole purpose of offering sacrifices to you. Accept the gifts I bring to you this day, and grant that I may share in your eternal feast of grace now and forever. Amen.

17 FEAST (MEAL)

Scripture: " . . . [G]et the fatted calf and kill it, and let us eat and celebrate." (Luke 15:23)

Reflection: The feast or meal that is an element of a theophany refers to a special repast eaten in the presence of God or with him. A feast serves to solidify the theophanic experience and bring about a unity among those who participate in it. The father who has his son back in Luke's Gospel directs that the fatted calf be slaughtered, that a feast be prepared, and that the family unity be re-enacted through the meal. The feast will reincorporate the members into a family. Meals become special at Thanksgiving, Christmas, Easter, Passover, etc. Those who share them are moved beyond themselves to see for a moment the greater unity that exists between those gathered around a table—and maybe even their connection to a group, neighborhood, city, or the world. A feast uncovers the force or energy that is common to all the members. Sharing food implies sharing people. When people share food, they become more than the sum of the members; they enter into a communion of subjects on multiple of levels. This is how God is manifest through a feast or meal.

Journal/Meditation: What recent feast or meal enabled you to be reincorporated into a family or a group? How were people shared through food? How was God present in the feast or meal?

Prayer: LORD God, from whom all good things come, grant that those with whom I feast may experience themselves in deep communion with each other and with you. May I one day eat and drink in your presence forever. Amen.

18 WIND

Scripture: "[The LORD] makes lightning for the rain, and he brings out the wind from his storehouses." (Jer 10:13b; 51:16b)

Reflection: While many people may not be aware of their biblical connection to air as the breath of life, the spirit of life, and the wind of life, the authors of Scripture link everyone and everything into one world. In other words, breath, spirit, and wind bring about an interrelatedness to which many people pay little or no attention. The air people breathe, the spirit that fills them, and the wind that blows around them come from God's huge storehouses. In the invisible place—wherever that may be!—the LORD keeps the wind until he is ready to open the doors and release it. The prophet Jeremiah's idea can be likened to a hot air balloon. As the air is heated by some kind of fire, it rises in the balloon and causes the balloon and its basket to lift up from the earth. When the storehouse of air in the balloon cools, it permits the large nylon balloon with its suspended compartment for the pilot and passengers to descend to the earth. While it is rising and while it is descending, the balloon is surrounded by air and pushed through the sky with wind, even as its pilot and passengers are breathing the same air! A hermeneutic for the theophanic element of wind might also be captured by the image of flying a kite. While the person holding the string is breathing the air surrounding him or her, the kite—a light framework covered in a thin, light material—is carried aloft by the wind. In its more violent forms, wind twists itself into tornados, columns of swirling, rotating air that pass in a narrow path over land; hurricanes, severe tropical storms with high winds; and cyclones, large-scale storms with winds that rotate counterclockwise in the Northern Hemisphere and clockwise in the Southern Hemisphere. When these latter types of winds arrive, people flee to their underground shelters, tie down their belongings, and cover the windows of their homes with wooden slats. Depending upon the point to be made, wind from a gentle breeze that shakes the outdoor chimes to a violent storm that can destroy life and property serves as a hermeneutic for wind in biblical texts about breath, spirit, and wind.

Journal/Meditation: What is your favorite experience of wind? After describing it carefully, what characteristics does it possess that are similar to theophanic wind?

Prayer: O LORD, you made the earth and the heavens. At your command the storehouses release the winds. Grant me a deeper awareness of your presence in the gentle breeze and the violent storm now and forever. Amen.

19 LIGHT AND DARKNESS

Scripture: "Remember your creator in the days of your youth, before the days of trouble come, and the years draw near when you will say, 'I have no pleasure in them'; before the sun and the light and the moon and the stars are darkened and the clouds return with the rain." (Eccl 12:1–2)

Reflection: Throughout all of life, there is the interplay of light and darkness. Most people see them as opposites of which only one can be chosen. However, as the author of Ecclesiastes states, youth may be associated with light and age with darkness, but they exist in one's life in paradox. Indeed, one cannot know the meaning of either without the other! Sometimes it is easier to see in the dark than in the light; and sometimes it is easier to see in the light than in the dark! The paradoxical rhythm is etched in wakefulness and sleep; one cannot be awake without first having been asleep; and one cannot sleep without first having been awake. And between the two opposites, there is a middle position where one is neither awake nor asleep! Even one's age affects this paradox, not to mention the shifting of the length of days and nights during the seasons of the year. Furthermore, an awareness of dawn and dusk, those in between times of increasing light and decreasing darkness or decreasing light and increasing darkness can create a hermeneutic from the biblical light and darkness paradox. The various streaks of the pinkish orange and bluish purple clouds on the horizon change rapidly with the increase and decrease of light. Like a painter's brush strokes on a fresh canvas, the paradox of light and darkness is displayed daily before one's eyes as a modern element of a theophany.

Journal/Meditation: Where in your life do you find the paradox of light and darkness? What modern image helps to display your experience? Explain. How can God be in the middle, between the opposites of light and darkness?

Prayer: Creator, as I remember the light-filled days of my youth, make me grateful for the dark-filled days of my older years. And as I enjoy the dark-filled days of my older years, make be grateful for the light-filled days of my youth. Grant that I may recognize you presence every day in light and in dark both now and forever. Amen.

20 JEWELS (PRECIOUS STONES)

Scripture: "The gates of Jerusalem will be built with sapphire and emerald, and all [her] walls with precious stones. The towers of Jerusalem will be built with gold, and their battlements with pure gold. The streets of Jerusalem will be paved with ruby and with stones of Ophir." (Tobit 13:16:cde)

Reflection: Tobit's hymn of praise, found at the end of the OT (A) book bearing his name, mentions sapphire, emerald, gold, ruby, and other precious stones. Most people have a jewelry box or jewelry drawer that contains precious or semi-precious stones purchased by them, purchased by others and given to them, or owned by a deceased family member and handed down to them. Jewels may highlight necklaces, earrings, rings, watches, etc. Stones are considered precious when they are hard to find in the mines in the earth. Tobit uses such rare stones to capture the wealth that the rebuilt city of Jerusalem will display. Because jewelry and precious stones remain rare today, they continue to serve as a hermeneutic for the same element in biblical theophanies. The rarest of valued stones are used as metaphors for the Divine Presence. Diamond, the most highly prized gemstone, should be added to the list and especially combined with that soft, yellow, malleable metallic element of gold, which is often the setting for diamond. Even though it is more readily available, silver might also be used. Tobit's use of precious gems and metals describes the glory of the rebuilt city. The same can serve today to describe the glory of the LORD.

Journal/Meditation: What is your favorite precious stone? What is your favorite precious metal? How can those serve as modern metaphors for the glory of the LORD?

Prayer: You have decreed, O LORD, that the gates of Jerusalem will be built with sapphire and emerald, and all its walls with precious stones. Its towers will be constructed with gold, and their battlements with pure gold. Its streets will be paved with ruby and gold. Grant that I may one day behold your glory in the new Jerusalem, where you dwell forever and ever. Amen.

21 DREAM (VISION)

Scripture: The LORD said to his people, " . . . I will pour out my spirit on all flesh; your sons and your daughters shall prophesy, your old men shall dream dreams, and your young men shall see visions." (Joel 2:28)

Reflection: Through the prophet Joel, God promises his people that they will experience the gift of prophecy, that is, the spiritual ability—new life and power—to reveal the will of the LORD through dreams or visions. What is interesting about the prophet Joel is that he declares that this gift will be given to all people. God will enter into a special relationship with people through his spirit. While dreams and visions are studied by many today—both those in psychology and those out—the unconscious is understood to work out whatever was not solved by the conscious. The phrase, "sleep on it," indicates that one will see or understand something differently the next morning after a good night's sleep. Some people consider dreams and visions to be more important than others. Furthermore, modern people know that their dreams and visions are not as vivid as biblical characters' dreams and visions, which have been enhanced through oral tradition before finally being recorded in written form. Without delving too deeply into physics, the concept of string theory might serve as a viable hermeneutic for the theophanic element of dream or vision. String theory postulates that beyond the usual four dimensions—height, width, length, and time—there are eleven (and most likely more) dimensions which cannot be perceived by people. These extra dimensions contain other worlds. Dreams and visions may be a way that limited, four-dimensional people can enter those other worlds and encounter the world of the Divine Presence. While string theory is just that—a theory—so is the understanding of dream and vision. Such questions—Where does one go when dreaming? Where does one go when unconscious? Where does one go when given an anesthetic?—are worth considering in an effort to create a hermeneutic today. In the Bible, God grants access to those other worlds in which one can see the glory of the LORD.

Journal/Meditation: Identify several solutions to issues or problems that you solved while dreaming. What is common to your experiences? How accurate were your visions? Did you see God?

Prayer: LORD God, you promised to pour out your spirit on all flesh so that men and women would prophesy, dream dreams, and see visions. Outpour the Holy Spirit upon me that I may determine your will through my dreams and enact it now and forever. Amen.

Bibliography

Baird, William. "The Gospel According to Luke." In *The Interpreter's One-Volume Commentary on the Bible*, edited by Charles M. Laymon, 672–706. Nashville: Abingdon, 1971.
Batchelder, David B. "Holy God, Dangerous Liturgy: Preparing the Assembly for Transforming Encounter." *Worship* 79:4 (July 2005) 290–303.
Beavin, Edward Lee. "Ecclesiasticus or the Wisdom of Jesus the Son of Sirach." In *The Interpreter's One-Volume Commentary on the Bible*, edited by Charles M. Laymon, 550–76. Nashville: Abingdon, 1971.
Bergmann, Sigurd. *Religion, Space, and the Environment*. New Brunswick, NJ: Transaction, 2014.
Betz, Hans Dieter. *The Sermon on the Mount*. Hermeneia. Minneapolis: Fortress, 1995.
Blenkinsopp, Joseph. "Deuteronomy." In *The New Jerome Biblical Commentary*, edited by Raymond E. Brown, Joseph A. Fitzmyer, and Roland E. Murphy, 94–109. Englewood Cliffs, NJ: Prentice Hall, 1990.
Boadt, Lawrence. "Ezekiel." In *The New Jerome Biblical Commentary*, edited by Raymond E. Brown, Joseph A. Fitzmyer, and Roland E. Murphy, 305–28. Englewood Cliffs, NJ: Prentice Hall, 1990.
Bovon, Francois. *Luke 1*. Hermeneia. Minneapolis: Fortress, 2002.
———. *Luke 2*. Hermeneia. Minneapolis: Fortress, 2013.
Brown, Raymond E., Donald Senior, John R. Donahue, and Adela Yarbro Collins. "Aspects of New Testament Thought." In *The New Jerome Biblical Commentary*, edited by Raymond E. Brown, Joseph A. Fitzmyer, and Roland E. Murphy, 1354–81. Englewood Cliffs, NJ: Prentice Hall, 1990.
Camile, Alice. "God's Great Collaborator." *U.S. Catholic* 81:9 (2016) 47–9.
Clifford, Richard J. "Exodus." In *The New Jerome Biblical Commentary*, edited by Raymond E. Brown, Joseph A. Fitzmyer, and Roland E. Murphy, 44–60. Englewood Cliffs, NJ: Prentice Hall, 1990.
———and Roland E. Murphy. "Genesis." In *The New Jerome Biblical Commentary*, edited by Raymond E. Brown, Joseph A. Fitzmyer, and Roland E. Murphy, 8–43. Englewood Cliffs, NJ: Prentice Hall, 1990.

Bibliography

Cody, Aelred. "Haggai, Zechariah, Malachi." In *The Interpreter's One-Volume Commentary on the Bible*, edited by Charles M. Laymon, 349–61. Nashville: Abingdon, 1971.

Collins, Adela Yarbro. "The Apocalypse (Revelation)." In *The New Jerome Biblical Commentary*, edited by Raymond E. Brown, Joseph A. Fitzmyer, and Roland E. Murphy, 996–1016. Englewood Cliffs, NJ: Prentice Hall, 1990.

Collins, Raymond F. "The First Letter to the Thessalonians." In *The New Jerome Biblical Commentary*, edited by Raymond E. Brown, Joseph A. Fitzmyer, and Roland E. Murphy, 772–9. Englewood Cliffs, NJ: Prentice Hall, 1990.

Cupitt, Don. "Eschatology, Globalized and Personalized." *The Fourth R* 29:5 (2016) 15–16.

Dentan, Robert C. "The Song of Solomon." In *The Interpreter's One-Volume Commentary on the Bible*, edited by Charles M. Laymon, 324–28. Nashville: Abingdon, 1971.

De Vries, Simon J. "The Book of Habakkuk." In *The Interpreter's One-Volume Commentary on the Bible*, edited by Charles M. Laymon, 494–7. Nashville: Abingdon, 1971.

———. "The Book of Nahum." In *The Interpreter's One-Volume Commentary on the Bible*, edited by Charles M. Laymon, 491–3. Nashville: Abingdon, 1971.

Dillon, Richard J. "Acts of the Apostles." In *The New Jerome Biblical Commentary*, edited by Raymond E. Brown, Joseph A. Fitzmyer, and Roland E. Murphy, 722–67. Englewood Cliffs, NJ: Prentice Hall, 1990.

Duran, Marek. "Memory, Morality, and the Joy of the Gospel." *Chicago Studies* 55:1 (2016) 68–82.

Faley, Roland J. "Leviticus." In *The New Jerome Biblical Commentary*, edited by Raymond E. Brown, Joseph A. Fitzmyer, and Roland E. Murphy, 61–79. Englewood Cliffs, NJ: Prentice Hall, 1990.

Gilmour, S. MacLean. "The Revelation to John." In *The Interpreter's One-Volume Commentary on the Bible*, edited by Charles M. Laymon, 945–68. Nashville: Abingdon, 1971.

Gray, John. "The Book of Exodus." In *The Interpreter's One-Volume Commentary on the Bible*, edited by Charles M. Laymon, 33–67. Nashville: Abingdon, 1971.

Guthrie, Harvey H. "The Book of Numbers." In *The Interpreter's One-Volume Commentary on the Bible*, edited by Charles M. Laymon, 85–99. Nashville: Abingdon, 1971.

Habel, Norman C. *The Land is Mine: Six Biblical Land Ideologies*. Minneapolis: Fortress, 1995.

Harrington, Daniel J. "The Gospel According to Mark." In *The New Jerome Biblical Commentary*, edited by Raymond E. Brown, Joseph A. Fitzmyer, and Roland E. Murphy, 596–629. Englewood Cliffs, NJ: Prentice Hall, 1990.

Hartman, Louis F. and Alexander A. Di Lella. "Daniel." In *The New Jerome Biblical Commentary*, edited by Raymond E. Brown, Joseph A. Fitzmyer, and Roland E. Murphy, 406–20. Englewood Cliffs, NJ: Prentice Hall, 1990.

Hiebert, Theodore. "Air, the First Sacred Thing." In *Exploring Ecological Hermeneutics*, edited by Norman C. Habel and Peter Trudinger, 9–19. Symposium Series 46. Atlanta: Society for Biblical Literature, 2008.

Johnson, Luke Timothy. *The Acts of the Apostles*. Sacra Pagina 5. Collegeville, MN: Liturgical, 1992.

Kee, Howard Clark. "The Gospel According to Matthew." In *The Interpreter's One-Volume Commentary on the Bible*, edited by Charles M. Laymon, 609–43. Nashville: Abingdon, 1971.

Knight, George A.F. "The Book of Daniel." In *The Interpreter's One-Volume Commentary on the Bible*, edited by Charles M. Laymon, 436–50. Nashville: Abingdon, 1971.

Bibliography

———. "The Prayer of Azariah and the Song of the Three Young Men." In *The Interpreter's One-Volume Commentary on the Bible*, edited by Charles M. Laymon, 581–2. Nashville: Abingdon, 1971.

Kselman, John S. and Michael L. Barre. "Psalms." In *The New Jerome Biblical Commentary*, edited by Raymond E. Brown, Joseph A. Fitzmyer, and Roland E. Murphy, 523–52. Englewood Cliffs, NJ: Prentice Hall, 1990.

L'Heureux, Conrad E. "Numbers." In *The New Jerome Biblical Commentary*, edited by Raymond E. Brown, Joseph A. Fitzmyer, and Roland E. Murphy, 80–93. Englewood Cliffs, NJ: Prentice Hall, 1990.

Luz, Ulrich. *Matthew 1–7*. Hermeneia. Minneapolis: Fortress, 2007.

———. *Matthew 21–28*. Hermeneia. Minneapolis: Fortress, 2005.

MacKenzie, R.A.F., and Roland E. Murphy. "Job." In *The New Jerome Biblical Commentary*, edited by Raymond E. Brown, Joseph A. Fitzmyer, and Roland E. Murphy, 466–88. Englewood Cliffs, NJ: Prentice Hall, 1990.

Marks, John H. "The Book of Genesis." In *The Interpreter's One-Volume Commentary on the Bible*, edited by Charles M. Laymon, 1–32. Nashville: Abingdon, 1971.

Marlow, Hilary. "The Other Prophet! The Voice of Earth in the Book of Amos." In *Exploring Ecological Hermeneutics*, edited by Norman C. Habel and Peter Trudinger, 75–83. Symposium Series 46. Atlanta: Society for Biblical Literature, 2008.

Matthews, Victor H. "Theophanies Cultic and Cosmic: 'Prepare to meet Thy God!'" In *Israel's Apostasy and Restoration*, edited by A. Gilead, 307–17. Grand Rapids, MI: Baker, 1988.

——— and James C. Moyer. *The Old Testament: Text and Context*. 3rd ed. Grand Rapids, MI: Baker Academic, 2012.

McKenzie, John L. "Aspects of Old Testament Thought." In *The New Jerome Biblical Commentary*, edited by Raymond E. Brown, Joseph A. Fitzmyer, and Roland E. Murphy, 1284–1315. Englewood Cliffs, NJ: Prentice Hall, 1990.

———. *Dictionary of the Bible*. Milwaukee: Bruce, 1965.

Milgrom, Jacob. "The Book of Leviticus." In *The Interpreter's One-Volume Commentary on the Bible*, edited by Charles M. Laymon, 68–84. Nashville: Abingdon, 1971.

Miller, David M. "Seeing the Glory, Hearing the Son: The Function of the Wilderness Theophany Narratives in Luke 9:28–36." *Catholic Biblical Quarterly* 72:3 (2010) 498–517.

Miller, Susan. "The Descent of Darkness over the Land." In *Exploring Ecological Hermeneutics*, edited by Norman C. Habel and Peter Trudinger, 123–30. Symposium Series 46. Atlanta: Society for Biblical Literature, 2008.

Moloney, Francis J. "Johannine Theology." In *The New Jerome Biblical Commentary*, edited by Raymond E. Brown, Joseph A. Fitzmyer, and Roland E. Murphy, 1417–26. Englewood Cliffs, NJ: Prentice Hall, 1990.

Murphey, Cecil B. *The Dictionary of Biblical Literacy*. Nashville, TN: Oliver-Nelson, 1989.

Murphy-O'Connor, Jerome. "The First Letter to the Corinthians." In *The New Jerome Biblical Commentary*, edited by Raymond E. Brown, Joseph A. Fitzmyer, and Roland E. Murphy, 798–815. Englewood Cliffs, NJ: Prentice Hall, 1990.

Neyrey, Jerome H. "The Second Epistle of Peter." In *The New Jerome Biblical Commentary*, edited by Raymond E. Brown, Joseph A. Fitzmyer, and Roland E. Murphy, 1017–22. Englewood Cliffs, NJ: Prentice Hall, 1990.

BIBLIOGRAPHY

North, Robert. "The Chronicler: 1–2 Chronicles, Ezra, Nehemiah." In *The New Jerome Biblical Commentary*, edited by Raymond E. Brown, Joseph A. Fitzmyer, and Roland E. Murphy, 362–98. Englewood Cliffs, NJ: Prentice Hall, 1990.

O'Day, Gail R., and David Peterson, eds. *The Access Bible: New Revised Standard Version with the Apocryphal/Deuterocanonical Books*. New York: Oxford University Press, 1999.

Ortlund, E.N. "An Intertextual Reading of the Theophany of Psalm 97." *Scandinavian Journal of the Old Testament* 20:2 (2006) 273–85.

Parsons, Mikeal C. "Exegesis 'By the Numbers': Numerology and the New Testament." *Perspectives in Religious Studies* 35:1 (2008) 25–43.

Perkins, Pheme. "The Gospel According to John." In *The New Jerome Biblical Commentary*, edited by Raymond E. Brown, Joseph A. Fitzmyer, and Roland E. Murphy, 942–85. Englewood Cliffs, NJ: Prentice Hall, 1990.

Pervo, Richard I. *Acts*. Hermeneia. Minneapolis: Fortress, 2009.

Pfeifer, Daniel J. "Which Came First, the Symbol or the Referent? A Study of the Historical Twelve." *Bibliotheca Sacra* 172 (2015) 433–49.

Pherigo, Lindsey P. "The Gospel According to Mark." In *The Interpreter's One-Volume Commentary on the Bible*, edited by Charles M. Laymon, 644–71. Nashville: Abingdon, 1971.

Raynal, Gordown W.G. "Time to Re-mythologize Jesus?" *The Fourth R* 29:4 (2016) 2.

Roberts, J.J.M. *First Isaiah*. Hermeneia. Minneapolis: Fortress, 2015.

Robinson, Bernard P. "The Theophany and Meal of Exodus 24." *Scandinavian Journal of the Old Testament* 25:2 (2011) 155–173.

Ryken, Leland, James C. Wilhoit, and Tremper Longman III, eds. *Dictionary of Biblical Imagery*. Downers Grove, IL: InterVarsity, 1998.

Savran, George. "Theophany as Type Scene." *Prooftexts* 23:2 (2003) 119–149.

Schwartz, Baruch J. "The Priestly Account of the Theophany and Lawgiving at Sinai." In *Texts, Temples, and Traditions: A Tribute to Menachem Haran*, edited by Michael V. Fox, et al., 103–34. Winona Lake, IN: Eisenbrauns, 1996.

Shepherd, Massey H. "The First Letter of John." In *The Interpreter's One-Volume Commentary on the Bible*, edited by Charles M. Laymon, 935–9. Nashville: Abingdon, 1971.

Shnider, Steven. "Psalm XVIII: Theophany, Epiphany, Empowerment." *Vetus Testamentum* 56:3 (2006) 386–98.

Thompson, Claude Holmes. "The Second Letter of Peter." In *The Interpreter's One-Volume Commentary on the Bible*, edited by Charles M. Laymon, 931–4. Nashville: Abingdon, 1971.

Toombs, Lawrence E. "The Psalms." In *The Interpreter's One-Volume Commentary on the Bible*, edited by Charles M. Laymon, 253–303. Nashville: Abingdon, 1971.

Turner, Marie. "The Spirit of Wisdom in All Things: The Mutuality of Earth and Humankind." In *Exploring Ecological Hermeneutics*, edited by Norman C. Habel and Peter Trudinger, 113–22. Symposium Series 46. Atlanta: Society for Biblical Literature, 2008.

Verman, Mark. "The Power of Threes." *Jewish Bible Quarterly* 36:3 (2008) 171–181.

Viviano, Benedict T. "The Gospel According to Matthew." In *The New Jerome Biblical Commentary*, edited by Raymond E. Brown, Joseph A. Fitzmyer, and Roland E. Murphy, 630–74. Englewood Cliffs, NJ: Prentice Hall, 1990.

Bibliography

Wahl, Thomas P., Irene Nowell, and Anthony R. Ceresko. "Zephaniah, Nahum, Habakkuk." In *The New Jerome Biblical Commentary*, edited by Raymond E. Brown, Joseph A. Fitzmyer, and Roland E. Murphy, 255–64. Englewood Cliffs, NJ: Prentice Hall, 1990.

Walsh, Jerome T. and Christopher T. Begg. "1–2 Kings." In *The New Jerome Biblical Commentary*, edited by Raymond E. Brown, Joseph A. Fitzmyer, and Roland E. Murphy, 160–185. Englewood Cliffs, NJ: Prentice Hall, 1990.

Williams, James G. "Number Symbolism and Joseph as a Symbol of Completion." *Journal of Biblical Literature* 98:1 (1979) 86–7.

Wright, G. Ernest. "The Theological Study of the Bible." In *The Interpreter's One-Volume Commentary on the Bible*, edited by Charles M. Laymon, 983–88. Nashville: Abingdon, 1971.

Zimmerli, Walther. *Ezekiel* 1. Hermeneia. Philadelphia: Fortress, 1979.

———. *Ezekiel* 2. Hermeneia. Philadelphia: Fortress, 1983.

Index of Major Biblical Theophanies

IN THE FOLLOWING INDEX, biblical theophanies and notations are listed according to the order they appear in the Bible. Chapters refer to the chapter numbers in this book. RCL:S refers to the Sunday(s) when the biblical theophany or a part of it is read in the Roman Catholic Lectionary. And CL:S refers to the Sunday(s) when the biblical theophany or a part of it is read in the Common Lectionary.

MORE SPECIFICALLY, IN THE RCL:S:

A1, 2, etc. = Advent Sunday 1, 2, etc.
L1, 2, etc. = Lent Sunday 1, 2, etc.
E1, 2 etc. = Easter Sunday 1, 2, etc.
OT2, 3, etc. = Ordinary Time Sunday 2, 3, etc.

P(P)S = Passion (Palm) Sunday
HWTHUR = Holy Week, Thursday
EV = Easter Vigil
BBC = Body and Blood of Christ
CK = Christ the King

MORE SPECIFICALLY, IN THE CL:S:

A1, 2, etc. = Advent Sunday 1, 2, etc.
C1, 2, etc. = Christmas Sunday 1, 2, etc.
E1, 2, etc. = Epiphany Sunday 1, 2, etc.
L1, 2, etc. = Lent Sunday 1, 2, etc.
Easter 1, 2 etc. = Easter Sunday 1, 2, etc.

P1, 2, etc. = Proper 1, 2, etc.
P(P)S = Passion (Palm) Sunday
HWTHUR = Holy Week, Thursday
EV = Easter Vigil

Index of Major Biblical Theophanies

Creation, Gen 1:1—2:25
Chapters 2, 6, 18, 19
RCL:S: L1, Cycle A; EV, Cycles ABC;
OT27, Cycle B
CL:S: Trinity, Cycle A; EV, Cycles
ABC; Baptism, Cycle B; L1,
Cycle A

Noah, Gen 6:5—9:28
Chapters 2, 6, 13, 14, 15, 16
CL:S: P4, Cycle A; EV, Cycles ABC

Tower of Babel, Gen 11:1-9
Chapter 1
RCL:S: Pentecost, Cycles ABC
CL:S: Pentecost, Cycle C

Abram/Abraham, Gen 12:1—25:18
Chapters 2, 6, 11, 13, 14, 16, 21
RCL:S: Holy Family, Cycle B; Lent
2, Cycles AB; EV, Cycle ABC;
OT16, Cycle C; OT 17, Cycle C;
BBC, Cycle C
CL:S: L2, Cycles ABC; EV, Cycles
ABC; P5-9, Cycle A; P11-12,
Cycle C; P14, Cycle C

Isaac, Gen 25:19—28:9
Chapter 3
CL:S: P10, Cycle A

Jacob, Gen 28:10—36:43
Chapters 1, 16, 21
CL:S: P11-13, Cycle A; P24, Cycle C

Joseph, Gen 37:1—50:26
Chapter 21
CL:S: E7, Cycle C; P14-15, Cycle A;
P19, Cycle A

Moses: Burning Bush, Exod 3:1—4:31
Chapters 1, 11, 14, 15
RCL:S: L3, Cycle C
CL:S: P17, Cycle A

Moses: Plagues, Exod 5:1—11:10
Chapters 6, 7

Moses: Passover, Exod 12:1—13:22
Chapter 17
RCL:S: HWTHUR, Cycles ABC
CL:S: HWTHUR, Cycles ABC; P17,
Cycle A

Moses: Red Sea, Exod 14:1—18:27
Chapters 4, 6, 18
RCL:S: EV, Cycles ABC
CL:S: L3, Cycle A; EV, Cycles ABC;
P19-21, Cycle A; P13, Cycle B

Moses: Horeb (Sinai), Exod 19:1—24:18
Chapters 1, 2, 3, 4, 5, 6, 7, 8, 9, 10,
11, 12, 13, 14, 15, 16, 17, 19, 20
RCL:S: L3, Cycle B; Pentecost,
Cycles ABC; OT11, Cycle A;
OT30, Cycle A; BBC, Cycle B
CL:S: L3, Cycle B; P6, Cycle A; P22,
Cycle A; Transfiguration, Cycle A

Moses: Ark and Tent, Exod 25:1—40:38
Chapters 5, 17
RCL:S: OT24, Cycle C; Trinity Sun.,
Cycle A
CL:S: P19, Cycle C; P23-24, Cycle
A; Transfiguration, Cycle C

Moses: Remember Horeb (Sinai), Deut
5:1-33
Chapters 1, 2, 3, 4, 5, 6, 7, 8, 9, 10,
11, 12, 13, 14, 15, 16, 17, 19, 20
RCL:S: OT9, Cycle B
CL:S: E9, Cycle B; P4, Cycle B

Joshua: Jordan Crossing, Josh 3:1—4:24
Chapters 6, 14
CL:S: P26, Cycle A

Joshua: Jericho, Josh 6:1-21
Chapter 9

Index of Major Biblical Theophanies

Gideon, Judg 6:1—8:35
  Chapter 13

Samson, Judg 13:1—16:31
  Chapter 13

Samuel, 1 Sam 1:1—7:17
  Chapters 3, 4, 13, 15
  RCL:S: Holy Family, Cycle C; L4,
    Cycle A; OT 2, Cycle B
  CL:S: C1, Cycle C; E2, Cycle B;
    P4-5, Cycle B; P28, Cycle B

Solomon, 1 Kgs 5:1—9:28
  Chapters 1, 10, 16, 19
  RCL:S: OT9, Cycle C; OT17, Cycle A
  CL:S: E9, Cycle C; P4, Cycle C; P16,
    Cycle B

Elijah: Mount Carmel, 1 Kgs 17:1—18:46
  Chapters 1, 2, 13, 16, 17, 18
  RCL:S: OT10, Cycle C; OT32, Cycle B
  CL:S: P4-5, Cycle C; P27, Cycle B

Elijah: Mount Horeb (Sinai), 1 Kgs
    19:1-21
  Chapters 1, 2
  RCL:S: OT13, Cycle C; OT19, Cycle
    A; OT19, Cycle B
  CL:S: P7-8, Cycle C; P14, Cycles AB

Elijah and Elisha, 2 Kgs 2:1-25
  Chapters 6, 18
  CL:S: Transfiguration, Cycle B; P8,
    Cycle C

Elisha and Naaman, 2 Kgs 4:1—8:15
  Chapter 15
  RCL:S: OT13, Cycle C; OT19, Cycle
    A; OT19, Cycle B
  CL:S: E6, Cycle B; P9, Cycle C; P12,
    Cycle B; P23, Cycle C

Psalm 18
  Chapters 4, 7, 10, 11, 12, 19

Psalm 29
  Chapter 3
  RCL:S: Baptism of Lord, Cycle A
  CL:S: Baptism of Lord, Cycles ABC;
    Trinity, Cycle B

Psalm 77
  Chapters 6, 7, 8, 12
  CL:S: P8, Cycle C

Psalm 97
  Chapters 5, 7, 8, 11, 12
  RCL:S: Christmas: Dawn,
    Cycles ABC; E7, Cycle C;
    Transfiguration, Cycles ABC
  CL:S: Christmas, Cycles ABC;
    Easter 7, Cycle C

Psalm 99
  Chapters 1, 5, 12
  CL:S: Transfiguration, Cycles AC;
    P24, Cycle A

Isaiah's Call, Isa 6:1-13
  Chapter 4
  RCL:S: OT5, Cycle C
  CL:S: Trinity, Cycle B

Jeremiah's Call, Jer 1:4-10
  Chapter 4
  RCL:S: OT4, Cycle C
  CL:S: E4, Cycle C; P16, Cycle C

Ezekiel's Call, Ezek 1:4—2:10
  Chapters 4, 20
  RCL:S: OT14, Cycle B
  CL:S: P9, Cycle B

Ezekiel and Dry Bones, Ezek 37:1-14
  Chapter 18
  RCL:S: Pentecost, Cycles ABC
  CL:S: L5, Cycle A; EV, Cycles ABC;
    Pentecost, Cycle B

Index of Major Biblical Theophanies

Daniel
  Chapters 5, 11, 21
  RCL:S: OT33, Cycle B; OT34 (CK), Cycle B
  CL:S: P28–29, Cycle B

Habakkuk 3:1–19
  Chapters 1, 6, 8, 12

Jesus' Conception and Birth, Matt 1:18—2:23, Luke 1:26–56
  Chapters 3, 4, 13, 15, 19, 21
  RCL:S: A4, Cycle A; A4, Cycle B; A4, Cycle C; Christmas: Vigil, Cycles ABC; Christmas: Midnight, Cycles ABC; Christmas: Dawn, Cycles ABC; Holy Family, Cycle A; Mother of God, Cycles ABC; Epiphany, Cycles ABC
  CL:S: A4, Cycle ABC; A3, Cycle AB; C1, Cycle A; Epiphany, Cycles ABC; Annunciation, Cycles ABC

Jesus' Baptism, Matt 3:13–17, Mark 1:9–11, Luke 3:21–22
  Chapters 3, 5, 6
  RCL:S: Baptism of Lord, Cycles ABC
  CL:S: Baptism of Lord, Cycles AC; L1, Cycle B

Jesus' Transfiguration, Matt 17:1–13, Mark 9:2–8, Luke 9:28–36
  Chapters 2, 4, 5, 15, 21
  RCL:S: L2, Cycles ABC; Transfiguration, Cycles ABC
  CL:S: L2, Cycles ABC; Transfiguration, Cycles ABC

Jesus and Wind, Matt 8:23–28, Mark 4:35–41, Luke 8:22–25
  Chapter 18
  RCL:S: OT 12, Cycle B
  CL:S: P7, Cycle B

Jesus and Sea, Matt 14:22–27, Mark 6:47–52, John 6:16–21
  Chapter 18
  CL:S: P12, Cycle B; P14, Cycle A

Jesus' Return on Clouds, Matt 24:29; 26:64, Mark 13:26–27; 14:62, Luke 21:27
  Chapters 5, 7, 9
  RCL:S: A3, Cycle C; P(P)S, Cycles AB; OT33, Cycle B
  CL:S: A1, Cycle B; A1, Cycle C; P(P)S, Cycles AB

Jesus Multiplies Loaves and Fish, Matt 14:13–21; 15:32–39, Mark 6:30–44; 8:1–9, Luke 9:10–17, John 6:1–14; 21:1–14
  Chapters 14, 17
  RCL:S: E3, Cycle C; OT16, Cycle B; OT17, Cycle B; OT 18, Cycle A; BBC, Cycle C
  CL:S: Easter 3, Cycle C; P11, Cycle B; P12, Cycle B; P13, Cycle A

Jesus' Signs, John 2:1—11:57
  Chapters 14, 15
  RCL:S: L4, Cycles ABC; L5, Cycles ABC; OT2, Cycle C
  CL:S: L4, Cycle A; L5, Cycle A; E2, Cycle C; P12, Cycle B

Mount of Olives, Matt 21:1–11, Mark 11:1–10, Luke 19:28–40
  Chapter 1
  RCL:S: P(P)S, Cycles ABC
  CL:S: P(P)S, Cycle ABC

Jesus' Death and Resurrection: Light and Darkness, Matt 27:45; 28:1, Mark 15:33; 16:2, Luke 23:44; 24:1, 50–51, Acts 1:9–11
  Chapters 12, 19
  RCL:S: P(P)S, Cycles ABC; EV, Cycles ABC; Ascension, Cycles ABC
  CL:S: P(P)S, Cycle ABC; EV, Cycles ABC; Ascension, Cycles ABC

Index of Major Biblical Theophanies

Pentecost, Acts 2:1–13
   Chapter 11
   RCL:S: Pentecost, Cycles ABC
   CL:S: Pentecost, Cycle ABC

Paul and Silas's Jail Escape, Acts 16:16–40
   Chapter 12
   CL:S: Easter 7, Cycle C

Other Books by Mark G. Boyer

History of St. Joachim Parish: 1822—1972; 1723—1973
Day by Day through the Easter Season
Following the Star: Daily Reflections for Advent and Christmas
Mystagogy: Liturgical Paschal Spirituality for Lent and Easter
Return to the Lord: A Lenten Journey of Daily Reflections
The Liturgical Environment: What the Documents Say
Breathing Deeply of God's New Life: Preparing Spiritually for the Sacraments of Initiation
Mary's Day—Saturday: Meditations for Marian Celebrations
Why Suffer?: The Answer of Jesus
A Month-by-Month Guide to Entertaining Angels
Biblical Reflections on Male Spirituality
"Seeking Grace with Every Step": The Spirituality of John Denver
Home Is a Holy Place
Day by Ordinary Day with Mark
Day by Ordinary Day with Matthew
Day by Ordinary Day with Luke
Baptized into Christ's Death and Resurrection: Preparing to Celebrate a Christian Funeral: Vol. 1: Adults
Baptized into Christ's Death and Resurrection: Preparing to Celebrate a Christian Funeral: Vol. 2: Children
The Greatest Gift of All: Reflections and Prayers for the Christmas Season
Meditations for Ministers
Waiting in Joyful Hope: Reflections for Advent 2001
Filled with New Light: Reflections for Christmas 2001–2002

Other Books by Mark G. Boyer

Lent and Easter Prayer at Home

Using Film to Teach New Testament

Waiting in Joyful Hope: Daily Reflections for Advent and Christmas 2002–2003

Waiting in Joyful Hope: Daily Reflections for Advent and Christmas 2003–2004

The Liturgical Environment: What the Documents Say (second edition)

Reflections on the Rosary

When Day Is Done: Nighttime Prayers through the Church Year

Take Up Your Cross and Follow: Daily Lenten Reflections

These Thy Gifts: A Collection of Simple Meal Prayers

Day by Ordinary Day: Daily Reflections on the First Readings, Year One

Day by Ordinary Day: Daily Reflections on the First Readings, Year Two

Mountain Reflections: A Collection of Photos and Meditations

Nature Spirituality: Praying with Wind, Water, Earth, Fire

A Spirituality of Ageing

Caroling through Advent and Christmas: Daily Reflections with Familiar Hymns

Weekday Saints: Reflections on Their Scriptures

Human Wholeness: A Spirituality of Relationship

The Liturgical Environment: What the Documents Say (third edition)

A Simple Systematic Mariology

Praying Your Way through Luke's Gospel and the Acts of the Apostles

Daybreaks: Daily Reflections for Advent and Christmas

Daybreaks: Daily Reflections for Lent and Easter

An Abecedarian of Animal Spirit Guides: Spiritual Growth through Reflections on Creatures

Overcome with Paschal Joy: Chanting through Lent and Easter—Daily Reflections with Familiar Hymns

Taking Leave of Your Home: Moving in the Peace of Christ

A Spirituality of Mission: Reflections for Holy Week and Easter

An Abecedarian of Sacred Trees: Spiritual Growth through Reflections on Woody Plants

www.ingramcontent.com/pod-product-compliance
Lightning Source LLC
Chambersburg PA
CBHW071231170426
43191CB00032B/1315